After Arson

Also by Gary Fincke

NONFICTION

The Mayan Syndrome
The Darkness Call
The Canals of Mars
Vanishings
Amp'd: A Father's Backstage Pass

SHORT STORIES

The Killer's Dog
A Room of Rain
The Proper Words for Sin
Sorry I Worried You
The Stone Child

POETRY

For Now, We Have Been Spared
The Infinity Room
The History of Permanence
Standing around the Heart
Writing Letters for the Blind

After Arson

New and Selected Essays

GARY FINCKE

Lake Dallas, Texas

FIRST EDITION

Requests for permission to reprint or reuse material
from this work should be sent to:

Permissions
Madville Publishing
PO Box 358
Lake Dallas, TX 75065

Cover Art: "Astonishment of Air" by Shannon Fincke
Author photo: Aaron Fincke

ISBN: 978-1-963695-21-2 paperback
978-1-963695-22-9 ebook

Library of Congress Control Number: 2025932098

For the "family," especially Liz, Derek, Shannon, Aaron, Gavin, Raea, Sabina, River, Cherie, and Judy

Table of Contents

New

ALL OF IT

The Start of It

A friend of D's wife G says there's been a bad accident. "That's all I know," she says, "except that it happened on Rte. 15 and Laurel Road." She lowers her voice as if she doesn't want to be overheard. "D is in surgery right now as I'm telling you this. G is at the hospital. Their kids are on their way."

A Bit of It

Hours later, a posted photo of the accident site on Facebook shows one car destroyed, the front end crushed, the rest damaged by fire. D's car is farther down the four-lane highway, twisted sideways and pressed against a guardrail. "Whoever was driving the less damaged car," the poster writes, "is the one who was seriously injured."

A Glimpse of It

In the comments that scroll below, a familiar name says she's so sorry she didn't recognize D's car as she was slowly passing by in the one open lane. "All I thought was how awful it must have been by the look of the car that hit him, how fast it must have been flying down that hill to have its engine explode like that."

Some of It

The following day, an electronic newspaper article reports that it's still undetermined how it happened, but the elderly driver of the car that was struck while attempting to cross Rte. 15 was entrapped for two hours, that after being extracted, he was life-flighted to the hospital.

"After extensive surgery, he is listed in critical condition. The other driver, nineteen, escaped serious injury even though his car was demolished and caught fire."

More of It

The detailed police report, when released a week later, is one short paragraph. In three sentences, it declares that there is no evidence that the uninjured driver was speeding. That he was not impaired by drugs or alcohol. It concludes by saying that the retired professor, who has died despite two major surgeries, pulled from a side road and attempted to cross two lanes of highway with "insufficient clearance."

The Rest of It

Because the retired professor was more than forty years a close friend, the report's absence of detail magnifies the immediacy of his sudden absence. There is nothing revealed about what was surely, mid-afternoon, on D's car radio—an NPR showcase of classical music. No reassurance that his seat belt lay snug around his waist and against his chest where his heart kept its reliable pace. No mention that his vision was recently recorded as 20/20 after being restored to perfection by cataract surgery. That his trained, historian's mind, supplemented by extensive research, was mid-way through producing another commissioned book. Not a word about the why of his choosing Laurel Road, the most unlikely route for haste or convenience or mileage saved. Not a phrase about his retiree's love of finding an unusual rather than a shortest route to anywhere he had to drive for the errands that were within thirty miles of his home. No investigation into October's temptation of leaves, D's annual self-guided motor tour where ash, sycamore, maple, and beech synchronize into Pennsylvania's spectrum upon one particular, brilliant hillside for a few hours, receiving the slanted light so perfectly that whatever errand D had could wait patiently in a neighboring town eight miles north of Laurel Road. No speculation about how, each autumn, one farmer sells cider by that roadside until October's end, closing his stand's produce season with something that might have held an old, faithful customer for conversation while he sampled a preview of the gallon discovered intact behind the driver's-side seat. How that highly likely give-and-take affected timing to the smidgeon of a second when fate exclaimed "Now" as D accelerated across those two downhill lanes, the high-speed rural-area traffic light and intermittent, even what could be called "spotty" just after three p.m., NPR's "Here and Now" begun, the sun behind him, the sky clear of clouds.

Word for Word

Inheritance, very often, dissolves us. A lifetime friend now looks exactly like his father when he sank through the stages of dementia. At times, he chokes on confusion or, word for word, repeats an anecdote. My wife, after forgetting some small, unimportant thing today, insists she's not as sharp as she used to be. "Or even a week ago," she finishes, sounding like her mother. "And I'm not exaggerating."

Immediately, I claim kinship to keep her company on this nearly imperceptible, but certain downslope. "I write things down now," I say, choosing my most obvious recent concession, the one I'd agreed to make after, within two weeks, I had arrived an hour early for an appointment and forgotten one completely.

I say nothing about how I've already neglected to check the calendar those appointments are written on, proving that system less than fool-proof. But at least I am more candid than my father was when he was losing touch with the world, sometimes belligerent with his refusal to acknowledge how he was changing.

"In his decline," my mother would have said about him at seventy-nine, my current age, someone who groused about sensing he was less respected for not keeping current with technology or worse, no longer the one who mowed his lawn or washed his car. She didn't get to use that phrase on my father because she died and left him a widower for twenty-one years. My father's phrase, for all of those years, was "You make do," relying upon the assisted living of resignation.

My father, for the last six years of his life, recited the Gettysburg Address multiple times when my wife and I visited. Before he began, he would hand me a paper upon which that speech was printed. "Check for mistakes," he would say. After a while, I could recite a few paragraphs, too.

However, once he'd mastered the speech, he insisted upon trying to match the speed of Lincoln according to his former high school history teacher. "Time me," he said, so serious about that memory from 1935 that I nodded a signal and monitored the sweep hand of my watch while he enunciated, sometimes six seconds long, sometimes seven short of exactly two minutes and sixteen seconds. "Don't lie," he would say. "Don't humor me." Twice, he finished only two seconds from duplicating what must be, at best, an estimate.

"Almost," he said each time, then readied himself again, as if arriving at the precise cadence in my presence would resurrect an accomplishment he had achieved privately. My father, who never wore a watch, must have rehearsed near where his single clock stood on the bedroom nightstand, orating to the ceiling, then turning to compare, keeping the inevitable at bay by mastering the unlikely.

The last time he recited, he was ninety and a few weeks from acquiescing to a nursing home. As always, he sat in his blue chair with the worn-through arm rests, a pillow stuffed behind him. The weather inside his closed windows suggested a ceiling of gathering thunderheads, but before sitting, he buttoned his sweater and closed the drapes like a magician ready to vanish the felled tree that had, for months by then, stretched nearly the width of his backyard.

After he finished, not missing a word, first coming within eight seconds, then within four, he let me pull the drapes aside and open one window. Outside, in August, the neighbor with seven children yelled the same blasphemy at all of them. Her husband was three years dead, the oldest boy smoking, the youngest in diapers. My father, nearly deaf, rocked himself to prepare to stand, failing, then rocking again while I concentrated upon keeping my arms still.

There's never enough preserving, never enough remembering. I've discovered, this morning, that the most common noun is Time

Scream: A Panorama

1

In the midst of the pandemic, Japan reopens its amusement parks, roller coasters, once again, climbing to precipices meant to terrorize. To prevent the spread of the virus, the government tells riders, "Please, scream in your heart." For a few weeks, on social media, that phrase is chattered about as if such screaming is rare. Yet, there are thousands of roller coasters, thousands of high suspension bridges over rivers and chasms, thousands of roads carved into cliffs guarded by nothing more than caution and mechanical soundness. And, of course, countless personal crises that end or continue privately and unheard in innumerable ways.

2

Home for the first break of my freshman year in college, I rode with a high school classmate until midnight, the radio cranked to speaker-threatening. The road we lived on was so familiar either one of us could have been speeding, but he was at the wheel when a car backed across both lanes from a garage. He braked hard, the car four-wheel-drifting toward a row of junipers that filled the side window as I gripped the door handle and braced, the world turning dark green just before it brightened, his father's car spinning and stopping so close to the other that I could see the shape of that driver's inaudible scream.

Neither my friend nor I made a sound during those moments of lost control. What I did do was reflexively reach for the door handle. My friend, when he talked, said, "Good thing I knew what to do" as we waited for the other driver to straighten and drive away. Good thing I didn't open the door, I said to myself. Out loud, I said nothing because I had no idea what it was he had done. We were a mile from his house, a quarter mile from the right turn to my house.

3

Perhaps the most well-known silent scream is the one portrayed in Edvard Munch's famous painting. Less well known is the inscription scrawled below the figure by the artist: "I felt the great scream throughout nature." The cryptic sentence is often said to refer to a walk Munch took near a fjord overlooking Oslo.

Many viewers of Munch's painting find the figure's scream is made more striking by the swirled, unusual colors of the sky. It has been suggested that the red-colored sky was inspired by a volcanic sunset seen by Munch after the Krakatau eruption in 1883 or by a sighting of nacreous clouds, ones that are rare and so high in the stratosphere that the ice crystals they contain refract light from a low-lying polar, winter sun.

4

My father, the night of the near-accident, was at work, my mother asleep. The neighbor's dog, chained outside, barked as I got out of the car. I crept to my room and huddled on my bed fully clothed. Long after I lay down, the neighbor's miserable dog kept up with its yammering. My quiet hysteria gradually faded. I silently made a vow of a future filled with caution, something that sounded, at once, like it had been copied like the answers to an exam for which I was not prepared.

5

Scream, a movie in which the serial killer wore a mask that reproduced the expression on the screaming figure in Munch's painting, was so popular that millions of that mask were sold. The film, itself, spawned a franchise of sequels.

6

Thomas Pynchon's Gravity's Rainbow opens with this: "A screaming comes across the sky." The arc of a V-2 rocket. The novel itself is long and complex. Doom swirls over and around that screaming. Pynchon goes on: "It has happened before, but there is nothing to compare it to now. Always, someone is trying."

7

One of the most recognizable images in silent films is the scream of the nurse watching the baby carriage tumble down tiers of steps while disciplined rows of soldiers brutally slaughter Odessa's population in Sergei Eisenstein's *The Battleship Potemkin*. The extended scene concludes with a famous close-up, the nurse's pince-nez shattered, her face contorted by agony and terror.

8

From 1949 on, some of the figures in Francis Bacon's series of *Screaming Popes* paintings replace the head of Pope Innocent X as painted by Velazquez with the screaming face of Eisenstein's wounded nurse. Bacon remarked that during the silent era, the image in films had tremendous force, "sometimes very powerful, very beautiful."

9

The beginning of the film *Don't Look Now* juxtaposes silent images of Donald Sutherland and Julie Christie having sex with the concurrent drowning death of their young daughter. It's the audience that screams in its heart while watching that sequence.

10

The Odessa nurse's gaping mouth distinctively informs Bacon's *Head VI*. The dangling pince-nez is echoed in *Pope III, 1951* and *Study for the Head of a Screaming Pope, 1952*. He explicitly uses it in a full-length nude, *Study for the Nurse in the Film Battleship Potemkin, 1957*.

11

The extended closing scene of *Don't Look Now* is nearly silent. When his throat is cut by the red-caped killer, Donald Sutherland's scream is barely audible. As he silently bleeds to death, the movie relies on nothing but a series of images while the sound track fills with the pealing of church bells—a reprise of the sex and drowning, the killer's silent celebratory face, Julie Christie's vulnerable throat.

12

Someone on my Facebook feed has posted a photograph of a thrill ride so steep and high it suggests that parachutes might be required for safety. Would you ride? she asks, and already there are two hundred and seventeen shares, thousands of comments that tally a landslide for NO. I silently and repeatedly agree, but I can't take my eyes off what looks to be suicidal.

13

The Internet is full of short films of cars and buses traveling narrow, uneven roads carved into cliff sides thousands of feet above where an accident would plummet the passengers to certain death. I always watch them several times, imagining the screams of the passengers if the bus tipped over the edge. The sounds are like comic book screams, ones that are silent yet meant to be heard in the imaginations of readers. They are almost always written in a series of vowels of varying lengths depending on the distance of the fall.

14

A vasovagal episode is the medical term for the effects on the body created by screaming in the heart. I learned that name after years of panic attacks, most of them endured in private. I also learned I wasn't unique. Not even rare. It is a routine medical phenomenon. I've experienced it multiple times during medical exams as simple as the taking of blood pressure. I've been given Valium to stop that silent scream. Once, an emergency room nurse gave me a brown paper bag and told me to breathe into it. "It's just hyperventilating," she said while I imagined ways of murdering her. When I calmed down, she handed me three new bags. "Keep them handy," she said. My wife drove me home.

15

I've screamed in my heart in a friend's jeep as he inched us along a road better described as a ledge overlooking, without guardrails, a fall of hundreds of feet. "You're not the worst," he said, referencing my terror. "I have a friend who curled up on the floor." My internal scream was nothing like a comic book wail. In my imagination, I was mute all the way to the base of that cliff.

16

A colleague, when I returned to work after knee surgery, asked how the procedure had gone. "I was awake," I said. "I watched it on a screen. The worst part was waiting for the spinal to wear off."

"Don't tell me anything else," she said. "I have problems."

I laughed. "So do I. I start to go cold and clammy."

"Oh God," she said, "excuse me." She backed through the door, so pale I expected her to sprawl in the hall. By the time I managed to lurch up, get the crutches under me, and swing myself to her office, she was sitting in her chair with her head between her knees.

I couldn't even slip away discreetly and hope she hadn't seen me. Swaying on the crutches, I said, "It's like second-hand smoke."

17

One late morning, in Italy, our tour visited a perfume factory, an inspection so boring some of us sat outside to voice indifference and smoke. A few minutes later, our bus driver, after a wrong turn, needed to reverse us. The road, narrow and without guardrails, was bordered by a plummet of several hundred feet to a town beside the Mediterranean Sea. More than once, the driver backed those in the rear seats to the rare space where "Poised over nothing" was translated by tears, prayers, and a scattering of screams. My wife and I sat near the front. I was transfixed within a mute, onomatopoeia for dying.

18

Throughout the tenth episode of the fourth season of the television show *Buffy the Vampire Slayer*, there is no dialogue until, as the show concludes, Buffy screams. The extended silence and speechlessness make that scream memorable.

19

Johnny Weismuller, the Olympic swimmer who made the movie version of Tarzan famous, repeated the same call of alarm in response to every jungle emergency. He had to learn to repeat it for public appearances. The sound was created by a combination of a camel's bleat, a hyena howl played backwards, plucked violin, and a soprano's high C added to Weismuller's own best roar.

20

The most well-known sound effect for personal disaster is The Wilhelm Scream. In 1951, in a scene from *Distant Drums*, a soldier pulled underwater by alligators utters a brief scream of terror. Nothing special about the sound, except that the makers of the 1953 film *Charge at Feather River*, when they needed a scream, reused it.

A man on horseback dawdles while an off-screen voice says, "Hurry up, Wilhelm."

"Yeah, I'll just fill my pipe," he says. Immediately, he's struck by an arrow and utters the scream of the man attacked by alligators. No matter that the arrow merely strikes him in the thigh. A moment later, a soldier who receives a spear in the chest emits the identical scream. He's not named. Wilhelm's scream soon becomes ubiquitous.

21

Roger Daltrey's scream near the end of "Won't Get Fooled Again" was used during the opening of the wildly successful television series *CSI:Miami*. By now, through both means, it has been heard billions of times.

22

It is estimated that the screams of the Beatles fans at Shea Stadium in 1965 reached a decibel level around 131dB. Translated, that means the screaming was louder than a low flying jumbo jet or a clap of thunder sustained for nearly an hour.

23

Although uncredited, Sheb Wooley is thought to be the person who recorded the Wilhelm Scream. He is best known for the popular novelty song "Purple People Eater" that he recorded seven years after *Distant Drums* was released.

24

The Wilhelm Scream has been used in over 400 movies of all kinds: *Star Wars, Indiana Jones, Reservoir Dogs, The Green Berets, Them!, More American Graffiti, Toy Story, Beauty and the Beast.* The morning I watched a YouTube compilation of examples, 2,442,984 viewers had preceded me.

25

Screams of distress are in the vocal spectrum least affected by age deterioration.

26

Arthur Janov's book *The Primal Scream* launched a psychotherapy based on recalling childhood trauma. Patients were induced to recall painful incidents and then scream in the most unrestrained way they could muster. Celebrities like John Lennon, James Earl Jones, and Roger Williams were advocates.

27

Frederick Douglass wrote about hearing his Aunt Hester scream while being whipped by a slave master.

28

In one Robert Graves' story *The Shout*, the scream is a weapon. "The terror shout" kills animals with sound. "My shout," the perpetrator says, "is not a matter of tone or vibration but something not to be explained. It is a shout of pure evil ... pure terror." It's left to the reader to imagine what that sounds like.

29

The elongated screams of women are a fixture of horror movies. The actresses cower and scream or stand paralyzed and scream or thrash and struggle and scream. In many of these cases, no help arrives. There is a film category, mostly filled with female b-movie stars, called "scream queens." Julie Adams struggles with the monster in *The Creature from the Black Lagoon.* Hazel Court is imperiled in a series of Edgar Allan Poe movies like *The Raven* and *The Premature Burial.* Famously, Janet Leigh's open-mouthed extended scream as she is stabbed in the shower scene from Alfred Hitchcock's *Psycho*.

30

Hitchcock eventually added shrieking violins to Janet Leigh's scream, but his first intention was to use no soundtrack at all for the scene. Hitchcock also used the sound of a casaba melon being stabbed for the sound of flesh yielding to a knife in that shower scene. He auditioned a variety of melons before settling on casaba. Because of the extraordinary scream recorded for the scene, that bit of realism can be overlooked.

31

One of the memorable tag lines in the history of movie advertising is "In space, no one can hear you scream." *Alien* was, indeed, frightening, especially when the crewman's chest was opened from the inside by a juvenile form of the monster that had incubated within him. That scene and none of the others of mayhem and death are embellished by piercing, elongated screams. The closing confrontation between Ripley and the monster is nearly entirely silent. Her repressed screams, the ones in her heart as she tries to outwit the Alien, are the ones the audience temporarily carries too.

32

One morning, at 5:38 a.m., my wife and I were startled out of sleep by a policeman knocking on our door. We were simultaneously terrorized by the belief that one of our three children, all of whom lived elsewhere by then, was at best seriously injured, or at worst, dead. Neither of us spoke through another flurry of fists to our door. How long had that policeman pushed our broken doorbell? At last, when my wife opened the door, we discovered he was serving a summons for us to be deposed for a legal squabble that the builder of our house was having with his former employer. Before the policeman left, my wife wanted to know why he would think to knock before dawn for something so petty. "My shift begins at 4 a.m.," the man said, omitting why he couldn't appear during one of the five daylight hours during which he worked.

33

My wife and I have rushed each of our three children to emergency rooms—a deep gash in the forehead of our older son at two, croup distress in our infant daughter turned to a whistle so shrill it could barely be heard, our younger son lapsing into the throes of pneumonia at five. Each time, my wife chattered and consoled and comforted while I silently drove.

34

The only times I have screamed aloud are while awakening from nightmares where I or my wife or my children are about to be killed, mostly by apocalyptic terrors. The scream always begins while I am asleep and continues long enough for me to hear myself make the sound of hopelessness.

35

My wife, in her nightmares, makes a whimpering sound that extends into a wail that raises gooseflesh on my body. I lie in the dark and listen, trying to somehow overhear the scene that is causing her distress. I've never learned what is happening. I've never seen her wake up wailing. I've never awoken her.

36

The most terrifying minute of my life happened in the library of the college where I was teaching. My son was three. The librarian, because she thought he was both adorable and well-behaved, gave him a lemon sourball that, a short while later, became stuck in his throat. What made it horrifying was his silence. No gasps. No coughs. I didn't say a word. Pre-Heimlich and panicked, I pounded on his back. When nothing changed, I turned him upside down and pounded until, at last, the candy dropped to the carpet.

37

Years ago, I wrote in detail about that experience. My son was so young that he has had only my storytelling to let him know what happened. How I screamed in my heart. How he must have too. Though, in his case, there's no way of knowing.

14

38

A few years after the near-disaster sourball incident, a neighbor girl ran up to me in our front yard to say that same son had tumbled from our backyard playhouse roof and wasn't moving. Without saying a word, I sprinted to where my son lay soundless and motionless. Just as I reached him, he pedaled his legs and moved his arms. My son stood up into my arms. He talked and talked. Now nearly eight, he said he felt like he wasn't inside himself. Neither, I said, do I. In the darkening west, stars were forming familiar shapes, blue going black near Buffalo, where schoolchildren my son's age were reported to be losing their balance near the environmentally disastrous Love Canal. From a distance, Buffalo's lights flickering on suggested news so terrible that there would be a community of screaming.

39

More than fifty years ago, one week after riding with me in my parents' station wagon, a girl speeding, by then, in another boy's new Corvette, was catapulted through its windshield when it crashed. Decades later, I used that girl's death to fuel a short story's conclusion. "What happened to your friend is not your story's truth," an editor explained, asking for a revision that avoided that inevitable tragedy. So, I saved her, though ambiguously, the choices she made perhaps maiming or killing her on another reckless evening. I left her being sped through expectancy, that thrilling car still unscathed, her body nervous, but excited. Unharmed. Screaming only in her heart.

OAK RIDGE: A CANTATA

The first brochure I pick up in Oak Ridge, Tennessee, is for a Public Bus Tour. "Extended Season! Now March-November," it reads. August has just begun. Tiny print at the bottom of the page says, "Must be U.S. citizen age 10 or older. Must have photo I.D. (18 years or older)."

When I ask, "Why now?" a woman behind a nearby desk tells me, "That's how it's been ever since the gates were opened in '49."

The second brochure I pick up mentions Ed Westcott, the twenty-ninth employee hired for the Manhattan Project in Oak Ridge, becoming the official government photographer there from 1942 to 1966. I expect his photographs to be an extensive display of propaganda. Instead, Ed Westcott's photos are an invitation to history without the viewer's proof of citizenship and age.

Oak Ridge Tour Fact: E. O. Lawrence won a Nobel Prize for inventing the Cyclotron, the predecessor of the world's first uranium enrichment processor at Oak Ridge.

WESTCOTT PHOTO #1: THE PERENNIALS OF OAK RIDGE

The trellises in the photograph appear to be handmade, vines and branches trained upward, beauty and comfort compatible, though temporary and brief like each sad emphasis on the end of this settlement no one mentions until privacy returns. Inside laboratories, riddles are whispered, answers unsolvable as the equation for heaven, but here, the stems climb their small increments of reassurance, leaves opening to drink up light. Annuals have been abandoned like promises of early surrender. In Oak Ridge's second summer, fast-climbing perennials. Possible, now, to believe in the sensuality of shadows cast by the rise of roses, the ascension of morning glories, or, at least, the small contentment of the narrowing latticework become a sieve that magnifies the spell of early evening before descending light diffuses into the indifferent drift to darkness.

Oak Ridge Tour Fact: One of the advertised hiking areas is named "Top Secret Trail."

In 1942, my father failed his Army physical. "This bum ear is why we're all here," he said to me more than once. "I went for my exam with my friend Al. He passed, and I didn't, and then he didn't come back." Every time he told that story he equated that outcome with the guarantee that he, too, would have been killed in action. And when his three brothers, all of them veterans, had opinions about the atom bomb, he stayed silent because, he said, he hadn't earned the right to express himself about military decisions.

One of those brothers was the navigator on a bomber that flew multiple missions over Germany. When, as an eleven-year-old who was planning on applying to West Point, I asked, "How many missions?" my father said, "More than enough, and don't you dare ask him."

I never did. Talking about the war seemed more private than sex. The only time my uncle mentioned anything about his experience in the war was to say, after a Memorial Day parade a few years later, that there were clouds over the Japanese city of Kokura, or else somebody else would have gotten theirs from the B-29 that day instead of the folks in Nagasaki.

Oak Ridge Tour Fact: The gates closed on April 1, 1943. Always, throughout the war, the guards at the Oak Ridge gates demanded photo IDs, no exceptions.

WESTCOTT PHOTO #2: SANTA CLAUS ARRIVES AT OAK RIDGE

Santa's made the trip by automobile. He's working day-shift, the reindeer pastured, but his Chevrolet is stopped like a spy's. Although Santa ho-

hos, the guards remain in character, serious as war while they rummage through two sacks, reminding him the red flag of his baggy suit requires a pat-down, including his shiny boots. He's scuffling now, stumbling like a hobo, that sack unwieldy with stocking stuffers, footing uncertain on the unpaved street as irregular as pieces of coal meant to terrify the worst brat polite. By the time he's surrounded by children, he's a mess of mud splatter, gasping brief white clouds like the ones the reindeer pant when the sleigh is miraculously loaded. Housewives on Saturdays, the Oak Ridge mothers have set aside an hour for Christmas among their chores. They've dressed for Santa Claus, the secret work of war set aside like a long novel, the place bookmarked by a small child's crayoned drawing—the stick figures of family and pets, an oval sun whose beams strafe house and yard. Near Santa's hardback throne, consequence lifts like tentative fog; the children form lines from the left and right, loud but orderly. The mothers retreat. Cameras taboo, they memorize the scene as if it were poetry: The bright marathon of wishful thinking, footballs and bicycles, dolls and board games, roller skates and air-rifles and all those perfectly detailed model Air Force planes.

Oak Ridge trivia: In 1902, John Hendrix, a local mystic, prophesied the construction of Oak Ridge.

My father-in-law had fought in World War II but, like my father's brothers, never spoke of it. In fact, he seldom spoke at all. All I ever knew about his silence came from his wife. "He was different before all that war business," she said from time to time. "He was a fun guy." My wife, once, told me she learned how much her father hated the Japanese when he became enraged upon learning she had been invited to the senior prom by a boy who was "half-Japanese." She already had a dress; the event was less than two weeks away. Her father, without ever meeting the boy, told her "absolutely not." He had fought in the European theater, but never expressed an opinion to her about my German heritage.

"There will be worse and more of it" was my navigator uncle's annual Thanksgiving reunion observation when the future was discussed. As if he expected the antecedent, measured in kilotons, to be remembered for decades, he never elaborated.

Oak Ridge Tour Fact: During the war, there were six beauty shops and two bakeries in Oak Ridge. They were never counted, but the estimate is there were tens of thousands of ashtrays.

WESTCOTT PHOTO #3: THE MIDTOWN FIRES, 1944

During the invasion of January, the year begins with the flickering firefights of uncertain outcome. Trailer flames, hutment blazes—every neighborhood in Oak Ridge lights up during that epidemic year, nearly a thousand alarms despite the trained caution of every resident. An hour or more, each night, some lie awake like watchmen for the burglary of fire. Children are slapped, sometimes, for carelessness. Out of love. Out of inevitability. Someone's hands always shake over kerosene, the fuel so necessary, the inexperienced are forced to defuse. As if daily sacrifice was required by the American version of God. As if the trailers were set on altars fashioned by faith, the temporary triumph of flame across a street or distant as an accidental Passover, the fortunate rising to reignite before walking to incomprehensible work with discipline, resignation, and yes, with joy.

Oak Ridge Trivia: During the war, the secret city had its own symphony orchestra.

The Air Force manual my uncle studied declared, "The navigator's primary duty is navigating his airplane with a high degree of accuracy. But as a member of the team, he must also have a general knowledge of the entire operation of the airplane. He has a .50-cal. machine gun at his station, and he must be able to use it skillfully and to service it in emergencies. He must be familiar with the oxygen system, know how to operate the turrets, radio equipment, and fuel transfer system. He must know the location of all fuses and spare fuses, lights and spare lights, affecting navigation. He must be familiar with emergency procedures, such as the manual operation of landing gear, bomb bay doors and flaps, and the proper procedures for crash landings, ditching, bailout, etc."

DUTCH

Theodore "Dutch" VanKirk, the navigator on the Enola Gay, attended Susquehanna University for a year, and yet I worked at Susquehanna for more than thirty-five years without hearing anyone mention "Dutch" VanKirk. When I asked a colleague who had written a history of the university what he knew about VanKirk, he said he'd mentioned him in his book, one that I'd bought five years before, skimming until I arrived at the years just before I'd been hired.

Oak Ridge Tour Fact: Without preference, the chapel served all the Protestant sects, Catholics, and Jews.

WESTCOTT PHOTO #4: SQUARE THROUGH IN OAK RIDGE

Each Saturday night, in Oak Ridge, Bill Pierce calls squares for workers out for a good time at the Midtown Rec Hall. Comfortable or clumsy, the couples keep following his lead. The city women have learned quickly from rural friends, but their men are as reluctant as boys at an eight-grade social. "Do-si-do," Pierce calls, "now four ladies chain." Behind him the fiddler has time to slip in a pinch of chew tobacco. Later, the fiddler has a sad solo when the dance turns slow and private, but now it's the simple refrains, the sound of shuffling and laughter as Pierce works old-timey into his calls: *Hey, all join hands and circle to the south, And get a little moonshine in your mouth.* This night, Pierce switches to wartime patter: *Now allemande left with a soldier's wife. If we finish our work, we'll save his life.* During a break, the fiddler tells Pierce he had misread a gauge into red earlier in the week. Thankfully, correctible, the danger brief and only to himself. *Luck is singing with a fiddle and bow. All move together now, and do-si-do.* Right now there's time enough to celebrate the unraveling of whatever's feared, a near-rhyme for urgency's solitaire with a single, mysterious lab task. Pierce calls three familiar couplets to close, and the fiddler holds the last note, then bows. There's a necessity in everyone performing the smallest share of production; any larger, it would be impossible to bear.

Oak Ridge Trivia: Besides a bridge club and a swim club, wartime Oak Ridge stabled horses enough for its residents to form a saddle club.

Absolutely, my father-in-law once said, we were right to drop the bomb, though he had been home for a year by the time Hiroshima and Nagasaki were decimated.

"Dutch" VanKirk grew up in a town across the river from Selinsgrove, where Susquehanna University is located. Anticipating the war, he left school to enlist before Pearl Harbor, becoming an Air Force cadet in October 1941. After the war, VanKirk enrolled at Bucknell University, twelve miles north of Susquehanna, and so he is listed there as a notable alum.

Oak Ridge Tour Fact: In all of the dorms of the Secret City, the ironing rooms were for women only.

WESTCOTT PHOTO #5: HUTMENTS COME TO OAK RIDGE

In Oak Ridge, the races were separated at the gate, the Negroes packed off to hutments in Gamble Valley, their jobs, by design, requiring nothing more than dirty hands, heavy lifting, and huge humility. Hutments, they learn, are sixteen by sixteen packing boxes. In each wall, one window without glass or screens, boards available to shut out flies, mosquitoes, rain, and light. What's more, Negro husbands are not allowed to live with wives, and though they visit each other like prisoners, in the evenings the wives are widows, the night as formless as Genesis. It's no surprise that more than half the Negroes refuse those cells, choose to commute daily from Knoxville, but always, like migrants, driven in by bus, rebroken like badly set, fractured bones, searched each morning for weapons, contraband, the remnants of reasons not to obey. Always, through the translucent, stained windows, they watch the guards gather as if woken by alarms set so low in frequency, they seem to insist from within like pulse.

Oak Ridge Trivia: Cigarettes were in such demand that long lines formed to purchase them.

Navigation is the art of determining geographic positions by means of (a) pilotage, (b) dead reckoning, (c) radio, or (d) celestial navigation, or any combination of these 4 methods. By any one or combination of methods the navigator determines the position of the airplane in relation to the earth.

About the time my uncle and "Dutch" VanKirk would have been ready to enter active duty, they would have read these lines by Marvin Peterson:

SILVER WINGS

"THE NAVIGATOR GRADUATE"

I've won the right to wear these Silver Wings
and see the many awesome sights of
which the poet sings.
I've earned a place among the gods of flight
under the sun's and moon's eternal light....

DUTCH

When "Dutch" VanKirk was interviewed about his role in the war, he said, "We were fighting an enemy that had a reputation for never surrendering, never accepting defeat. It's really hard to talk about morality and war in the same sentence. Where was the morality in the bombing of Coventry, or the bombing of Dresden, or the Bataan Death March, or the Rape of Nanking, or the bombing of Pearl Harbor? I believe that when you're in a war, a nation must have the courage to do what it must to win the war with a minimum loss of lives."

Oak Ridge Tour Fact: Gaseous diffusion plant K25 was, during the war, the world's largest building under one roof.

WESTCOTT PHOTO #6:
THE TRAVELING LIBRARY IN OAK RIDGE, 1946

The children are eager for more pictures. They scramble for warriors and princesses who will sometimes meet and love each other before or during or after battles. Illustrated or not, none of the books mentions Oak Ridge, where those children's parents have begun to learn how they ended war with obedience, discipline, and care. Because science is a workday subject, because research never ends, these children will remain, three years yet, before the gates will open, all of them with time to learn the new definition of infinite. One of the boys is returning a book of horses, its gold-bordered cover torn through two pintos whose faces his mother has taped while he sobbed out apology. Now, 11 before the librarian reshelves those horses into circulation, she inspects for the interior damage of marginal notes, things scribbled as code. Satisfied, she runs her finger along the tape before pressing it to the boy's damp forehead as if she were knighting him.

Oak Ridge Trivia: In September 1944, test runs were conducted with dummy bombs simulated to be the top-secret weapon. They were painted orange. The bomber crews called them pumpkins.

After leaving the displays behind, I drive to the Chapel on the Hill, where services were held on Saturdays and Sundays throughout the war, one after the other to cover all of the denominations who were represented among the people who lived in Oak Ridge. It looks like a movie set for a musical about Oak Ridge, one starring a perky Doris Day and a handsome Gordon MacRae.

Enola Gay memorabilia is highly valued by collectors. The detailed chart carried by copilot Robert A. Lewis was sold, in 2005, for $72,000 at Christie's auction house. In 2016, Sotheby's sold the navigational charts detailed by "Dutch" Van Kirk for $372,500.

Oak Ridge Tour Fact: Cattle exposed to fallout from the A-Bomb test in Socorro were shipped to Oak Ridge for study.

Westcott Photo #7: The New Mexico Cattle, 1946

What's striking, at first, is that every cow inside the rough-hewn corral is facing the camera, curious as just-discovered political prisoners. Slatted fencing reveals an open landscape unlike where those cattle absorbed the consequences of the first atomic bomb. Scientists are listening to *Inevitable*'s preliminary report. Everything they observe and record is essential, vital work, heavy with imperatives. Not one of them has ever touched a cow, but now they will care for them, especially the yearling in the foreground who confirms there is no limit to our emptiness.

I once had an atomic bomb ring that cost 15 cents and one Kix box top. My mother bought the cereal, but I had to part with three nickels. "See atoms split to smithereens" and a mushroom cloud were in the advertisement. Like everything that I could buy with less than a week's allowance, it was disappointing.

During the 1970s my father-in-law showed me the blueprints for a cooling tower. He was an engineer, and what he let me glimpse was the outline of a job for him to complete. When I asked him how he felt about the complications, what to do with nuclear waste, the hazards of working with something so dangerous, he said all of that was on someone else's plate, but if everyone did their job, there was no cause for worry.

Dutch

"Dutch" VanKirk became the last surviving member of the Enola Gay crew. He was 93 when he died in 2014. Included in his obituary were details of that famous mission:

> In the predawn hours of Aug. 6, 1945, the Enola Gay, piloted
> by Col. Paul W. Tibbets Jr. and carrying a crew of 12, took off
> from Tinian in the Mariana Islands with a uranium bomb built
> under extraordinary secrecy in the vast Manhattan Project.
> Captain VanKirk spread out his navigation charts on a small
> table behind Colonel Tibbets's seat. From that spot, at the end
> of a long tunnel atop the bomb bays, he took the plane's bear-
> ings, using a hand-held sextant to guide with the stars.

At 8:15 a.m. Japan time, the Enola Gay reached Hiroshima, a city of 250,000. The bombardier, Maj. Thomas W. Ferebee, said, "I got it," announcing that the Enola Gay was over his aiming point, the T-shaped Aioi Bridge. Captain VanKirk, who had familiarized himself with Hiroshima's landmarks, leaned over Major Ferebee's shoulder and confirmed he was correct. His navigating skills had brought the Enola Gay to its target only a few seconds behind schedule at the conclusion of a six-and-a-half-hour flight.

Oak Ridge Tour Fact: The gates to the city reopened with a parade on March 19, 1949.

WESTCOTT PHOTO #8:
THE GIRL SCOUTS VISIT OAK RIDGE, 1951

In full uniform, neckerchiefs and hats, the Girl Scouts enter what's billed as sacred, but the roads are unpaved, and though it's June, they're muddy from recent rain, the ruts filled with standing water, the ridges gooey. The story ends, they all know, the summer before they started school, the final year August didn't swirl toward apprehension. Their leader, this morning, has related how, during her junior year, the high school closed over Christmas vacation, saying, "Just like that. No warning. Disappeared. Gone." Look, right now they are afraid for their shoes, or worse, the misery of sudden slip. The tour is just beginning, and Miss Spatz would never excuse anyone, not when they have traveled thirteen miles, not after the careful arrangements for permission to examine, first hand, where the world changed. Half of the girls love Frank Sinatra; half have been raised on Hank Williams. Four of them have televisions with snow-plagued channels in their houses, and one has a father who tracks the frequency of A-bomb tests in Nevada, the site remote as Mars. Russians, he's said, know the end-time secrets. For Christmas, her mother gave her dancing lessons; for her birthday, she renewed them like a subscription. When water covers her ankle, she leaps and squeals like science.

Oak Ridge Trivia: After the war, Oak Ridge residents watched a film of its story, "The Beginning or the End?" at the city's own Grove Theater.

One of the brochures I carried home with me features a walking-tour that I followed for more than an hour, the paths pleasantly landscaped. The brochure touts how Oak Ridge's leading-edge technology continues to earn the United States the title of "Super Power."

DUTCH

One version of "Dutch" Van Kirk's obituary ends this way:

> "The plane jumped and made a sound like sheet metal snapping," Mr. Van Kirk told the New York Times on the 50th anniversary of the Hiroshima raid. "Shortly after the second wave, we turned to where we could look out and see the cloud, where the city of Hiroshima had been. I describe it looking like a pot of black, boiling tar."

HANDS: A MEMOIR

MODELING HANDS

My great uncle, for decades, was a hand model. His right hand alone or both of them together displayed in magazines and newspapers. He always took such good care of his hands, my mother said more than once. According to my father, my great-uncle's hands looked as if they had never done a day's work. Like they had never touched anything but themselves.

WORKING HANDS

Five nights a week, my father's hands were white with flour they were dusted with to ease the handling of one pound sections of bread dough and for rolling smaller bits of dough into spheres. Hundreds of times each night, with both hands, he shaped that dough into sandwich buns and Parkerhouse rolls.

CROSSED HANDS

I was five when one of my uncles died from throat cancer. He was thirty-one, a heavy smoker who consumed three packs a day. He was laid out for viewing in a coffin in the living room of my grandfather's house. His hands were folded one over the other just below where his suitcoat was buttoned. Like he was waiting for something.

CHANGED HANDS

During a break in the viewing hours for all of the close relatives to eat lunch in the kitchen, I had to pass through the living room to reach the stairs that led up to the bathroom. With nobody else around, my uncle looked different. Like the body wasn't his. I touched his hands. They felt like the hands on my sister's dolls. My first secret. One I kept.

Praying Hands

Two years before I entered first grade, I started attending Sunday School. The teacher showed us how to make a tepee with our hands when we prayed. Only our fingertips touching. To encourage us, she taught us to flip our hands and thrust our right-hand fingers up between those on our left hands while we chanted a song that went "Here is the church/ There is the steeple/Open the door/And see all the people."

Modeling Hands

"You can't have any broken fingers, no scarring, no moles and no marks," my mother said when she mentioned my great-uncle's hand modeling. "And the fingernails have to be perfect. He's always kept them nice even after he stopped modeling." My father said, "If he let his nails grow longer, his hands would look like a woman's."

Praying Hands

When I was in second grade, my mother said, "You're a big boy now. That's enough of the steeple song. Just press one hand against the other just below your chin when you pray."

Working Hands

Week after week, when I was twelve, "He's Got the Whole World in his Hands" was the Number One song on the radio. The singer sounded as young as I was. The song never identified who "He" was, but even a five-year-old would know it was God.

Both Hands

Boys had to climb hand over hand up thick ropes in seventh grade gym class. Half way to the ceiling, exhausted and struggling, barely inching up, I grew terrified I would fall. "Whatever you do, don't slide down," the gym teacher said, but that's exactly what I did. My hands were fierce with heat. "What did I say? Get that taken care of," the teacher said. Blood seeped from where the skin had broken. "Take a shower first," he added. "That's an order."

Working Hands

That same year, in history class, during our six days with myths, Atlas held all of us in place, using his legs and back. His hands helped to balance the planet, but he looked unhappy in his labor, like a hard-working man underappreciated by his boss.

Changed Hands

After our Boy Scout meeting, David Dorner grabbed me by the arm and held up a section of pipe. "Pretty cool, huh?" he said. I stared at the pipe. It reminded me of sinks and toilets, but I didn't say anything. "If you want to blow something up, all you have to do is light the fuse and boom!" I nodded, but didn't act excited. Dorner went to a different school. He was nobody I had to impress. A few days later, I heard that when he lit the fuse, the pipe blew up in his hand. I wondered what his screaming sounded like. My father said Dorner had lost three fingers. He never came back to Boy Scouts.

Both Hands

My father's cousin had a son who was two years younger than me. Once, when we were playing together, he said he was so tired he had to sit down on the ground. He held his hands against the sides of his head, his mouth falling open like the man in the poster the art teacher had shown us. Like he was screaming to himself.

Crossed Hands

When my Sunday School class was mostly thirteen years old, we were confirmed on Palm Sunday. Before that ceremony, we learned the perfect position to receive the body of Christ, kneeling to lay our open left hand upon the right. We were supplicants and learned the proper way to reach for wine, letting the blood of Christ be passed down to our half-raised hands from the minister's tray of tiny cups. Communion was like pity on the part of God, his charity approaching us with a patronizing snack. A man from the congregation followed the minister with an empty tray so we could return those cups.

Modeling Hands

My mother said, "Your great-uncle wore gloves when working around the house and tried avoid intense cold or heat." When I asked what a hand model was needed for, she said, "To sell watches and sport coats and cuff links and ties."

Working Hands

That year, I started to work in the bakery for a few hours on Friday nights. When I helped with rolling sandwich bun dough, I could only make spheres with my right hand. "Just make circles," my father said, but none of the pieces of dough cupped in my left hand turned into anything but small white turds.

Both Hands

My second cousin, the boy who held his head, had leukemia. After he died, my father told me I was to be a pall bearer. The job was more than lifting the coffin with both hands. "You have to use just one hand to help carry," my father said. I made sure to stand on the side where I could use my right hand to grip a handle. Two of my cousins were older. Another was a man with small children. They took most of the weight of the coffin while I held on and tried not to trip and fall.

Working Hands

"Wash hands after using" was taped above the rust-stained sink beside the terrible bakery basement toilet. Bacteria closed bakeries. They hid inside the near future like failure.

Modeling Hands

My mother had a small scrapbook of clipped ads that featured my great-uncle's hands. Here, she said, are his, and there, too. It was like taking an IQ test. Which of these are identical? Which one of those doesn't belong?

Both Hands

The pall bearers rode to the cemetery in a limousine. My left hand was as soft and unmarked as ever, but a white groove slashed across my right hand. As we rode, the groove darkened to red. When I looked while we stood by the grave, the mark had vanished. Silence shouldered in among us on the way back to the funeral home. No one talked about the inconceivable or any of the other in- words: incomplete, incurable, inconsolable, incensed. As if I'd stolen them from my aunt's black handbag, I kept those words to myself, afraid to spend them.

CROSSED HANDS

A new minister decided that the wafers were to be laid directly on our tongues. Our hands, unoccupied, gripped the railing as we knelt or were clasped for a pose of piety while we waited for wine to sip from the common cup wiped dry after each upraised mouth had altered it. All of us were infants at the rail, our hands used only for balance as we rose, steadying ourselves, returning to the hardwood pews, Christian families with histories, ready to sing the recessional hymn, verses releasing us into weather that waited outside, regardless of communion and prayer, fathers retrieving their cars like valets, their wives and children waiting in the doorways like the wealthy.

WORKING HANDS

Years before, bare-handed, a man who worked for my father had pulled a pan of sandwich buns from the oven without burning himself. My father, some Fridays, would tell that story whenever miracles were mentioned. As if we needed faith, as if that man never again forgot his insulated gloves.

BOTH HANDS

Before sleep, my hands loved the brief pleasure they made, my body remembering the beautiful parts of girls from my invisible place in their lives.

PRAYING HANDS

Except for pretending in church, I gave up praying. In order to be convincing when I lip-synched the familiar prayers, I gripped my hands together in front of my chest.

MODELING HANDS

My mother said that moisturizing was important to my great-uncle. "He used to moisturize a dozen times a day," she said. "About once an hour."

WORKING HANDS

My mother worked in the bakery for twelve hours every Saturday. Just before closing, she scrubbed pans while steam spread around her. Her hands, when she finished, were always red.

BOTH HANDS

"What small hands," a girl told me, "for someone your size," and I pulled them away from where she had been running her fingers over my palms, tracing what she called my life lines. I wondered if she knew what that assessment meant. Every boy in the high school did.

PRAYING HANDS

My mother, for years, had a set of dish towels embroidered with praying hands, the palms pressed together in a way that was unmistakable.

BOTH HANDS

Half of the basketball team could palm the ball with either hand. I didn't even try. I dribbled away when they swung an arm around, the ball firmly in one hand.

THE HUNS OF TIME

There's no escaping the Huns of time, my great-aunt said, or seemed to, her teeth badly fitted. The Huns of time, she said, are never satisfied, no reasoning with them, intending, I thought, to make me see the ways the Huns could invade me. Some afternoons, when I was doing nothing but slouch in front of our small television, I thought I could hear the Huns of time muttering among themselves outside. Some evenings, when the Huns slipped inside, I could tell they'd quit school, that they moved a lot because they couldn't hold jobs. Always, though, the Huns were having fun, more of it, at least, than parents like mine who were punctual as dawn. The Huns of time laughed a lot. They swallowed beer and wine in gulps. Wasn't there always plenty of time? And didn't it return the next day? No wonder the Huns looked so happy. Their families were sure to join them, coming from over the horizon where they pillaged like darkness or light.

BOTH HANDS

I was never able to master using my left hand in basketball, not for dribbling, not even for an uncontested layup.

CHANGED HANDS

During my senior year, there was a student teacher who had a prosthetic hand. Although I never saw him use it, the hand seemed perfectly formed, something like a mannequin's hand, only soft and pliable.

WORKING HANDS

Once I had a driver's license, I began to work in the bakery on Friday nights from ten o'clock to five-thirty. My father left the front door open until after the bars closed at two a.m. Occasionally I waited on men who believed, leaving the two nearby bars, they needed cupcakes or cookies or small pies. Afterwards, before returning to my regular work, I had to go downstairs to the sink and scrub my hands after handling the small bills and change I had to touch.

CHANGED HANDS

I read about a woman born with three fingers who experienced, after amputation, a phantom hand with five fingers. As if those bones had needed years of weather to expose them, an old crime revealed from a life lived long before this one.

WORKING HANDS

Though rare, there were nights when a woman, drunk, would lean across the glass counter, a loose blouse falling open as if she was inviting my hands. My trip downstairs would include private pleasure before I scalded my hands before finishing the work I owed my father. Afterward, I slept until noon, waking to lunch without washing, holding a thick, pressed meat sandwich, stuffing it down my throat because now I wasn't working for anybody but myself.

Both Hands

When, at last, a girl touched my body with her hands, I inhaled so sharply I sounded like someone I didn't know.

Changed Hands

Although rare, there have been cases of men and women who bite off fingers from their own hands. Often, they beg to be restrained. If left alone, they disfigure themselves.

Both Hands

After working in the bakery for five years, I still could not roll sandwich bun dough into spheres with my left hand.

Praying Hands

When my wife learned she was pregnant with our first child, I went with her to the nearest gynecologist. Both of us stared at the half dozen posters of praying hands framed and hung on the waiting room walls. There were pamphlets that explained that the doctor would always save the baby rather than the mother if a choice had to be made in the delivery room. The doctor, when we met him, confirmed that. "My faith guides that decision," he said. That same afternoon we sought out a different doctor.

Working Hands

I learned to type with more than two fingers. My hands sped over the keys except for my little fingers, which refused to work. A magazine article declared the world smaller, the globe shriveling from the cold of technology until it fit in the soft palms of the wealthy. By then I thought that the world wasn't as simple as that. It was more complicated, something worse.

Modeling Hands

My great-uncle lived forty years beyond when he hand-modeled. A few months before he died, he visited with my parents the same evening my wife and our first child were there. His hands were mottled and liver spotted, but they looked to be nearly wrinkle-free. When we shook hands before he left, his hands were soft, even delicate despite his age. As if he had never ceased caressing them with lotions and creams.

Both Hands

My daughter, an artist, teaches anatomy to small children, beginning, each year, with the hands. Her daughter, at six, drew my hands like a camera. At eight, she sketched my face so perfectly I feared that my secrets could be revealed through her accomplished hands.

HEADLIGHTS

1

At twilight, driving Route 8 north of Pittsburgh, my father often refused the headlights, saving, he said, the bulbs. Sixty-five years ago, that road near our house had three lanes, passing a dare on the straight stretches on the way to Butler. Nearly always, the oncoming cars would flash the simple code for anxiety or, more likely, anger, but still he blinded us, intent upon hoarding a few more minutes without headlights and challenging the darkness to prove, by the mile, he could see well enough to drive by passing the brightly lit.

2

My father, if he knew, never mentioned that cars, at first, didn't even have headlights. Maybe it seemed obvious that traffic was sparse, that the roads were terrible and the cars moved slowly and hardly ever, for good reason, at night. But by the time I sat in the two-tone Bel-Air on those trips, the speed limit on Route 8 was 50. Later, when he opted for a two-toned Chevrolet station wagon, the limit was 55 and the road still not widened.

3

A confession—when I began to drive, shortly after the all-beige station wagon replaced the red-and-white one, I was as reluctant to turn on the headlights as my father. Because we had only that one car and both of my parents worked, I didn't have many opportunities, and hardly any of those were at night, so I was a college freshman when, on Route 8, as I passed a slower car at late twilight, an oncoming one pulled into the passing lane, then abruptly swerved back in, its horn blaring. The danger, I discovered, was less my inability to see, it was in being unseen by other drivers. That oncoming car seemed to explode into view so close neither of us would have had a chance without his reflexes saving us. I understood my father's folly. I pledged to be seen clearly and from a distance both day and night.

4

Not for long, of course, were cars without headlights. Common sense demanded them. Automobile headlights fueled by acetylene or oil were introduced in the late 1880s. Acetylene lamps were popular because the flame was resistant to wind and rain. The road was illuminated by fire, an improvement that carried an obvious qualifier. Speeding was self-evidently a poor choice. After dark, the roads, as traffic passed, were torch-lit. From a distance, medieval.

5

Briefly, early in that freshman year, I had a girlfriend who regularly attended a Lutheran church. My parents, lifelong Lutherans, were thrilled. She visited our house twice, both times on a Saturday, and once my parents discovered she sang soprano in a church choir, they seemed so pleased by my good fortune that they never tried my room's closed, but unlocked door. My mother, after dinner, turned up the television volume to better hear Lawrence Welk's champagne music makers, her habit covering the barely suppressed shrieks we made pleasing each other with our urgent hands.

After her second visit, when I parked in the nearby game lands before driving her home, she flicked the headlights of my father's car on, then off, creating, before I opened her blouse, the evening and the morning of the first day. She told me we were alone as Adam and Eve, reciting the passages about births from clay and rib, God's recipes so simple, yet perfect, flicking the lights again as if she wanted God's finger pointing at us. I found her breasts in the dark, secretive as the newly created, in love with the knowledge of her body, saying "yes" to whatever she believed about dirt and bones.

6

What seems crazy is that electric headlights took a while to become widespread. But there were reasons. A big problem was the short life of the glowing filaments. Operating conditions were far less than ideal. Headlamps mounted to the front of the vehicle had problems of surviving any sort of bump, and it was difficult to produce batteries small enough, yet powerful enough to produce sufficient current. The lights, for years, were unreliable.

7

I'd driven for three years before I learned there was a headlight game called Padiddle. A new girlfriend punched my arm as I drove and called out Padiddle. When I said "What?" she explained that a Padiddle was a car with only one working headlight. Whoever called out first got to punch someone. It seemed immature and stupid, but I let it pass every time I felt her body pressing against mine as I drove the newest family station wagon. I was a second-semester college freshman, and she was a high school senior, my "vacation" girlfriend—spring break, a weekend or two, summer. It was nearly ninety miles to where I attended college. and I had no car of my own.

8

In 1912, six years before my father was born, technology had progressed enough that the Cadillac division of General Motors integrated its vehicle's Delco electrical ignition and lighting system. Roads were better, too. Speed increased. Headlights, necessarily, were standard.

9

Sophomore year, another high school girl visited once. It seemed to excite her to be among older boys and drinking beer and walking down a frat-house hallway that resembled the layout of a motel. But she had to be home for Sunday morning Mass. She had to be in her own bed, secretly returning by two a.m. so she could say, if caught, that she'd overstayed a nearby party instead of confessing to riding a bus late Saturday afternoon.

That midnight in February was below-zero-brutal. I borrowed a friend's car. On a two-lane road, halfway back to Pittsburgh, a set of headlights approached us in our lane. "Look at that," I said, and she did, leaning forward as if a few inches provided a better view. Those oncoming headlights didn't leave our lane. I took my foot off the gas, the car slowing until I decided, last second, to swerve into the oncoming lane, almost avoiding the car that caught the right front bumper and spun us to a stop. The driver of the pick-up truck was drunk. His passenger, less drunk, negotiated a settlement that excluded the police. We were a Padiddle car now, some other teenage girl punching her boyfriend as we passed, but I had $80 and a gun. More than that car was worth to give to my friend. A few months later, my roommate and I bought it from him for $50.

10

In 1940, modern sealed beam headlights appeared. My father, twenty-two by then, did not yet own a car, walking everywhere or else riding a streetcar or bus. For seventeen years, the government mandated the seven-inch size of the lamp and stifled innovation, but in 1957 the law changed to allow different size and shape lights as long as they illuminated the road properly.

11

During spring break, twilight settling in as we drove on a familiar two-lane road, that second high school girl said, "Do you ever think about turning the headlights off when it's dark?" She slid closer, her right hand resting on top of mine where it gripped the steering wheel. "Try it," she said, breathing the words. Her breasts pressed against my side, and her breath in my ear made me keep my hands still even as she put more pressure on my hand. The road was empty and dark and straight, exactly the conditions I hoped would last until she started to talk about something that didn't bring the sweat up out of my armpits and palms. "No headlights," she said, "would be such a rush." She put her tongue in my ear, and I stared up the highway until I was convinced she saw a car without its headlights on. "Go ahead. There's nobody coming." I switched the lights off and counted to five before pulling them back on. She sat back against the passenger door, and I thought, for a moment, that she was satisfied.

39

12

By that time, the halogen headlight was popular in Europe. It used bromine surrounding a tungsten filament. It had a much longer filament life and illuminated the road more brightly. Despite that advantage, the tungsten incandescent headlight was still standard in the United States.

13

That girl wasn't satisfied. "Ok," she said. "This time, wait until there's a car close and coming our way. Let's find out how it feels to be invisible in traffic." I checked the speedometer and saw it had slipped to fifty, her voice bringing me under the speed limit. When a set of headlights came over the horizon, she rested her hand on my leg, her fingers kneading the inside of my thigh with so much pressure I nodded, watching the headlights until they looked like they were 100 yards away before I switched my lights off. "Yes, like that," she said when, seconds later, I had the lights on again. But even as her hand slid higher, I stayed soft and she looked at me. "You were afraid," she said. "You didn't get turned on at all." She kept her hand on me as she nearly whispered, "You know what would be really exciting? Driving in the oncoming lane without headlights as a car approached."

14

Four years later, I married. We moved five times in six years. We had three children. The headlights on our cars changed from incandescent to halogen. Nearly fifty years, it had taken, for the technology of headlights to improve in the United States.

15

Every time my family was in the car at twilight, I pointed out the approaching drivers who had not yet turned on their headlights. "Idiot," I would say. "Moron." For a while, when my children were young, they'd call out "Moron" or "Idiot" before I did. As if it were my family's version of Padiddle. When it was so fully dark that there were no more idiots or morons approaching, they would switch to calling out idiot and moron when any car with one headlight appeared.

16

The car we owned just before our sixth move was a Dodge Omni. It was so unreliable that I wasn't surprised when the alternator proved to be defective. The third time it failed, the radio, as always, disappeared first, the halogen headlights dimming as I drove a two-lane rural road. I sped up to a car and tucked in close behind to use its headlights to guide me through what felt, at once, like the middle of nowhere, little or no shoulder on either side. A few miles, I told myself, and I'll be close to something, and then my lights went out entirely. I hugged those taillights, but before long, the Omni's engine stopped running. The car I was tailing pulled away and disappeared. I put the Omni in neutral, but there was no place to drift to that had a shoulder. I coasted just over a slight grade, happy, for a moment, to roll a few more feet on the downslope before surrendering two tires onto a narrow strip of mown weeds that was bordered by a shallow ditch. Then, common sense returning, I tried to guess how likely it was that an approaching car would see mine as it crested the rise and decided "not long enough." I scrambled out the door. I had no flashlight. The moon was a thin crescent and clouds drifted past it. The first car swerved so dramatically that I nearly screamed, but the driver blew his horn and sped away. I hurried to the crest of the hill and prepared to wave. Three sets of headlights, all with the yellowish glow of halogen bulbs, passed before someone stopped.

17

Nobody in our family car called out "Idiot" or "Moron" when a car without its headlights on sped past just as I was pulling out from a stop sign. It was nearly nine-thirty at night. Not a time of year with Daylight Savings Time. Everyone did nothing but breathe.

18

My father, even years after I'd left home, would give "driver advice" when he rode with me. "You should have used your headlights to signal that fellow to slow down because of what we just passed. That fellow, too. You're not listening." What we had passed was a deer or a disabled car parked safely off the highway and abandoned.

I had an uncle who believed in using headlights to communicate with other drivers. One flash—check your headlights; two flashes—check your speed; three flashes—danger ahead. "Too many signals," my father said. "What if one means something different to the other guy." At least half a dozen times, he brought up the moth effect, how drivers can be mesmerized by flashing lights and head in the direction they are looking.

19

After my father turned eighty, I insisted on driving when I visited. The older he became, the less he talked in the car. Especially at night, he scanned the road as if he could make out "problems," his failing eyesight somehow an early warning system. One night, where my father and I were, rain threatened to overwhelm the back road we traveled. A channel opened beside us. For a short stretch, wires were down. The squall smothered my headlights. Pulled over on the shoulder, flashers on, I asked Siri for directions. *Please repeat*, she said, *I do not understand you.* My father, eighty-eight, whispered, "Who is that, someone you know?"

20

By then, LED (light emitting diode) headlights were being talked about. Our next new car, I told my wife, will have them. I was having night-driving issues of my own. They were definitely much brighter, it seemed, a technology advance that might keep me safe for a few more years.

21

The last time I drove my father somewhere at night, he complained about the high beams of an oncoming car. "Thinks he's smart," my father said. "His luck will run out if he keeps high-beaming people."

I could tell by the light that the car had been equipped with LED headlights. "Probably a Lexus, Dad," I said, having read that the newest models of that luxury car were equipped that way.

"So, he's a rich fool?" my father said.

My father was ninety years-old. For several years, I'd allowed every possible argument pass. "Those aren't his brights," I said. "They're called LEDs. Even on low, they're brighter."

"They're dangerous is what they are."

"Maybe so," I said, letting that one pass as well.

22

As I write this, I discover there is another contemporary headlight—HID (high intensity discharge). It uses xenon gas and throws an even brighter, whiter beam than the LED. My father, if he were still alive and squinting at the road to save us from disaster, would be incensed when a car equipped with LID headlights approached. He'd bring up the moth effect again.

23

A short while ago, I pulled off a nearby four-lane highway while my car, including its LED headlights, was running properly. I had time to make sure the shoulder was wide. There are Amish families who live in the area. They drive their buggies along this road, and yet I picked a spot where an open field seemed level enough to take my right-side tires as insurance. When I opened the door, there was plenty of clearance from the highway's nearest lane. Though it was dark and I have reached the age of caution, I did not switch on the flashers.

I had stopped where a boy, bullied at a local school for years, had stepped in front of a speeding truck. The posted speed limit is 55, but most traffic exceeds it. His death was as certain as if he'd leaped from the roof of a high rise, but his method required timing. He had to will his body to move far enough to be crushed and torn and disfigured. Being bullied didn't seem enough to step into that sort of slaughter, the thought which had driven me there even though I understood that I was, at best, a voyeur for doing so.

When there were no headlights in the two oncoming lanes, I walked onto the road and stood in the middle of the inside lane. As a truck and a few cars sped by in the opposite direction, the asphalt felt as if it could trip me somehow if I decided to run to safety. At the first sight of distant, oncoming headlights, I felt foolishly selfish. Whatever my reason for stopping seemed indefensible. Soon, I could tell from the headlights that the approaching vehicle was a truck. I stayed in place, started counting, and reached three before I scrambled over the shoulder and into the field, hearing the truck pass as I stopped. When I turned, a second truck was passing. It did not slow. Shaking, I hurried to my car. Once inside, I saw headlights filling both lanes in the mirror, so much brilliance I held my breath as if expecting to be crushed.

Selected

KICKING ASS

From: *Amp'd: A Father's Backstage Pass* (Michigan State, 2004)

"COULD THESE GUYS KICK ANYMORE ASS? NO!"—GINA, A FAN.

Four women in front of me, four women in back, and every one wears skin-tight leather pants and a black, sleeveless halter-top that says "candy girls" in the same size and font style as the official logo for "Strangers With Candy." The line to get into the club lurches forward, and the words rise and fall, shaped by the size and rhythm of their breasts.

All of them have IDs in their right hands and cigarettes in their left, and all of them look thin and a touch too haggard for women in their 20s. "I'm on the guest list," I say to one of the two women taking six dollars from everybody in the line.

She peeks at her guest list sheet, then looks me up and down, repeating to herself, I imagine, that maybe I'm someone other than a rock band fan because I'm twice the age of nearly everyone who's passed by her this evening. "Name?" she says, and I give it, but without glancing down again, she says, "I don't see it."

I force a smile. I feel an elbow jolt against my back and see all eight of the Candy Girls rush to the front of the stage, arranging themselves two-deep between two burly men who look as if they've just finished a six-month regimen of bench presses and steroids. They all lean forward as if the show has already begun, and then two push themselves up and head toward the bar. "My son plays guitar for Strangers With Candy," I say, imagining him missing notes, distracted by all those ankle-high breasts, and the woman lifts her index finger in the air, setting one of the broadchested men into a walk-with-purpose stride toward us. STAFF, it says on his T-shirt, the letters three times the size of the lettering on "candy girls" but still not crossing his chest. Over his shoulder I see my son step through the door behind the stage, and I wave.

The woman turns, and Aaron gives her a thumbs up. She shrugs like somebody learning from her television that another African country has declared itself free from the ruling military junta. "Ok," she says, dropping her hand. The security guard squints at me, but he turns back to the stage, mingling among the hundred or so fans, mostly male, who, though it's over an hour until Strangers With Candy goes on, are packing themselves together near the stage, drinking fast, smoking, jittery and bouncy. The two Candy Girls push their way through the men, each holding four bottles of Coors Light.

"It's getting crazy since the MTV thing," Aaron had said earlier in the week, "but I can get you into the dressing room before the show, and there's a place to watch from that's out of the crowd."

"What's crazy mean?" I'd said.

"You'll see."

"I LISTEN TO THEIR CD 25 TIMES A DAY AND WATCH THE MTV BATTLE EVERY DAY 5 TIMES A DAY."——CRIMSON, A FAN

The music my son's band plays attracts a mass celebration of controlled violence called moshing. It's not new. Neither is stage-diving. Neither is crowd-surfing. But now it is my son and his music driving the fans of Strangers With Candy to share this odd combination of joy and danger.

By the time Aaron finishes his sound check, the crowd is twenty-deep, packed to the sides of this club where a large banner proclaims COORS LIGHT WELCOMES MTV'S STRANGERS WITH CANDY. On a nearby sign, in smaller letters, is the warning NO MOSHING.

"The NO MOSHING signs are bullshit," Aaron says five minutes later. "They're like NO TRESPASSING signs or NO LOITERING signs. They make people do it. If the bouncers don't do their job, they don't mean anything, and this place looks like it doesn't have enough musclemen to take care of things."

I think of enormous barking dogs or occasional police rounds. I look around and see four huge men wearing STAFF shirts within twenty feet of us, and remember Aaron's excitement the week before.

"The club had seven bouncers," Aaron had said, when I'd called to ask how things had gone in New Jersey. "When we played there last month they had one." MTV was better than yeast, I'd thought. Strangers With Candy had won the title of MTV's Ultimate Cover Band three weeks before, and every place they played had suddenly swollen with fans. "The only thing that sucks," Aaron had said, "is that we'll have to change our name if we get signed. You know, Comedy Central started that stupid show with the same name."

"You have any ideas?" I'd said. "We're making a list. Right now, Driver's in first place." Now I follow him up a short flight of stairs and into an abandoned kitchen that looks as if it could audition for *The Shining II*. Huge, gleaming bowls haphazardly stacked on counters and the floor. Juice machines prone on countertops. Cutting boards, sauce pans, a griddle large enough to fry a small child on, everything strewn as if it had been arranged by the tumbling bodies of drunken fist-fighters.

The door we go through next is unmarked. Behind it are a couple of old couches, a half-dozen chairs, and a countertop on which sit two tubs of ice, one stocked with water bottles, the other with beer. Otherwise, the room is empty. "Pretty nice, huh?" Aaron says, and I shrug, gauging how stale the air is, thinking of my asthma, the inhaler in my pocket. He opens another door and we step into an old railroad car. "You can get through all that crap and check things out through a window," Aaron says. "You'll be right on top of us, but out of reach."

We turn back, and Aaron fishes Yuengling Lagers out of the ice for both of us. The rest of the band files in, and I shake hands. Chris, the drummer, has played with Aaron since they were in tenth grade. I had him in class at the university where I teach. I've met Mark, the bassist, and Nick, the singer, three times before. "This is Tony," Aaron says, and I shake hands with a twenty-two year-old who calls himself DJ Worm and wears, even now, a ball cap with its bill angled, I'm sure, exactly where "cool and current" is located, somewhere between the ordinary of facing front and the worn-out hipness of reversed.

"Water or beer?" Nick says, standing between the ice buckets. "Beer," Tony says. "Water makes me piss too much." "You got a set list?" Nick says to Aaron. "Let's do Korn first," Aaron says. "'Blind' and 'Falling Away from Me,' maybe some Rage, and then some of our shit."

"OH MY FUCKING GOD—WHERE DO I EVEN START? THEY ARE JUST FLAT OUT GORGEOUS."—BUTTERFLY, A FAN

I tell Aaron I want to stay in the crowd for a while. He rolls his eyes. "Go for it," he says. "As long as you know how to get to the safety zone. I'll see you later." On the club's floor a railing splits the long room in half, separating the bar area from the open pit that stretches back fifty feet from the stage. By now the crowd reaches nearly to the end of the bar. Up front, I count a dozen more Candy Girls. The woman at the door, as I work my way past her, shouts to one of the bouncers, "We're running out of wristbands." Just in front of the railing is a space that reminds me of an air pocket, and I slip into it, leaning against the railing to make sure nobody gets behind me. A minute later, the stage lights go up, the spots running through red and blue and back again, everything flashing so rapidly Strangers With Candy looks as if it's arranging itself inside a pinball machine. Aaron machine guns the opening riff to "Blind," and the audience unanimously recognizes it and roars, surging forward, opening five feet of space in front of me as they pack closer to the stage. Aaron repeats the riff again and again, the crowd heaving, and then Nick takes the mike and growls, "Are you ready?" driving what looks to be fifty of the closest fans to bounce and then, a few seconds later, to slam into each other.

Not so bad, I say to myself. The space in front of me fills, but this far back, the modest, early violence doesn't quite reach me. However, it's already so smoky I start to panic about my asthma, and I tell myself five more minutes and I'll work my way to that railroad car. "Blind" ends, and Aaron chimes the opening riff of "Falling Away from Me" as another hundred fans sweep around the railing into the surging crowd. "I want to see all you motherfuckers go crazy," Nick yells, and a few seconds later, when the song explodes, they do, the original fifty and a few dozen more just behind the two rows of Candy Girls slamming into each other, forearms and shoulders fending off other forearms and shoulders, a swirling pit that looks as if it could suck the crew of the *Pequod*, Ishmael included, through the club floor.

I walk past a bouncer who seems remarkably placid and go backstage, through the kitchen, lifting a second beer from the ice bucket and beginning to squeeze myself through hills of trash toward the front of the railroad car.

"There's a lot of shit in the way, so watch out," a voice I recognize says from near a window.

"Hey," I say, and sidestep my way toward where Derek, my other son, is standing with Keri, his girl friend. He's understating. Broken furniture. Unknowable metal fragments. Swaths of insulation. Old banners from previous shows: Bad Hair Day, 40 Lb. Head, UUU. I imagine the Strangers With Candy banner hanging above the heads of the crowd being shoved into the pile by a janitor. I imagine a COORS LIGHT WELCOMES DRIVER sign. I imagine myself tripping on the way back out and being impaled.

"We walked right by you," he says. "You were so into it I didn't have the heart to break the trance. Anyway, Aaron said he was going to put you up here. He knows what happens down there in the pit."

The window of the railroad car sits three feet above the heads of the craziest fans. Keri leans out, taking pictures with a camera I hope comes in a sturdy, crush-proof case. By now the mosh pit has become a tornado of chaos. It looks as if over 100 fans are slamming into each other, and I fix on one man whose eyes glitter unnaturally. He hurls himself against other bodies with ferocity. He punches the air so close to the faces of other moshers I nearly flinch. But I pick him because he's bleeding from a cut above his eye, blinking against the dripping even while he lunges toward the nearest group of frenzied fans as Nick screams a Rage Against the Machine chorus, "Lights out, guerilla radio, turn that shit up."

And then things settle a bit. The band plays its most melodic original and covers a long, complicated Tool song that keeps the moshing to a minimum. Forty minutes later the last song of the first set is Filter's "Hey Man Nice Shot." The crowd, knowing a break is imminent, launch themselves into a frenzy with each extended wail of the chorused title, but when I turn to my son and say, "It's not so bad," he grins.

"This is the wimpy set," he says.

The three of us work our way back to the lounge. Nick and Mark and Aaron are so sweat-soaked they change shirts. Chris opts to go shirtless. When Derek asks Nick to explain the set list strategy to me, he says, "We try to keep it just a little crazy for a while, but the second set is all the heaviest shit. They'll go fucking nuts."

"The bouncers get a workout," I say, and he laughs.

"Fuck, yeah," he says, helping himself to a beer, passing a bottle to everybody who's within arm's reach.

Sitting on the couch, the mosh-pit bleeder is getting attention, a girl in leather and leopard skin holding a compress to his eye. Aaron sees me staring. "This is Butch," he yells, waving me closer. "He's our professional fan."

We're introduced. Butch shrugs and shows me where he's taken stitches above the other eye a few weeks ago. "Three shows in three nights," he says. "There's bound to be damage, but fuck me, my fucking shirt's ruined."

He pulls up his blood-spattered, black Strangers With Candy T-shirt. I wore mine when I watched the MTV show three Saturdays ago, drinking beer and eating nachos with Derek, Keri, my wife, and my friend Tom until the credits rolled up two hours after it began. Butch had worn his black shirt to the taping in New York's Roseland Ballroom. That night, the Strangers With Candy version of "Guerilla Radio" had lasted 45 seconds because of the format of the show, yet the camera had picked up a small, spontaneous mosh pit forming almost immediately. I think of going back to the tape I made and watching those moshers again, looking for Butch. Now, satisfied that the bleeding has stopped and the band-aid is stable, Butch strips off the shirt and pulls on a red Strangers With Candy shirt. "I cut the band's hair," he says and laughs, pulling Nick under his arm. Their haircuts are nearly identical, jagged and short and a sort of glow-in-the-dark blond. Nick sports a new lip piercing, a tongue piercing, something shiny through his nose, but as far as I can tell, in the six weeks since I've last seen him, my son has restricted his piercings to multiple rings through his ears.

"This is John," my son says, and I shake hands with a beefy guy who's shaved his head to cue-ball slickness. He grins. "Aaron's Dad," he says, "good to fucking meet you." Though he's sweating and breathing heavy, he's not bleeding. "Butch is crazy," he says. "I try to exercise a little damage control out there. That's what comes from being a prison guard." He laughs again. "Lackawanna County Jail. You end up there, you look me up."

The people who wander into the room look my way, take in my age, the way I'm dressed, and then return to whatever they're doing. Their behavior tells me how non-threatening I look, so far out of line with anyone else I couldn't possibly be an undercover cop, so ordinarily dressed I couldn't be a record company executive.

Nick smiles when I tell him I remember him fronting a band when he was 15. "I was 14 when I started," he says. "Those guys were in their 40s."

"Like a Hanson brother playing with his father and his friends."

Nick laughs. "It was a fucking hair band," he says. "I had shit way down my back. Those guys were way too fucking old after a while." I go back to my beer. Those guys, like me, are in their 50s now.

A girl with pink hair is holding her side. "The pit's crazy tonight," she says. "The bouncers are sitting on their asses. Nobody's getting tossed."

She weighs, at most, 110. She's drunk, but so are 500 other women in the club, and only a couple of dozen are in the pit.

"We can't get really hurt," she says. "It's like roller derby. You walk away with your shit still together."

Butch lifts her off the ground. "And we always stop to pick you up when you get your ass kicked."

She squirms and mock-punches at him. "The mosh pit rules," she says. "You fall 500 times a night, but the music's so fucking mad good you stop counting."

I settle into one of the couches, figuring the smoke for being less threatening closer to the floor, and a few seconds later three girls with astonishingly similar cleavage flop down beside me, throwing their heads back like pole dancers in a strip club. I consider the chances of my son getting one or more of these girls pregnant, but I skim past that worry to the possibilities of disease. I feel like asking each of them for one of those clean-health IDs some prostitutes carry like a union card. Suddenly, with thighs rubbing against me from either side, I'm turning as paranoid as any typecast father in a 50s juvenile delinquent movie.

Tony barely gets back to the band lounge before the last set is scheduled to start. He grins and launches a fast-talking story full of tight pants and large breasts. "I kept trying to walk away, but my dick kept talking."

"Those chicks are dumb," Nick says. "They kept getting hotter every time they said something stupid." "Dumb's not good enough," Aaron says. "They're real dumb." Tony laughs. "You don't fuck their brains." He points at me. "Hey," he says, "you all seen his ride? Fucking tight. When you going to give me that?" "If you can spell it, you can drive it home," Nick says. Tony hesitates as if he's mulling it over. "I can spell *toy*," he says. "What the fuck is *ota*?" I think of the university parking sticker on my new Celica parked two blocks from the club, how far Tony must have wandered in pursuing the hot, dumb chicks, how easily that car had turned his head. I realize I'm waiting for any one of the three girls on the couch to whimper even the smallest protest.

"Spell Tylenol," Butch tells him. "That and all the fucking beer we can swallow is what keeps us out there rocking." Tony doesn't change shirts. Twenty minutes outside in early March has chilled him down. One of the girls leans forward, flaps her top to create a breeze over her exposed breasts. She's so at ease with the motion I understand I'm the only one in the room who's aroused.

"THESE GUYS ARE THE SHIT."—SYL, A FAN

At the university, earlier in the week, I hosted a visiting writer, a poet. On the way to campus after dinner, I slid the just-released Strangers With Candy CD in. Despite the fact that he was ten years younger than I am, it was so much like playing the music for my father that I turned the volume down. We were back to campus before one song ended. "If it wasn't your son playing, would you be listening to this?" he said.

I shrugged the way I do when the president of the university where I teach asks me, in passing, "How are things?" I've never said anything but "OK" in twenty years, and it didn't please me then to acquiesce to politeness because he was a visiting writer, a peer, someone who writes poems and publishes them in the same journals I do.

I knew what I'd do after his reading—slip in Rage Against the Machine or Tool and turn it up so loud I couldn't hear an ambulance if it was approaching my intersection from a ninety degree angle. The paper would say I was inexplicably broadsided; the autopsy would show no traces of drugs or alcohol in my system.

The truth is I've been driven to the loudest, most aggressive music since I started listening to rock and roll—Little Richard, James Brown, Blue Cheer, Iggy and the Stooges, Korn.

At school I can't say, "I want the music to kick ass." I'm educated, a professional, and every colleague I know talks about classical, jazz, or Broadway musicals. None of those genres fucking rules. None of them brings hysteria and chaos, thousands of people transfixed to physical risk. Truth be told, none of the literary writing I or that visiting poet encourage in our workshop classes will be cranked up to jet-takeoff decibel level. Strangers With Candy is "mad good," not profound.

"I WANT TO FUCK AARON'S BRAINS OUT."—CINDEE, A FAN

Nearly all the women I meet backstage have names like dolls: Tiffany, Kandee, Starr, Angel. Seemingly without exception, they smoke, and every one of them is thin. When I lean out of the railroad car window a few minutes after the second set begins, I verify that smoking and thinness runs through the fifteen rows closest to the stage. Just behind them, the heavier women, most of whom don't light up, bloom here and there as if ChemLawn stopped spraying for weight thirty feet from the stage. A few rows later, there's no distinction among fat and thin, smoker and nonsmoker, and I'm suddenly sure the names change to Sarah and Erica and Stacey.

By now the room looks as if it's gone beyond capacity. Derek and Keri move to the end of the window closest to the stage, and the woman in leather and leopard, standing just below us, yells up that the club ran out of wrist bands at 1000, but let several hundred more people jam inside. Past midnight, yet there's still a line filing past the woman checking IDs at the door. The mid-room railing looks vulnerable. I start to think of famous soccer crowds, fans crushed against restraining fences. The club seethes. It ripples from front to back and side to side. The pit swells to well over a hundred, but the rest bounce and pump their fists. I can find only those four bouncers, all of them by the stage, and none of them seems inclined to wade into the crowd. Their job, apparently, is to protect the band. Everybody else, for tonight, is on their own.

I recognize the opening riff of another Rage song. "Wah, wah, wuppa, wah, wah, wuppa wuppa, wuppa…" Aaron has enough foot pedals on his sound board to take his guitar from bells to jackhammers. Girls are passed across the top of the crowd. One in particular, Asian, wears a black tank top and pants that call up memories of the stylized stripes on Cincinatti Bengals' helmets. "How many times do you think she'll be groped," Derek asks me, and I watch, beginning to count, comparing the numbers of hands on her breasts to those that find themselves high on her thighs.

"As many times as possible," I say.

The Candy Girls don't mosh, but while Butch slams and punches the air, other women throw themselves into the pit, slamming against the men, stumbling and falling. True to Butch's word, the moshers stop each time somebody falls. They lift the prone to their feet and then slam again.

"Bulls on parade," Nick repeats, his voice more hoarse each time over the relentless hook. By now every person in front of the mid-room railing is fist-pumping and screaming along. I'm leaning far out of the window, mouthing the words, head bobbing until the song ends and I say a "Fuck, yes" to myself, a great, silent orgasmic yelp that keeps me fixed on the sweaty shuddering of the nearest women.

Aaron launches the next opening riff, back-to-back Rage, this time "Know Your Enemy." Delivering the vocals, a fusion of rap and roar and melody, Nick looks as if he wants to skewer the complacent on his out thrust, corkscrewing fist. I watch his feet, which seem to sense the last inch of stage he can occupy without tumbling into the turmoil of the pit, and then I concentrate on his staged anger, more convincing, despite his slight build and smooth face, than the theatrics of a professional wrestling villain. The women just below him look as if they'd welcome his hurtling body, ecstatic under the careening weight that would snap them down to the floor.

It's all I can do to notice my son, who's adopted a "look, no hands" sort of showmanship, running through the sound effects and lightning-fast fingerings as if he were strumming rhythm guitar in a folk band. He looks bemused, and the women below him gape with the astonishment of sex-charged school girls who would volunteer to be sawed in half by hands so deft.

"All of which are American dreams," Nick screams over and over, referring to *ignorance*, *brutality*, and *the elite*, among others, and then the song abruptly ends without me even seeing Chris or Mark or Tony.

Suddenly, Butch climbs on stage. Nick introduces him as their "craziest motherfucking fan," and when the band launches into its own song, "Idiot," Butch rocks back a step, then flings himself forward into the crowd.

"Fuck me, I'm fucked up anyway," Nick sings. "Nothing's gonna change me," and the moshers fling themselves into the air, twirling and slamming forearms and shoulders into whoever is closest, roaring the lyrics, Butch swept over the heads of the crowd followed by a girl modestly holding her blouse against her chest as she's flung, legs in the air, from the front to the back of the mosh pit.

One beefy guy, so sweat-soaked his hair sprays the moshers nearest him when he spins, forearms a woman to her knees. When he bends to help her up, he's pushed on top of her in a way that takes the breath out of me. I lean forward, watching, and know I expect serious fondling, that I wouldn't be surprised if his hand ran up her thigh and wedged itself between her legs. And suddenly I understand that if I drifted off and stood by myself, every gesture would turn as sordid as rough-sex pornography.

It slips away, this feeling. The woman, if she believed herself threatened, is laughing it off. "If you start to analyze, you'll have to leave," I hear Derek say. He passes me a beer as if it was penicillin for uneasiness.

Derek turns, and I follow his look to see two women working their way through the trash stacked on either side of the narrow path through the boxcar. Because they're both smoking, I rethink the old insulation, the paper, how a fire would surely kill us all. They climb onto the window ledge and scream at the nearest moshers. They're planning to dive into the crowd, but Keri, still holding her camera, taps one on the shoulder and points to where the wooden ledge is beginning to separate itself from the side of the car. "Fuck," the woman says.

"Shit." She backs down and puts her feet on the floor, still leaning, and screams at the crowd again. Half inch sections of four nails are visible, and her friend, when she finally turns her head, screws her cigarette into the ledge, drops it over the edge, and skids back into the car. "Fuck it," she says. "Thanks."

They disappear through the trash as "Idiot" ends, but a moment later I see the second woman come up behind Aaron and begin to climb the speaker stack beside him. It teeters a bit, but she manages to stand on the top, her feet level with Aaron's head. Six feet plus three feet of stage, I think, the speakers swaying as she pumps both fists. "The roof, the roof, the roof is on fire," Nick begins to growl, and the bouncer underneath the speakers looks up like everyone else as she lifts her arms as Nick screams, "We don't need no water, let the motherfucker burn." She arcs into the crowd, a dozen hands reaching up to catch her, then pass her overhead until she rolls sideways and drops to the floor as feet-first as any house cat.

A steady stream of stage-divers follows, none of them chancing the speakers, thank God. The idea, after all, is to nearly get hurt, not to be crippled. You get talked about as a "crazy motherfucker." You get known among the faithful. You log onto the official Strangers With Candy web site with pen names like Full Metal Jacket and CandyCum and type in messages that proclaim how last night's show "kicked fucking ass" and you would "fuck you guys every day if at all possible."

At 1:20, knowing the last set is half-over, I leave Derek and Keri in the window and make my way to where I'm almost back on the floor, standing at the shallow end of the ramp that leads to the old kitchen, keeping the railing between me and the crowd pressing near the stage.

The railing and the ramp fence off the crowd on my side, the railroad car wall controls the other side, but every time the moshers heave forward, the Candy Girls and twenty other women sprawl from the waist up onto the stage, arms flailing over the monitors. And then they're up again, fist pumping, pogoing until they're hurled, caught at the thighs by the edge of the stage and folded forward.

A half hour of this—Deftones, more Korn—and then Nick announces they're finishing with three Strangers With Candy originals. The crowd recognizes the first one, yelling out the lyrics—"You bore me, now what am I supposed to do?" When the song blows up in the middle, Aaron turning his guitar to chainsaw volume, they launch themselves into attack mode, bodies flying, women flailing to the floor, lifted, then falling again.

The second original calls up more sing-along—"Come to my room, to my bed," and then, when Nick bellows "What do you want?" the moshers slam against each other so ferociously three women and one man lurch to the floor almost simultaneously, the pit breaking into jagged, smaller groups, reforming, swirling, until, finally, at quarter to two, the moshers pause for maybe five seconds while Aaron cranks out the opening riff of "Heave."

Nick roars, "So, get the fuck up," and suddenly the mosh pit is so enormous it swells nearly to the bar, a couple of hundred people caught up in what everybody knows is the last song. Bodies bounce off the railing in front of me. I watch a girl hurl herself, both feet off the floor, against two guys at the base of the ramp. She staggers back, then hurls herself again, screaming a second time, along with Nick, "So, get the fuck up."

There can't be more than five minutes of music left, but the smoke, down on the floor, is tightening my chest, so I go back up the ramp, through the empty kitchen, and lift a beer from the huge ice bucket, nodding at a guy with his feet up on a couch. I slip into the deserted kitchen to listen from the relatively smoke-free zone. "Who the fuck are you?" I hear, and I turn to see that the stranger from the dressing room has followed me.

"Aaron's Dad," I say, and he brightens.

"Really? Fucking great. I'm Chris." He extends his hand and tells me he's the brother of Corey, the band's new manager.

"Part of the entourage," I think, and as soon as "Heave" ends, we hear screaming from out front—"More. More. More."

"Fuck, yeah," Chris says, and the stage lights go dark.

"More. More. More," the crowd yells, and a moment later, we hear the opening riff of "Break Stuff," and the stage lights go white as a Fourth-of-July sparkler. They snap on and off as Aaron repeats the riff. "Check it out from back in here," says Chris, and he leads me through a door that opens onto the back of the stage. We stand and watch, shadowed in that doorway. The girls in front are still leaning forward, pressing hard into the stage as if it was made of foam rubber. They throw their fists at the band, screaming the Limp Bizkit exhortation "Break your fucking face tonight" as if they wanted to bring mayhem and harm to the owner of the nearest suspect expression, parting only when, the song ending, a tower of vodka shots is passed up to the band.

"They're going to get signed," Chris says. A roar goes up as all five band members tip their heads and drink.

"And turn into Driver," I say.

"Strangers. Driver. Whatever. They're off the hook," Chris says.

"THERE ISN'T A GIRL ALIVE WHO WOULDN'T TAKE CANDY FROM THEM."
—SUNSHINE, A FAN

In the lounge, I slump in a chair that has surely been in the room since rockabilly bands performed here. It takes less than a minute for me to disappear into the furniture as if I were Plastic Man, that old comic book character who transformed himself into any object. A group of women who look as if they'd paid a group rate for fake IDs surround the band. One of them is having her red Strangers With Candy shirt signed.

"How dope are these guys?" one of the other women says.

"They kick serious ass," another says. Both of them are wearing identically tight white pants and black tank tops. Both have short, cropped, neon-bright magenta hair.

The girl with the signed shirt twirls for the others. "How dope is that?" she says.

"That fucking rules," one of magenta twins says.

"I can't wait for the middie-shirts to come in," the other says. "Wait until they sign that." I focus on her flat stomach, how it will look bared, the Strangers With Candy shirt cut so short the band will have to sign on the back or else scrawl across her breasts.

"These guys make Wilkes-Barre a cool place to live." "Yeah, Pennsylvania isn't bore-state anymore." Derek and his girlfriend are staying. Neither of them has asthma or fifty-four years to carry. I shake Aaron's hand and nod at the rest of the band. "You guys are good," I say, "real good," as close as I can get to "fucking rule," and then I duck through the stage entrance, fighting the urge to check who might be seeing me as someone made interesting by my access to the stage.

When I step outside, the first thing I hear is "Boring" blasting from the open window of a passing car. It's the first cut on the new CD. Two cars later, I hear "Boring" again, and I wonder how close those CD players are to being in sync, everything about this night so completely "mad good" I open the sun roof of my silver Celica and crank my copy of the CD. It's early March, but I can stand the cold for a few minutes. My ride is so fucking tight I watch women as I roll slowly by them, imagining my age halved, getting laid through the double aphrodisiac of sleek car and kick-ass music.

Six blocks, and then nobody is walking. I roll shut the roof. The CD sounds even louder now, but there's such a ringing in my ears from the show I keep it cranked as if the noise can send my ambivalence into remission. I can listen to the CD three times before I get home. There are miles enough to nearly memorize each song before I crawl into bed at 3:30 and fall asleep to the shrill white noise of tinnitus.

THE CANALS OF MARS

From: *The Canals of Mars* (Michigan State, 2010)

When Mrs. Sowers, during the first week of sixth grade, showed us the canals of Mars, she traced the straight lines of them with the rubber tip of a wooden pointer. "Think of the Erie Canal," she said, holding the stick against the poster-sized map of Mars. "Better yet, think of the Panama and the Suez," she added, starting a list we were to memorize for one week's worth of geography.

"It's very likely," she said, "there were countries on Mars that fought over their technological marvels," and then she named, for our current events lesson, the nations threatening war for the Suez Canal, hissing out the names Nasser and the U.S.S.R., explaining the possible domino effect to the A-bomb.

The map, Mrs. Sowers went on to explain, had been drawn by Percival Lowell, a respected astronomer who had calculated the locations of Martian infrastructure. I believed her because up to that point I'd been relying for my information about Mars on a handful of science fiction movies I'd seen and a comic book Dave Tolley had brought to school the year before.

Through early September, before she brought us up to date on the Suez crisis, Mrs. Sowers ran a series of experiments for science. She demonstrated the water cycle; she wowed us with magnets and electric current that stood our hair on end.

Nature lessons were another matter. We fidgeted through two weeks on Pennsylvania plants. None of us like the taste of the sassafras tea she brewed from a small tree on the hillside behind our school. It was like drinking the chewing gum our parents preferred to the sweet pleasures of Double Bubble and Bazooka.

What my friends and I wanted to know about were killer plants. Venus Fly Traps, for instance, or Pitcher Plants, or most of all, the whereabouts of those wonderfully gigantic man-eaters from the double features we watched on weekends at the Etna Theater.

All those enormous leaves. The suffocating, hair-trigger, relentless vines. Those plants were as dangerous as the giant squids created by atomic tests leaving excess radiation in the ocean. If even one of their million fine-threaded leaves were brushed by careless explorers or women who wandered off from jungle camps against the advice of the guide, the horrible gulping would begin.

After one of those movies, a new Tarzan with Lex Barker, Charles Trout, the smallest boy in our class, was tossed into brambles behind the Etna theater by boys we didn't know because our parents had saved enough money to make down payments on houses rather than stay in Etna, where the steel mill and railroad yard were showing signs of shutting down for good. "See?" my father would say, running his finger over his newly painted bakery. "See what Etna does to white?" And I nodded, thinking I could write my name and the names of all my friends with my finger through the soot.

Charles Trout laughed it off. None of us lived in Etna anymore. We never saw those boys on the streets where we lived. And no matter, we couldn't get enough of those movies. We looked for plants in the neighborhood that might thrive on blood, dropped ants by the hundreds into any flower that grew wild, but never once did one close on the insects. It was as hard to find a carnivorous plant as it was to find quicksand. Apparently, we thought, you had to live in some steamy, forbidding place to watch anything being eaten by flowers.

Mrs. Sowers told us plants couldn't possibly get that large. She said we didn't study the Venus Fly-Trap because there weren't any in Pennsylvania. We were right, though, about one thing—they lived in bogs where other flowers seldom live. Worse, she insisted there weren't any within hundreds of miles of us.

That weekend Dave Tolley and I hiked to every marshy place we could find. It was late September, the weather, we thought, still warm enough for those traps to be working. Now that we had an important clue, we wanted to prove Mrs. Sowers wrong.

Meanwhile, we were glued to *You Asked For It,* where every Sunday on television we could see the impossible come true. Sooner or later, we thought, somebody would write in and ask to see a man-eating plant, but later that fall we settled for a man who could catch a bullet in his teeth.

While Dave Tolley and I watched, a bullet was marked by a witness from the audience so the rest of us would know it had really been fired. The camera, while the bullet was loaded, showed us the audience, all of the studio guests sitting up straight. They looked as if they were holding their breath. Every man was wearing a coat and tie; every woman a dress, and all of them were as old as our parents or older.

Even the man who could catch a bullet in his teeth was wearing a coat and tie as if he were going to church to pray for perfect timing. He furrowed his brow. He squinted. He concentrated. The marksman aimed carefully and fired. Across the studio stage the man was still standing. The camera panned in to show us it was the marked bullet he pulled from between his teeth, and we immediately set out to attempt a sort of beginners' lesson for bullet catching.

In Dave Tolley's refrigerator were bunches of green, seedless grapes. His parents played Canasta on Sundays; they wouldn't be home for hours, and we threw those grapes across the living room at each other, never once catching even a lob toss between our teeth.

There were over a hundred grapes on the carpet. "Either he's a fake," Dave Tolley said, "or we're spastic." I shrugged. We had to pick all those grapes up and wash them, eating enough to make it look as if we were helping his parents rather than using their grapes as ammunition. Twenty grapes into that bowl, we decided to try one more time, and when Dave Tolley, a few minutes later, caught one of my tosses between his teeth, we shut up about impossible and decided that if somebody practiced longer than the ten minutes we'd just spent, maybe it could be done.

After all, Richard Turner, another boy in our class, could already juggle three balls. He'd learned to do it in one afternoon from his father. We thought of four balls, then five; we thought of swords and flaming sticks; we thought of increasing the speed of grapes until we could take on a bullet, how we could perform a feat so incredible nobody would believe it.

Mrs. Sowers, of course, was no help. On Monday morning, when we told her, she said it was a silly thing to try. "Oh, that's just impossible," she said, even though we described the careful ways the program had made sure the whole thing was genuine. She shook her head and started current events, beginning with the Soviets invading Hungary. "For a few days there, the Hungarians thought they were free. Nothing's the way it looks," she said, "when it comes to Communism."

She went on and on about misuse of power, how France and England had invaded Egypt. They equated power with authority, she explained, and everybody in our class wrote it down.

Dave Tolley and I had some authority. We were patrol boys. We directed traffic for a few minutes in the morning and the afternoon. I loved wearing that belt and the crossed white strap that sported the patrol badge. It showed Mrs. Sowers approved, that I was responsible and trustworthy, that even the low-readers from the Locust Grove trailer court had to wait for my signal to cross. The badges we wore were like magic that warded off danger. None of those thuggish boys had ever threatened us.

The Invasion of the Body Snatchers arrived at the Etna Theater. We'd been waiting so long, every boy in our sixth-grade class but Jimmy Mason, who was thirteen and lived in the trailer court, watched it on Saturday afternoon. The Body Snatchers, it seemed, were plants. None of us could figure out how they'd changed the first human victims, but after that, people carried the big seed pods for them, placing the pods near the sleeping who woke up transformed into aliens. Sure enough, all the people in the movie who changed acted like plants. They didn't have emotions. They did anything they were told.

Just like in the Tarzan movies, it seemed scarier to be threatened by plants. You could recognize which animals were threatening. You stayed away from them. But plants? Except for poison ivy and the thorns on berry bushes and roses, there wasn't anything to be afraid of. Trees, bushes, flowers, weeds—if some of them could attack, we'd be out of luck because we were surrounded.

In the middle of November, Mrs. Sowers took Dave Tolley and me aside. "Listen, boys, she said, "I've come across a story you might enjoy. In England, a man came across a large meadow completely covered by sundews."

She looked at us for a moment. "Sundews are carnivorous plants," she said, and both of us started paying attention.

"There were a million plants," Mrs. Sowers said, and all of them, as far as the man could see, had just swallowed butterflies. An enormous flock of them had decided to settle on those flowers, and they had paid for their mistake, millions of them simultaneously eaten in minutes."

Dave Tolley and I nodded like carnival dolls. "Imagine," she said, "a whole field of insect-eating plants." We did, but like everything we wanted to see, the butterfly eaters seemed as far away as Mars.

"And as for *The Invasion of the Body Snatchers*," she said, "and all that big seed pod business, that's the Communists. Did either of you see *The Thing* a few years back? The alien in that movie was a vegetable that drank blood—it was a Communist, too. Korea and Red China—that's what all the to-do was about then. This thing in Egypt might be over for now, and all the Communists have to show for it is a canal nobody can use because it's full of sunken ships and broken bridges."

The last day before Christmas vacation, beginning at lunch, was our party—the gift exchange, games with candy bars as prizes, mothers bringing cookies and potato chips and Coke—but first, Mrs. Sowers said, she had a surprise, flinging her arm toward a man in a dark suit who had materialized in the doorway.

"Who can remember their canals?" Mrs. Sowers said. The stranger smiled while we chorused Panama and Suez, and then pieced together the canals of Pennsylvania, pleasing Mrs. Sowers by conjuring Main Line, Schuylkill, Delaware, Lehigh, and Morris.

The man in the suit, Mrs. Sowers said, had helped build the Pennsylvania Turnpike. That road had been completed, a wonderful success, nothing like that old dream we had studied in September, the Chesapeake and Ohio Canal, which was supposed to come right from the Bay to Pittsburgh and the beginning of the river seven miles from where we were sitting.

It turned out, after we had passed her retest, showing we remembered the long-closed canals of Pennsylvania and the still-open canals of the world, Mrs. Sowers was having that engineer show us a film on the first turnpike in America because part of that road ran through our county. And when Charles Trout, looking at the map of the turnpike, everything else in Pennsylvania blacked out, said it reminded him of the canals of Mars, the engineer told our class those lines on Mars weren't canals at all. Nobody said anything. Nobody looked at Mrs. Sowers. The engineer kept going, telling us those lines were just Martian forests that flourished on either side of the canals, how irrigation would show itself to approaching spacecraft, how growth along our own lengthening turnpike system would tell the monsters coming our way we could think.

So that settled that, we thought. Mrs. Sowers wasn't wrong, but she wasn't infallible. If we knew who to ask, he'd lead us to carnivorous plants; if we talked to an expert, we'd learn to face a one-man firing squad and live to hear the applause. But when she told us, just before the gift exchange, that the troops were withdrawing in the Middle East, we all smiled because the inevitable atomic war had been postponed a while longer.

I gave her a gift-wrapped box my mother said contained a pair of stockings. "Thank you," Mrs. Sowers said, and I nodded, embarrassed, because I hadn't even seen the stockings before my mother wrapped them. Anything could have been in that box, as long as it lay flat, was light, and was less than ten inches long and six inches wide.

Because it was Friday, I got off the bus two miles from my house where a path between the Atlantic station and a car dealership made a short cut to the Locust Grove trailer court. I walked, on Fridays, from the Atlantic station to my father's bakery in Etna. It was a mile, maybe, from that bus stop to the bakery, all of it along heavily-traveled Route 8, but there was a sidewalk most of the way, or parking lots to cut across, and I'd been walking that route once a week since fourth grade, during all that time talking to nobody who got off the bus there except Jimmy Mason after he flunked sixth grade and ended up in my class instead of the junior high school.

My mother worked until six o'clock on Fridays, but on that first official day of winter it was cold and gloomy and already nearly dark at four p.m. Instead of going up the path like he always did, Jimmy Mason fell in beside two older boys I'd never seen. All three of them caught up to me as soon as I crossed the Route 8 bridge where Pine Creek ran under the highway.

Jimmy Mason said the three of them had a job selling Christmas trees in Etna. He cut in front of me and walked backwards, slowing us down. If I had any money, he said, I should buy a tree from them, or better yet, just give the money to them and they wouldn't bother me anymore.

"I don't have any money," I said, telling the truth.

"Not on you," Jimmy Mason said, but the other two boys bumped against me from either side.

"What's that badge for?" the biggest said. "You play cops and robbers at your school?"

"Safety patrol," I said. He turned and put his forearm against my chest, resting it across the badge. I noticed he had a mustache.

"You keep the babies safe?"

I didn't say anything. I already wished I hadn't said a word or had the stupidity to wear that patrol gear outside my winter coat. "Patrol boy," he said. "I want to cross here. Why don't you step out and stop those trucks?"

I cut to the inside, afraid he'd push me into the highway. I kept walking, down to the last section of my trip, a quarter mile of crushed cinders sidewalk, Pine Creek ten feet below us on one side, a hundred-foot cliff running down to the highway on the other.

All three lanes were patch-iced, the traffic one step from where he waved his arms. I could see the stop light where businesses, including my father's, began. My mother would be wrapping bread and sandwich buns. In a few minutes, she'd start looking out the window to see if I was coming.

He snapped the white straps crossed over my red jacket. "Safety patrol," he said. "Pussy." The badge blinked from the early sets of headlights. He pulled on a pair of black leather gloves. "Give me that badge," the boy said, "or I'll beat the shit out of you, patrol boy."

He shoved me toward the guardrail, and I looked down the hillside at the creek I could see moving beneath the thin ice. "Don't move," he said, sticking a blue pen in my face. "Patrol boy, you write this down: 'I died here, December 21,' and then he shoved my arm toward the guardrail that made that pen skip along the metal's white and rust until I stopped where a string of *fuck yous* began.

"More darker," he said, and I went over and over the letters. "So the police," he said, "can read it when your body's found—now walk."

All four of us skidded down a path through the trees that lined the creek bank. Anybody driving a car along Route 8 couldn't see us anymore. On the other side of the creek an identical thick set of scrub trees covered a bank that sloped up and stopped where the leveled slag of the parking lot for National Valve began. Anybody in that factory, even if he was taking the time to stare out a window instead of shaping and cutting pipe, couldn't see us. Only someone overhead in a helicopter or a hot air balloon could have watched what was happening.

"You ever seen it hard, patrol boy?" he said. "You can fight back right now or else you can kneel and suck it." I checked the bank on the other side of Pine Creek for an opening among the trees. For all I knew, nobody worked at National Valve after four o'clock. When he cocked his fist, I stepped into water that ran over my shoes. "Cold?" he asked. "Wet?"

I watched his hands as I backpedaled to knee-high, the ice collapsing under me, and then I turned and slogged to the other side, eleven years old and dying at 4:15, December 21, in Pine Creek, all three of those boys screaming "Safety Patrol" across that ditch of factory run-off as I scrambled to the almost-empty lot where two cars were parked so near the edge, so close together, I thought, before I began to run toward the bakery, one driver was kneeling for another or both of them were waiting to kill me.

The Ass-End of Everything

From: *The Canals of Mars* (Michigan State, 2010)

"I want to find the farm where The Prince fell off the silo," I tell my father as we cross Route 8 and head into territory I haven't visited in nearly thirty years.

"A farm like that won't be there after all this time," he says.

Passing another new housing development, I see the sense of his caution, but I say, "Let's find out."

We drive for almost an hour, taking each of the through roads, looking for where The Prince, my grandfather, lived for nearly fifteen years in a sort of halfway house between a dissolved marriage and the charity home where he spent the last two decades of his life. We cross and then recross the Pennsylvania Turnpike, so I know we're close because I remember my father pointing and saying how that road, just completed, was the first of its kind in the United States. The third time we pass over the Turnpike, I remember the mink farm we drove by just before we arrived. I never saw those minks, but each time my father would announce it—"There's the mink farm"—and I'd stare at the long, low buildings expecting to see women in brand new luxurious coats saunter out the doors.

"Turn up here," my father suddenly says. "This is it, right across from what's left of that orchard. That's where Huggins' Farm was." The sign, when I crest the hill, says Treesdale, which turns out to be a luxury golf course and expensive houses. "My guess is out there somewhere is Huggins' Farm. Maybe a half-dozen of those holes and some of those mansions."

The golf course looks perfect, as if nobody plays on it. As if it were there for scenery from the windows and decks of the half-million dollar houses set back to shank-distance from the fairways. Were he alive, the Prince, skillful with a knife, could have carved miniature sets of clubs from balsa wood or, more profitably, from soap. Those wealthy enough to belong to this club would refuse the wood, but they would buy soap shaped like the head of an oversized driver or the grooved face of a sand wedge.

I slow down, but we keep moving, leaving the fairways behind. "I thought it was Rabold's Farm," I say. "I never heard of Huggins' Farm."

"The Prince lived at Huggins'."

"But we visited Rabold's?"

"Yes. Your mother walked to Huggins'. It was almost next door. The rest of us didn't visit The Prince. I worked for Rabold when I first started in the bakery."

"They had a retarded kid who scared me."

"Down Syndrome," my father says. "So did the Huggins'."

Walking distance. Less than a mile apart, then, those farm houses, and two Down Syndrome boys of nearly the same age. Coincidence? Something in the water? When I ask my father, he says, "Nobody talked about such things in 1950." But it's no wonder I was confused. The Down Syndrome double play is the sort of detail that makes a story implausible. In fiction, I would strike one of those retarded boys. And I would make the Prince worse.

"So I just think we were visiting The Prince. We really weren't?"

"Oh no. Never."

"But he was within walking distance?"

"Well, call it what you want."

It was absurd, of course, that my father, my sister, and I visited one farm so my mother could visit with her father at another. And it was miraculous that The Prince tumbled off the top of a silo and not only lived, but walked away unharmed, relaxed as a cat, according to Aunt Margaret, my mother's oldest sister, by alcohol. "He looked like Little Boy Blue in that haystack," Aunt Margaret would say every time she told that story. "The s-o-b. Only an old stew would live through a fall like that."

He fell in 1950, the same summer my parents took my sister and me with them to visit Bethesda Children's Home, the orphanage overseen by a friend of my parents. We took a tour around the spacious grounds and ended up entering the dining hall when hundreds of children of all ages were sitting down to Sunday dinner. "Children," the Director said. "I have someone to introduce to you. These are the Finckes, Judy and Gary. Welcome them to Bethesda."

The children clapped, but I had just turned five years old and became terrified by the last sentence. *My sister and I were staying!* She waved and smiled like an idiot who was happy to move into Bethesda, and I began to cry, convinced I was about to be led to a seat along the benches.

I took a step forward and turned to plead with the Director just as he extended his hands. "Aren't you feeling well?" he said, leading me up the stairs into daylight. My parents were sitting in chairs talking with the Director's parents. "Did you fall?" my mother said.

"No."

"What's wrong then?"

"Nothing," I said, and I smiled so broadly I could have blossomed into my own version of Down Syndrome, goofy and congenial. I had another year before I started first grade. By that time The Prince was taken in by the St. Barnabas Home, where, at first, he worked for room and board before becoming, like all the other residents, an outright charity case.

My father, earlier in the afternoon, handed me the hospital bill for my birth. "You might want this," he said, and I followed the numbers down the column to the total: $95.96. After deductions for his "subscriber savings," my birth cost him and my mother $15.80.

Remarkable, considering my mother and I both stayed in the hospital for ten days in July 1945. $6.00 a day for my mother. $1.00 per day for me.

So I came cheaply into this world, but I'd been asking my father for information, not about my mother's son, but about her father, and he finally handed me a handwritten letter from July 1920. The volunteer fire company had passed a resolution congratulating my grandfather on the birth of his daughter Ruth and wished to thank him for "the box of cigars presented to the company."

Now I was getting somewhere. Soon I had pictures, newspaper clippings, and a series of anecdotes my father was willing to tell, nearly all of them preceded by the qualification, "I never told your mother this, but…"

Because all of the stories had alcohol in them. Because all of the stories featured waste of some kind—money, jobs, friends, family, respect.

"He made some sort of mistake with the furnace," my father said, explaining how my grandfather lost his job as the high school janitor. "A dangerous one."

I understood the mistake to have risen from alcohol. I understood that without a job, sixteen years after the firemen had congratulated him, my grandfather was lost, eventually becoming a farm hand for room and board, and then, at last, becoming a destitute resident of a charity home. There was no divorce, an action unthinkable to my grandmother, but my mother's family had locked him out of his house for good.

Tracing a family tree is often a leisure time activity like collecting stamps or coins or all the commemorative plates replicating *Gone with the Wind* characters advertised in the Sunday paper. Often, it's a matter of "roots," trying to get at the place and culture of family origin.

Because it's not a matter of all the "begats" of family history, where my ancestors lived, what church they went to, their politics or ethnicity. It's a matter of behavior. It's a matter of values. It's the passing down of fears and ambitions and weaknesses.

A student in one of my writing workshops had told me, the week before, how she'd found a bottle of vodka in every drawer in her father's bedroom. Among underwear, between shirts, under sweaters, even beneath a sheaf of bills saved for income tax deductions.

Another student had begun his memoir with this sentence: "'Matt, make me another fucking drink,'" my father said every time we were home together at night during my senior year in high school." My grandfather, however, never drank in his house. Which is why, my father says, as we drive back to Etna, he lasted as long as he did.

I knew about the private club most often frequented by my grandfather. I knew the DOH ("Doors of Hell," according to my Aunt Margaret) and its bar had survived the sixty years since my grandfather had leaned on it. I'd met a few of the old-timers who still talked over beer and bratwurst there, but nobody was ancient enough to remember specific stories about The Prince first-hand. The best I'd gotten was, "I heard he was a real character." If I wanted to know first-hand what was behind the "doors of hell," I needed, sooner or later, to enter the DOH.

I take us through Etna to the Circle Bar (you could see it from my grandmother's porch), but now it's somebody or other's sports bar, one of those places with two pool tables, a dart board, and dual televisions tuned in to ESPN and ESPN2 below a display of Pittsburgh sports memorabilia and a sign advertising fifteen cent wings during Monday Night Football. Late afternoon on a weekday, it's deserted except for two men simultaneously watching an equestrian competition and a dog show. "You're too late for all this," my father says. "You should have been this interested when your mother was alive."

I look up the street and see Ogrodnik's, the funeral home where my grandmother was laid out more than forty years ago. Nothing else looks familiar, but I let the car idle until my father says, "You want to see what you don't remember?"

I nod, and he tells me to drive down an alley, and there, in the town a few miles north of Pittsburgh where I grew up, is an entire neighborhood I never knew existed. "What's all this?" I say.

"The Prince was a regular at Tomashek's," my father says. "It's down this way."

I remember the name. "Hell itself," Aunt Margaret called it.

"I never told Ruthy this," my father finally says. "After a softball game—The Prince was sitting on the curb outside Tomashek's. My friends asked him to sing. You know, because he was feeling good."

"He was a character by then. I started dating your mother just after that. I never went back to Tomashek's."

I understand this story illustrates public humiliation, but my father simply relates it and then tells me to turn into an alley of decrepit houses. He shows me three houses from his Meals-on-Wheels route, one where a man has just lost a leg to diabetes. When we turn into the last street, the freeway bypass looms over our heads.

Miraculously, the field my father played semi-pro football on is still here, level and hard-packed. "Millvale, Arsenal—the fields were used so much and baked so hard that the grass only grew over by the sidelines," my father says. "You knew you'd played a game when you came off a field like that."

I stop and get out. My father sits in the car. Well past eighty years old, he's grown as small as The Prince sitting on his bed in the St. Barnabas charity home.

"You go on," he says, meaning for me to believe he isn't going to follow. I walk, listening for the click of the car door latch, and when I hear it, I make myself keep walking so he can get out in his own good time.

I don't have to look back to know how he puts his hands to both sides, how he swings both legs outside and then pushes off slowly with his arms, gritting his teeth until the short, tight lift of his head means the pain is running through the bone-on-bone contact in his knees.

It's level here. After a few breaths to settle things down, he's able to shuffle. I give him a minute, and he manages twenty feet or so, far enough that, when I turn, he can stop as if he's decided that patch of packed earth is the perfect spot, right there, along the third base line. He can look around as well from there as I can from the outfield.

I stare up at the bypass from underneath, remembering when traffic backed up the entire six miles to Pittsburgh during rush hour because tens of thousands of people who worked in the city had moved to its northern suburbs after World War II. By the time this bypass had been built, Etna, a small, steel-mill town, was a bottleneck. A year after the new highway was opened, Etna was a town without a steel mill that people passed rather than visited.

Tomashek's, when we finally reach it, is closed, its beer and whiskey signs replaced by boarded windows and a padlocked door. The building is three times larger than the ones that house the other local bars. That size would doom any sort of reopening in this decaying neighborhood.

"My football coach got himself killed in there," my father says. "Drinking and money."

I look again at the shut-down building and the deserted street. "Fats Skertich. He made a bet and there were words spoken about paying.

Fats slapped a man, and that man went home, got a gun, came back, and killed him right there in Tomashek's." My father stares at the door as if he expects to see Fats Skertich walk out with his arm over the shoulders of The Prince. "A baseball bet. It was summer."

"Fats Skertich was a man you listened to," my father says, and then he adds, "You know, I always thought there were reasons The Prince had problems. A man gets married and moves into his wife's house. It's a hard thing. He and your grandmother sleeping in a room between her parents and her brothers, all four of them still there when they were starting out."

I remember the layout of the rooms in that house, how there were doors that connected those bedrooms, how you'd have to lock them if you wanted privacy. Or leave them unlocked as a sign of trust.

"The Prince fixed things around the house. All those men lived there, and none of them could fix anything but The Prince. Right up to the end there were still two brothers and the father plus his own five children, all old enough to have a mind of their own. The house was never his."

I drive us through Etna, past the long-closed steel mill, across the railroad tracks. "The Prince went out to Huggins' Farm before the war," my father says as we reach the block where his bakery had stood. He stares at each building as if he expects to see someone he knows standing in a doorway. "You might want to know this, too," he says. "When the war started, I didn't want to go in the service. I had deferments for a year— married, a baker, and then they just needed too many to not call me up."

I turn down the alley that I remember curling behind the bakery. Large patches of its bricks are missing; a chunk of concrete, displaced from an abandoned garage, sits so far into the alley I have to squeeze by it. Weeds that have grown door handle-high scrape against the car as I creep past them. When a section of newspaper, caught among a patch of thistle, flutters open, I expect to see headlines about Kennedy's assassination.

"I went down there with Al Kopniski, who played football with me," my father keeps on. "He went through the line and passed. I got taken aside because of this bum ear. We didn't talk about it. Al went and I didn't. And then he didn't make it back. So neither would've I. And then where would we be?"

It's been a mistake to drive my father here, I think. It's like his high

76

school reunion gone bad—classmates unchanged, just older and uglier and bunching up in the same way they had nearly seventy years ago.

Behind where the bakery had stood, I stop and let the car idle. "It's the same," my father says, "only worse."

He's right, I think. Except for the bakery being leveled, the area looks untouched by the last thirty years. "You can see the ass-end of everything from here, that's for sure," my father says. "Your mother hated to even park back here."

The shale hillside seems dotted with the same sparse sumac and burdock that grew there when I was a child. What I remember is the summer before second grade and the first time I left the sidewalk in front of the bakery where I was supposed to stay "no matter what" while my mother worked inside. I'd been trying to sell paper for a penny a sheet from my Rainbow Pad tablet in front of Miller's Tavern. For fifteen minutes, nobody passing by gave in to my simple sales pitch of "One-cent paper here." Then, instead of walking back to the bakery along the sidewalk, I took the path over the hill beside Miller's, ending up where the back door opened into the alley beside the railroad tracks.

From the rear, the six buildings between Miller's and the bakery appeared to be in danger of tumbling backwards down the hill. A train heading toward Pittsburgh looked enormous hurtling on the downgrade arm's length from where I stood staring at it. As soon as it passed, I noticed the dogs, two of them emerging from under the loading dock behind Hoburg's Hardware.

I started to backpedal toward the bakery, and when they snarled and began trotting toward me, I clutched my tablet, turned, and ran, one of those dogs catching the cuff of my pants, tugging me sideways toward the tracks until my mother, who hated pets of any kind, swept down the shale hillside with the stiff-bristled brush she'd been using on baking pans. "Go to hell," she screamed, and those dogs retreated to the tracks where I thought hell would find them if they didn't watch out. And then I closed my eyes, waiting for my mother to use that brush on me because I wasn't allowed where you could see the ass-end of everything.

"This isn't about The Prince anymore," I say, "but that's ok."

My father shakes his head. "The Prince always came up this way," my father says. "Afterwards, you know. When he hitched a ride to town from the farm. He'd slip out the back door of Miller's down there at the end of the block so nobody would see he'd been having a few, and then he'd come down the alley here and up between the bakery and the beauty parlor."

I nod, remembering the narrow passage between the buildings, just wide enough to walk through without turning my shoulders. "The Prince would slip through there, then turn the corner fast and open the bake shop door to get inside. He thought he was fooling somebody."

I back up and work the car slowly down the alley toward what's now Huntz's Tavern. Though Hoburg's is long gone, the loading dock, rusted and cracked, still stands, and I look in the shadows beneath it for the descendants of those snarling dogs. My mother had simply told me not to cry. She'd sat me on a folding chair and told me to settle down while she finished scrubbing. After a few minutes, she said, "Did you learn something just now?"

After I pull out onto the highway that takes us back to his house, my father says, "Like I was telling you, the Prince was handy with his hands. Let me see if I can find what I'm thinking of when we get to the house, and I'll show you something. It should only take me a second."

I sit in the living room while he's gone for a second and then a hundred more. I hear him rooting through the closet in my sister's old bedroom. When he reappears, he carries an old Gimbel's box. "Look at these," he says, and he dumps a dozen pairs of wooden pliers on the table, each set slightly larger than the next until one sits full-size. I open and shut three of them. Each works as if oiled, and I try to figure the method my grandfather used to create a hinge in one piece of wood.

"I've never taken a drink," my father says. "You know that." I pinch one of the smaller sets between the claws of the largest, lifting it, waiting. "I was afraid," he goes on, "I wouldn't be able to stop."

"The Prince wasn't your father," I say. I lay the small set of pliers back on the table before I open the claws.

"Take one if you want it," my father says. As soon as I pick up one of the smaller ones, he gathers the rest, returns them to the box, and closes the lid. "Good," he says, carrying the box down the hall, closing the door to my sister's room, returning that box to wherever he wants it to sit until he dies.

The Handmade Court

From: *The Canals of Mars* (Michigan State, 2010)

Building a tennis court was a dream I shared with my father. Constructing it ourselves was his dream alone. But it seemed so easy standing beside him in the middle of June near the edge of the twenty acres of land he'd just bought as an investment in his distant retirement that I estimated the end of July, August tops, and the two of us would be spinning out lime along the boundaries, getting things ready for play. He had me captive, because tennis was all I had wanted to do since May when I'd reached the quarter-finals of the biggest junior tournament in Pittsburgh, my rocket-flat serve and forehand good enough to be successful in the 15-and-unders, even against the kids nearly two years older, the ones lucky enough to have birthdays a month or two after the cut-off date of October 1.

The nearest house was a hundred yards away up a dirt road, and my father said there weren't any zoning ordinances that discouraged using your land any way you pleased. "Look at all that clay," he said, and I agreed it looked like we could hold the just-finished French Open right there on our new property if they had postponed it until September. "And this place is nearly level to begin with. We just push this bank over to there, fill in this low spot here, roll it, get some fence, and we're in business."

"All right!" I blurted. I was willing to give up a month of weekends to shovels and wheelbarrows and the heavy, water-filled roller that the residents who rented that nearest house allowed us to store in their garage. This was going to be country club stuff: a clay court, privacy, hours of play without some jerks wearing street shoes telling me and my friends to "get the fuck off the court," meaning any of the only three public courts in Shaler Township in 1959.

Three weeks earlier, my first time in a tournament, I was dressed in plaid swimming trunks and the same white t-shirt I wore under dress shirts on Sunday morning. Up until that Saturday I'd never worn shorts to play tennis because I didn't own any. I played in old black chinos faded to near-white at the knees, mostly with my father, who wore his green work pants to the pay-by-the-hour county courts ten miles from where we lived.

I wore a pair of black high-top tennis shoes, and the first morning at the tournament I learned that "tennis shoes" was a figurative expression. I wasn't allowed on the clay courts where the youngest entries were being shuttled, so I had to wait (and so did my angry opponent) for a default on one of the hard courts for us to play. Tennis shoes, I was told by the tournament director, had flat soles. They were low cut and lighter, and they weren't black like my Keds.

I had two tennis rackets at least, the ones my father and mother used. They were right off the discount store counter, pre-strung with string so cheap it shredded into what looked like unraveling cardboard. No one else in the Pittsburgh Metropolitan Tennis Tournament wore shorts that weren't white.

Where I played tennis with my friends, there were nets with holes so large they resembled the webs torn by the struggles of victims captured by giant spiders in the movies I watched on late night television. Men in blue jeans who used the same skinhead balls all summer would lean on those nets to swill beer after thirty minutes of loping around bare-chested. By the end of May, even if the park service repaired the worst holes in April before they put the nets back up after a winter in some storage garage, the net strings would tear away from the tape that ran across the top so you might, every once in a while, skid a shot through a hole without fluttering a bit of cord. If your opponent wasn't paying attention, the point continued.

For placing legitimate shots, however, cross-court was best. Although there were times we found the net pulled straight across by men who thought it needed to be the same level from side to side, it always sagged, when we lowered it, into a sad, shallow U because there was no center strap to adjust for tension.

The second day of that tournament, I added a cardigan sweater that was a cheap knock off of what Perry Como wore on television every Saturday. It had red and blue cuffs and a similar stripe where it buttoned up the front. I'd noticed that the better players had v-neck sweaters; they had racket covers and strings that were gold or clear. And their rackets said Wilson and Bancroft rather than Best Craft like mine, the least of my worries, because when I laid my mother's racket on the ground by the net post, it wobbled slightly from being warped. Worse, one of the strings was broken and tied off, how my father saved a few dollars, waiting until at least three strings broke before he took the rackets to the Honus Wagner store in Pittsburgh where they were replaced with those same woven-nylon shredders.

The second time my opponent served he looped a short, under-handed shot into the service box that I caught on the second hop. I thought he'd lost track of the score and was slapping the ball my way until he moved to the other side of the court to serve. During the next game, standing six feet behind the baseline, I caught a ball still in the air like I always did so I wouldn't have to chase it. "My point," my opponent said, and he walked so casually to receive my next serve that I was sure he was right.

"Don't be discouraged, son. He's seeded #4," the man who collected the used balls said from outside the fence. I didn't say anything. I didn't know what "seeded" meant. Ten minutes later, when that boy sprained his ankle, I took my default win and moved on. My mother, when I got home, presented me with a pair of white tennis shorts and a shirt with a collar to wear the following day.

I won that match, too, defeating a boy who was as unseeded as I was. He threw his racket over the fence four times during the match. His mother retrieved it each time. When we finished, he dragged his v-neck sweater by one sleeve, sweeping a path from the net post to the gate.

Fourth of July weekend, a couple of days before my fourteenth birthday, I found myself starting the first work I'd ever done that amounted to anything other than earning an extra dessert or the dollar-an-hour I received for greasing pans. As soon as I filled one wheelbarrow and hauled the clay to be dumped, I was sweating. In half an hour I had blisters, and there was no sign of an ice-cream break.

My father's new property was farther from our house than the county courts. Once we'd taken the forty-five minutes to drive there, my father was committed to a full day of work. After another half hour of digging and dumping, the only antidote to pain was planning lines I could use on girls when the muscles that would surely come from the hardest work I'd ever done bulged and rippled beside every swimming pool I could get myself invited to. I had reason for my hope. I'd just been invited by Janet Cook, who lived near Mt. Royal Boulevard, to a semi-formal dance at the club her parents belonged to.

Another half hour passed before I nearly speared myself as my shovel struck rock. "Dammit," I said, and my father spun around with his shovel loaded. I ducked, thinking I was eating a face-full for swearing. "Sorry, Dad," I said, when the dirt stayed put.

"What's the problem?" my father asked, so tolerant that I turned nervous.

"It's like there's a road under here, a big rock or something."

"Work around it. Find the edge and pry it out. Nobody said there wouldn't be any rocks. You can't expect everything to be simple."

I poked around with the shovel blade, and when I'd measured the perimeter of the rock, I understood that we were not going to finish this court in time to help my chances in the 15s. "Dad," I said, "it's four feet across; it's twice that around."

My father stood staring at me, performing a quick mental assessment of the personification of his genes. He didn't look like he was enjoying the evaluation. "You work over here, if that's what you want," he finally said. "No boulders over here. No mountains."

"Really," I said, "there's no moving this thing."

"There's always moving. It doesn't go down forever like a hole to China."

"You'll see."

"Over here, then. Over here so you can at least be shoveling while I get the Himalayas out of your way."

I didn't back off very far. This was an opportunity to rest for a minute. My father was about to recognize that this project was a disaster. He'd cancel the remainder of the work order before he'd remember to complain about me standing around. "Looks as if you're going to learn what real work is," my father observed after he'd probed long enough to make it look like he'd done the measuring. "Get the pick from the garage."

I was in the quarter-finals. This boy was seeded #2, but by now the strings on my father's racket were frayed so badly it looked, from a distance, as if there was a hole in the middle. During the last game of the first set three strings broke during one point, my last forehand slingshotting over my opponent's head as if I'd imagined him Goliath. I picked up my mother's racket, my ready-made excuse for losing in the one-sided fashion you might expect if you used a lightweight racket that was warped and missing a string.

The truth is I would have lost even with a Wilson Jack Kramer Autograph Model in my hand. I had a fast, flat first serve and a forehand I hit harder than any boy my age. But I ran around every shot to avoid my backhand, and then dashed back to a makeshift middle I created five feet to the left of center. It was easier to sprint to wide forehands than to run around backhands, and my opponent had made certain I was doing both on every point.

The other boy's father, sympathetic perhaps, took me aside to explain that I was using what was called a playground grip, the same grip my father used. I could only slice a backhand. If I tried to hit a backhand hard, the ball traveled directly into the bottom of the net. "You get yourself some lessons," the man said. "Learn how to play the game."

It was the same summer one of my father's brothers took me aside after church and said it was time I stopped tying my tie in a "nigger knot" like my father did if I was going to a semi-formal dance at the private tennis and swimming pool club where Janet Cook's parents and their friends had two well-kept courts for themselves. He stood me in front of a mirror in the men's room and had me master the Full Windsor. "There," he said, and he left the rest to my memory without saying a word about the origin of the name of the knot I vowed never to tie again, the same technique he'd used a few years earlier when he'd taught me to play chess. "You think you're ready?" he'd said, and when I nodded and moved my first pawn, he proceeded to checkmate me in four moves. "That's called the fool's gambit, Gary," he'd said. "You remember that the next time you think you know something."

I walked into that dance with confidence in my tie, but I didn't need my uncle to explain to me that I was badly dressed when none of the boys was wearing a sport coat like the one I'd gotten that week. "Just like new," my father had said, but my cousin had worn it for the past two years, and before that his older brother had worn it for three more.

It didn't matter that it was a good fit. The difference between being new in 1954 and 1959, from lapel width to pattern design, was clear.

Walking away from my struggling father, I maintained a steady cadence up the lane toward the garage by telling myself it was worth it having to split stone like I was on a chain gang just so I didn't have to hear again how stupid I was for claiming the rock unmovable. Nevertheless, I took as long as possible finding the pick. I wasn't in a hurry to swing anything that had the feel of the John Henry legend about it.

I lugged the pick back down the lane. The head of it looked to me like it had been forged in the 19th century and dragged across Pennsylvania while its owner had to scour the countryside for Indians. Though it was the only pick I'd ever handled, I was suddenly sure my father owned something from the Iron Age. I carted it across the clay to the monstrous rock, and before my father could start instructing, took what I thought was the correct stance, swinging the ancient tool up over my head the way I'd seen it being done in all those *Boy's Life* features on diligence and fortitude.

The heavy head slid down the shaft and split open two of my fingers. "Dammit, shit!" I yelled.

"Being ignorant doesn't mean you have to be stupid," my father said. "You ought to count yourself lucky you had one hand up so high, or you'd need more than swearing to cure you. You break your hand and there's no point in us finishing this thing here."

"I'm hopeless," I said. "I'm too dumb to live."

"Sarcasm doesn't help anybody."

"I need leg irons. I need a striped suit and one of those beanies."

"You go for a walk," he said. "You get your head clear while I take care of this." And I did, walking to where the people who lived in that nearest house were watching television on their porch. As soon as I paused to look over their shoulders, they invited me to sit down. The Pirates were on. I watched five innings while my father swung that pick against rock.

My next tournament, in early July, was entirely on clay courts, but by then I had real tennis shoes. Like the big tournament in May, it was held in an area of Pittsburgh where the streets were shaded and the yards were professionally landscaped. The mothers who sat along the fences were dressed in stylish skirts and blouses, and all of them wore sunglasses. The fathers who watched all wore dress shirts and ties, their suit coats left on hangers that were hooked to the inside of their cars.

By now I had a knit shirt with a collar to wear and a Bancroft tennis racket (with lousy spiral-nylon strings because my mother had bought it pre-strung). My father, foregoing sleep before his night shift in the bakery, stood throughout the two matches I played before I lost in the round of 16 to an unseeded player, double-faulting fifteen times because I was trying to serve with the proper grip. Both days my father wore a white T-shirt and his dark green work pants. Those courts were so perfect that when I saw a set of small green leaves pushing up through the clay at the base of the fence, I bent down and uprooted them.

The next weekend my father and I worked on the court, we discovered another stone stretched out like the continental shelf. I decided to give logic a try: "I say we give this up," I repeated three times, hoping that the tumblers in my father's brain would fall. I saw that the summer was going to disappear while we slaved in this rock garden. The weekend's late afternoons, when I should be perfecting the shots that would bring me trophies, were going to repeat themselves as times for physical exhaustion.

"We did one giant, we can do two," my father added, using an inaccurate personal pronoun.

I didn't see the proof for his syllogism. "The first one's still in the way," I pointed out.

"It's almost done," he said. "It's a day's work now."

I estimated how many times we'd have to split the newest discovery in order to size the pieces for carrying. "You keep at it with the shovel," my father ordered. "I'll work the pick. An extra weekend or two is all. You'll see."

My mother was the one who drove me to the next tournament because its starting times were in the morning and early afternoons on weekdays. Even at ten a.m., though, there were fathers in ties at the courts. What did they do, I wondered, that let them sit charting shots at every tournament?

My mother had sunglasses at least. She brought a folding lawn chair because, she explained, she knew how long these matches could take. But after one round I drew the #1 seed, and even with half as many double faults as I'd had in the previous tournament, I won three games altogether. "He's a year older," my mother consoled me. "He'll have to play with the older boys next year."

I shook my head. There was only one more tournament before school started, and it was played at a country club my mother had described as "snooty." It didn't matter. I lost in the first round to the best player in the 13 and unders, a skinny boy who was playing the 15s, his mother told mine, "for the experience."

By the third week of August the tennis court project was a shambles of strewn rock from seventeen boulders we'd found. On the next-to-last summer weekend, I stood among them, not one trophy in hand for my first year in the 15s, and I was thinking about how useless my work had been, how flat and unstable my ground strokes still were, how every court but the ones I practiced on had nets that rose, as they should, six inches higher on each side.

The stunted beginning of a stone wall ran along one side of the court. "It will get high enough we won't even need fence on that side," my father explained. "People can sit on it while they're waiting to play. Your friends, if they have a mind to come out this far for a day of tennis."

"Nobody wants to sit on a bunch of stones, Dad," I said.

"They do it all the time. In parks. On hikes."

"In old clothes they don't care about."

"You play tennis in a suit?"

"White shorts, Dad. Think about it."

"I'll sit on it then. Your friends from the swim club can stand. They can make sure they don't sweat, too."

My mother, after I told her I wouldn't go anywhere ever again in my lousy hand-me-down sport coat, said, "Only if it doesn't fit."

Because our church wasn't air conditioned and there hadn't been another dance, I hadn't worn the coat in over a month. I put it on and concentrated on the sleeves, extending my arms to give them every chance of being too long.

"They're ok," she said, but she tugged the fat lapels together and frowned. "It's tight in the chest," she said. "You'll look silly in this before you know it."

I inhaled before she could let go of the material. "Ok," she said, "but don't tell your father. It'll be our little secret until the weather turns cooler. All that digging in the dirt must be doing you some good."

Over Labor Day weekend I watched my father loop a chain around one of the thirty leftover fragments from the biggest stones we'd found, a mid-size one that was going to be a test. I followed his face while he worked, noticing how his jaw jerked, how his lips and teeth told secrets

87

about self-absorption. Each time my father yanked at the chain, the stone heaved and slid a few inches. It could have been the cornerstone for a pyramid. "See," he said. "Just a little bending of the back is all it takes. Just some elbow grease."

It took my father five minutes to stop and start his way thirty feet to where the stones stretched along the lane. I watched him walk backwards and tug, walk forwards and pull, horse-like, and I grew certain that I wouldn't be able to shift one of those stones more than the length of my body, that my father was going to be forced to remove every one of them unless he expected me to kneel and push each boulder from behind while he was dragging it with the chain.

During the first week in ninth grade geography, we studied farming practices, how different cultures worked to prevent erosion, and as I looked at the pictures of ruined crop lands, I could see how the tennis court was going to wash away with each rain because water poured over the bank we'd cut and the knobbed end of another huge stone we'd exposed, a delta of small channels branching into where a service court would be.

I knew I needed a backhand, too, and a second serve that had enough spin so I could accomplish something besides pushing it into play next year and having kids who understood plane geometry smash it back past me for winners.

"See?" my father said the next weekend, pointing to how only a half-dozen stones were left on the court surface. "You see how things get done?"

"Sure," I agreed.

"And see how high that wall's gotten? A fence would be a waste there."

"I don't know, Dad."

"How many balls you miss-hit high off to the side like that? Two, three, a match?"

"Something like that. Maybe more. It depends."

"You're fourteen already. Maybe next year you won't miss-hit more than one or two balls a match. Maybe none."

There were networks of furrows from the dragged stones. My father saw me looking at them. "You get to them with the roller and it's good as new."

"Yeah."

"We're playing here in two weeks. We don't have to wait until everything's perfect for that. It's not a country club we're building here."

I calculated how much of an advantage it would be to serve toward the end where the water was eating at where the service court would be. My father jerked at the chain he'd wrapped around one of the last boulders. Somewhere in one of the trees across the lane there were squirrels I couldn't see scrabbling along branches, but my father was straining so close to where I stood that I started to count his steps. He stopped and started twenty-three times before he worried the rock to the wall, never taking more than three choppy steps on any lunge.

THE FACES OF CHRIST

From: *The Canals of Mars* (Michigan State, 2010)

I sat in the audience, once, while a professor explained the Shroud of Turin to a hundred senior citizens. He had slides and sources. He waved a wand of light to trace the face of Jesus in case someone didn't see it. "Look," he said, "the eyes, the curve of lips exactly the same as in the pictures you know of Christ."

He ran overtime with the possibilities of belief. Except for the professor and me, there wasn't a person in the room under sixty, and I was betting myself that very few of them would stay for the second half of the program, a poetry reading I was giving to publicize my latest book, *Inventing Angels*.

That week a patient had discovered the face of Christ in the grain of a hospital door, and the citizens of a nearby town had witnessed Jesus on the side of their municipal water tower. People gathered, some of them joyful, some of them apprehensive about the inevitable skeptics.

Those aren't the only sightings. Certainly, they're not the oddest. For instance, Mrs. Edward Rubio, in 1979, in New Mexico, discovered the face of Christ seared into a burrito she was cooking for her husband. She enshrined it in a room in her house—flowers, votive candles—and worshippers and the simply curious came from all over to look long and hard at that burrito.

If my parents had lived in New Mexico then, they would have come to see that miracle on any day but a Sunday, something that explains why the first movie I ever saw on a Sunday was *El Cid*. I was nearly sixteen years old. My friends were going, and some of them had convinced me this was a movie not to be missed. My mother, when the car pulled into the driveway, told me she was disappointed; my father refused to speak to me.

I was uncertain then, and still am, about the logic of such belief. All the way until her death, I had always understood my grandmother's disapproval. She refrained from card playing and restaurants as well as movies on Sundays, but my parents played Canasta without a care and ate out every other Sunday after church. They had no difficulty watching television, which showed films of its own to their approval, so I'm left with the image of Charlton Heston as the dying Cid propped on his horse to lead his inspired men to victory and the sense that I took one step closer to damnation because I sat in a Pittsburgh theater on a Sunday afternoon.

Our family, in the years preceding my defiance, went regularly to the movies on Saturday night. There's hardly a film from the 1950s I don't vaguely or vividly recall. We saw whatever films happened to be showing in Butler or East Liberty, depending on whether we went north or south. If there was a choice, my parents opted for Biblical epics, costume dramas, westerns, musicals, or comedies. What I missed, I've discovered, were B-movie thrillers and film noir dramas. If I saw them at all, I saw them on Friday nights with my Great Uncle Bill, who didn't even know what was playing at the Etna Theater, except it was Friday and seven p.m., so off we went, walking in mid-feature, or near its end, no matter, because we just waited it out to watch until the story returned to the point where we'd come in. For years, I thought this was how everyone went to the movies, knowing the endings before the beginnings. For *El Cid*, my friends and I were seated during a set of previews. I didn't know about the Cid's heroics until the final fifteen minutes.

Certainly, I didn't know there were film critics, production budgets, or films in foreign languages, but I knew movies on Sundays were sinful, and I knew a film that showed the face of Christ was blasphemous. After the first one we saw of these, my father had had enough. He started reading about movies to insure it wouldn't happen again.

The movie that changed our viewing habits was called *Day of Triumph*. For the first time, the actor playing Jesus turned to face us instead of looking at crowds of disciples and followers who gazed at him in awe while we stared at his back and flowing hair. The actor's name was Robert Wilson. It was 1954, but it was the first crucifixion and resurrection film since Cecil B. DeMille had made a silent in 1927, so my parents had sought this one out, not knowing Jesus, played by an actor who looked old enough to be playing Joseph, was going to face us.

From then on, my father refused to sit through another film that showed the face of Christ. Christ was a flowing robe and outstretched hands; he was a beatific voice and sandals. No actor could possibly take on the role of Christ if he allowed himself to be filmed from the front.

It was worse than nudity. It would be doubly worse on a Sunday. In 1959, five years after *Day of Triumph,* we went back to a film that featured Christ called *The Big Fisherman* because Jesus was depicted as the sleeve of a white robe and one blessed hand.

Howard Keel, a singer who starred in some of the benign musicals my father loved, played Simon Peter; I don't know, even now, whose arm, clothed in baggy white, rose and fell, but watching that film, years later, I noticed a vaccination mark on one of the women, something of a miracle.

My father started choosing the films for his family more selectively. We passed on *King of Kings* the same year I saw *El Cid* because Jeffrey Hunter, unlike previous film Christs, acted as if he were just another character, facing the audience, turning in profile, but worst of all, acting as if he were an ordinary human being.

A year later, when, as a family, we had nearly stopped going to the movies altogether, we sat through a film called *Whistle Down the Wind.* It featured Hayley Mills, so wholesome, in my father's view, anything she starred in was a safe choice.

Instead, it centered on a character played by Alan Bates whose identity was ambiguously linked to Christ. Hayley Mills and enough other children to suggest the twelve disciples begin a sort of cult after they find him in a barn. So strongly does it appear that the vagrant Bates plays is Christ-like that there are scenes that prod us to remember the three denials of Peter. My father grumbled. He leaned over and whispered to my mother, but we didn't walk out. There was uncertainty, after all, although my father, after that, refused any movies unless he knew the entire story for fear he'd be subjected to blasphemy by metaphor.

Since then there has been a family in Texas who saw the face of Christ in swirls of plaster on their ceiling, and there was someone in Ohio who saw that countenance on the side of a soybean oil tank. In 1983, a woman named Josephine Taylor saw the face of Christ on her bathroom floor in Ontario. Three thousand people came to witness the miracle, although someone from the church eventually concluded the face had been formed from the scars of old linoleum adhesive. Regardless, Arlene Gardner, in 1987, in Tennessee, saw the face of Christ on the General Electric freezer sitting on the front deck of her trailer. Her neighbor's porch light, apparently, caused a bearded face to appear, so it took a bit of inadvertent teamwork to generate that miracle.

Now, when I visit my father, we watch whatever's on one of the two channels that come in clearly on his television. No cable, no antenna—he lives on a hill near Pittsburgh, or there would be no picture whatsoever. I've sat through soap operas and made-for-television movies where the characters could have used the behavioral adjustments a sighting of the face of Christ might bring. My father never criticizes the sins of these characters; he doesn't say a word about violence and sexual innuendo. The brightness and contrast on his television are nearly gone. The color is the kind I remember from the 1950s—fields of primaries washing into each other. Everyone is garish in a sort of colorized comic book effect. In these shades, all of the women look tawdry, all the men threatening—if the face of Christ appeared on his television, it would be sponsored by NBC or CBS, and it would appear as unnatural and unconvincing as Jesus on a burrito or wood paneling.

Last night, on one of the tabloid shows that intersperse with the melodramas, I saw a photograph of a tumor excised from a woman who had somehow denied its presence and growth for years. She had dressed and lived her life until it sickened her irrevocably, and the excision had made no difference. "Look at it closely," we were told, "and what do you see?"

"Death," I said at once, and immediately described to my father the literal apparition of a troll-like figure, his arms and legs spread in a sort of frenzied jig of triumph, like Hitler in France, his face set in the bearded leer of the satyr.

"The face of death," the announcer said, but I didn't need anybody to corroborate what I was witnessing. That woman's tumor, malignant or benign, was clearly anthropomorphic. Immediately, I thought of all the faces of Christ, the hysteria and worship. I reminded myself of foolishness, turned away, repositioned myself, and looked back on the same troll still dancing with the glee of success.

My father didn't say a word about trolls and cancer, but he can see the recent history of weather in a field where I'm busy with insects and thorns and poisonous leaves. He understands the effects of variations in rain and heat; he names the plants that thrive or decline accordingly. If the face of Christ appeared in that field, created by design or accident, he'd say blasphemy or miracle, depending on which technique proved to be at its source.

He told me, later that evening, the story of Saint Wilgefortis, the patron saint of women who wish to be rid of beastly husbands. She prayed for deliverance from her forced marriage to the brutal King of Sicily and sprouted, on her wedding day, a full black beard and mustache. She was crucified by her father, the king of Portugal, who had arranged the marriage for all of the standard reasons of wealth and power. "What do you think of that?" my father said, and I told him it sounded like another face of Christ story, most likely, a man dressed as a woman, the explanatory story fabricated by the church to accompany it.

"You'll see some day," he said, and though I kept my silence, I think my father was right about the face of Christ on film. By the time I watched a Jesus movie on my own, Christ, once veiled and awe-inspiring, then mellow and human, had become flawed and worst of all, silly.

Just out of college, I sought out *Johnny Got His Gun*, in which Donald Sutherland portrays Christ as a sort of hippie, laid back and unable to intervene in any meaningful way in the miserable lives we lead. Two years later, I watched *Jesus Christ, Superstar,* the film version of the rock opera, and a man named Ted Neeley opened and closed his film career by singing badly and suggesting, by the fixed expression he carried throughout, that Jesus was stoned for most of his waking hours.

There were other full-frontal Christ films released within a year. One of them was seriously pious, but unintentionally stupid. Johnny Cash, the country singer, made a film called *The Gospel Road*, which featured a non-speaking Jesus played by a non-actor named Robert Elfstrom whose deep meditations are interrupted by Country/Christian tunes written and sung by Cash himself. My father would have demanded his money back.

Shortly thereafter, a film called *Him* was released with the promotional line: "Are you curious about his sexual life?" My father would have picketed the movie theater that showed this one, a film featuring a homosexual Christ, crosses gleaming, in the advertisement, from his aroused eyes.

Watching the holy hand of Christ in *The Big Fisherman* had been ludicrous in its own way, something like watching, during that era, the papier-mache hand of Allison Hayes, the enraged housewife in *Attack of the Fifty-Foot Woman* or the one movable claw which represented, in close-up, the terrible threat of the giant vegetable space invader in *It Conquered the World*. Just like those monsters, however, Christ had more power when I couldn't get a glimpse of him. The fifty-foot woman is stupendously comical when we see all of her; the terror from outer space turns out to be physically challenged, obviously pushed forward on wheels when it decides to attack. Seeing too much is risky.

I've never told my father about any of these blasphemies, the religious and the artistic. I tell him, though, about the face of Christ that was seen in the construction site for a bridge a few miles from where I live. Some of the landscape slashes have merged into cheekbones; some have turned into hair and a beard running toward the Susquehanna River.

Planes appeared overhead, people paying fifty dollars to judge that symbol for themselves. Below them, they claimed, was a face in the Rushmore soil, and many of those who witnessed it said the bridge was better left unfinished because it would surely collapse.

For a brief time, I lived near where progress paused while priests debated whether we had been handed a shrine that would surely erase itself regardless. The bridge, of course, was completed, but what I believe now is we need a sighting of the face of Christ turned away from us. There, the witnesses will say, is the back of his head, trusting in instinct reinforced by faith. We look away and turn back, and still we see. We change angles and distance, and continue to believe. And when the back of Christ's head crumbles or caves in or is erased by wind and water, we know that underneath us the ridges and troughs go on aligning themselves in persistent, suggestive ways.

SHIBBOLETH

From: *Vanishings* (Stephen F. Austin, 2013)

1

Three days before my first year of graduate school began, my father helped me lug two suitcases and a few boxes up the stairs to the room I'd rented in a house owned and refurbished by a psychology professor. A month earlier, when I'd signed the lease, I'd been relieved to find a room that came with a kitchen to share, but with my father standing in the room, it began to shrink.

The room had been small and shabby, and now it was tiny and miserable. My father opened the single window that looked out over the back yard. Below it and to the right was a small roof over the entrance to the back door. "This is your way out of here if the house catches fire," he said. "You won't have much time. This place is a tinderbox."

I concentrated on hanging my half dozen oxford shirts in the small closet, but he wasn't finished. "How many boys you say will be living here? Seven? That's a lot of boys to rely on not being stupid."

Before he left, I told my father everyone in the house was a senior or, like me, a graduate student. He nodded as if 21-and-over made no difference in the odds on a house fire.

2

Al, one of the seniors who lived downstairs spotted me in the IGA Market later that week. When he approached me, smiling, I was happy he found me a guy he liked. Al pointed to the two checkout lanes in the

96

small store. "Make sure you get your Cleveland Indians game card when you pay," he said. "It could be worth something."

He walked back to the house with me, and I handed him my game card. When he peeled it, there was the face of 3B Max Alvis. "Another Alvis," Al said. "I already have six of him and four of this one," showing me C Duke Sims.

We were closer to Cincinnati than Cleveland, but the promotion was more about luck than rooting interest. Back at the house Al showed me the six players he had multiple cards for and explained the game. He would win $5000 in the *Cleveland Indians Lineup Game* if he completed the infield. A complete outfield would earn him $100; a full battery won instant small cash.

"The season's almost over. The Indians suck like they always do, but if you want to help me win this, I'll cut you in for half."

All he needed was a first baseman or a center fielder or a pitcher. If I distracted the checkout woman, he'd steal a stack of game pieces from under the other checkout lane counter. "They're always sitting there," he said. "There's never women in both lanes at the same time in the afternoon."

We ran the routine three times, maybe 150 game pieces in less than a week before Al decided somebody must have noticed. "It's like three years-worth of trips to the grocery store," Al said. "It's like we've gone to the IGA three times a day every day since the contest began."

After we opened the first twenty game pieces, I could see this was hopeless. We found four more of Max Alvis and five more of Duke Sims. We found doubles of SS Larry Brown and 2B Pedro Gonzales. In fact, every one of the first one hundred we opened matched the six players Al already had. We needed 1B Tony Horton, CF Vic Davalillo, or P Sam McDowell, but they weren't anywhere in that stack of 150 game pieces.

"Not even instant cash," Al said. "Not even ten lousy dollars."

But he had forty-six of Duke Sims and thirty-nine of Max Alvis. "It's fixed," Al said.

"You bet it is," I said right away.

"I hate the fucking Indians," Al said.

3

A month into the semester Professor Agnew, the Chair of the department, called me into his office. He taught the development of the English novel, Tuesday evenings from 6:30 to 9:30, and I'd written my first seminar paper on social climbing in Samuel Richardson's *Pamela*. "Mr. Fincke," Professor Agnew said, "what you've produced here is an example of literary shibboleth."

He paused, but I couldn't even muster an "oh" of surprise. All I had to go on was the tone of his voice. I wasn't about to admit I'd never heard the word before, and he wasn't explaining.

Incredibly, Professor Agnew had a copy of all eleven books I'd cited piled upon his desk. He lifted four, bindings facing away from me, pushed them to his left and said, "You need to distinguish which scholars are valued and which are unreliable." He didn't give any clues as to how this was to be accomplished, and he didn't reveal which books had become the goats in his re-enactment of Revelation.

He handed me my paper, which was so thick with marginal notes on the first page I began to feel like throwing up. "Learn from this," he said and began to busy himself with some sort of record keeping that signaled I was to get out.

When I left I hoped another student would be waiting, that Professor Agnew was right that second producing another stack of books researched carelessly. But the hall was empty. If someone else was guilty of literary shibboleth, he had spaced the interviews widely.

I had a C+. I'd never received a grade lower than A- for anything I'd written. That success was why I was an English major in a Masters degree program, that and Vietnam, which was waiting for me if I didn't stay in school and keep my student deferment. Two Cs or one D and you were dismissed. I'd learned that from a second year student after an early class. When I asked if that actually happened, his answer was "frequently." The week before I'd asked him why he wore a coat and tie to class, and he'd told me he taught a composition class for his assistantship, an arrangement that I'd somehow never heard of because I hadn't sought help from professors when I'd applied only to three schools, the same procedure I'd used to apply to college when I was in high school.

I looked up *shibboleth* in the thick, unabridged dictionary on display in one of the seminar rooms. There were plenty of entries:

> A word or saying used by adherents of a particular belief or sect usually regarded by others as empty of real meaning; a widely held belief; a truism or platitude; a custom or usage regarded as distinguishing one group from another. From *Judges* 12:6 as a test for distinguishing Gileadites from Ephraimites.

It looked as if my sin was not recognizing that what I thought were my ideas had already been recorded often in books and articles, so often that they'd become hackneyed.

For years, stretching all the way back to elementary school, I'd written perfectly punctuated, grammatical sentences based on borrowed ideas. In fact, I'd begun by simply copying from the encyclopedia for my fourth grade report on Chicago, and later, in junior high school, term papers on volcanoes and alcohol that I'd at least borrowed from three or four books, abandoning the encyclopedia my mother had bought over a period of a full year, volume by volume discounted by the grocery store as a way to induce customers to spend a bit more to reach the minimum purchase for the discount on their receipt.

4

All of us had girlfriends who lived somewhere else. Beginning around two o'clock, whoever was home began looking for the mail, which, for a month, arrived around 2:30 every day. When, for two days in a row, it arrived at 4:45, Ken, one of the seniors confronted the mailman. "You used to bring the mail before three and now it's almost five. Why are we your last stop now?"

"We're sorry for your inconvenience," the mailman said and turned away.

"We know why you're late. We know where you live."

I was struck by the mailman's unbroken stride and the collective pronoun Ken was using. A half block from where we were standing, the houses were almost entirely occupied by black families. The small black neighborhood of this college town began less than a hundred yards away.

My parents had insisted I bring a Bible with me, and one night in October, with my second paper soon due in English Novel, I lifted it out of the cardboard box where it lay under sweaters in makeshift storage. I turned to *Judges*, chapter 12, to see what the source of shibboleth was all about. There it was, in three verses. The Gilead army, victorious, guarded the Jordan River to catch any fugitive Ephraimites that were trying to return home. According to the story, the men from the opposing armies looked so much the same that the Gileadites devised a way to identify who wasn't one of them: they asked the man to say Shibboleth.

The men from Ephraim had no sound for "sh," and they would answer Sibboleth. The consequence? "Then they took him, and slew him at the passages of Jordan: and there fell at that time of the Ephraimites forty and two thousand.

Some test, I thought. I was glad that I hadn't even repeated the word in front of Professor Agnew, let alone attempted to argue for a higher grade.

The guy across the hall lived in the other single room, but his was nearly 50% larger. He was about to complete a thesis for a masters in psychology, and he offered to give me a test for depression—unofficial, of course, he said, just to give you a feel for what I did for my thesis.

I was depressed, all right, guilty of *shibboleth* and 300 miles from home with no car and a $10 a week budget for food that led me to stuff myself with mac and cheese, baked beans and ground meat. My luxury was orange juice, which I drank with every meal, hoping the vitamin C would keep me healthy.

Mildly depressed, Lando, the bulky, blond Swedish about-to-be psychologist, said after he scored the test. I was disappointed. I wasn't even threatening craziness. "I thought was worse."

"That's what I sensed," Lando said. "You talk like somebody who's depressed, but you're a long way from worse."

A few weeks later he would be gone, I thought, and I'd move into his room for the second semester, gladly paying $20 more not to be embarrassed by the tiny size of my room. I saw that the porch roof was to my left now. I was sure I could reach it.

The last Tuesday in October there was a B- at the end of my paper on satire in Henry Fielding. "Somewhat better," Professor Agnew had written beside it, but I understood that I remained a borderline failure.

On the reverse side of the last page, Professor Agnew had printed what he titled "a brief note of advice"

"Much of the class often laughs when you speak during our discussions, but there are those who think you funny in a way that you may not imagine. For example, you twice use the word 'e-pit-o-me' within your paper, but in class you pronounced it 'ep-i-tome'. Consider your language when you speak as well as write."

8

In early November, I stole a cube steak from Ken, who was watching a movie upstairs, the late show hosted by some aging celebrity who ad-libbed beer commercials, displaying empty Schoenling bottles as if he drank while watching, like us, a double feature of chillers, three hours of giant insects, mutant reptiles, and even, one weekend, deadly, oversized, ravenous rabbits.

It had been more than a week since he'd jammed a banana in the box for the black mailman he considered slow delivering letters from his girl friend. He'd promised "coconut next time" in case the postman missed the point, and I'd rebuked nothing about his rant of slurs after he found banana mashed on the doorstep, footprints leading to the next rental's box.

It was satisfying to swallow that heavily salted meat, though even then I couldn't claim eating that steak a formal protest, not half-drunk past midnight, overspending my paltry budget by three dollars for two six packs, that mailman likely asleep because he looked to be forty or more, married according to the ring he wore on the hand he'd used to wrestle that fruit from the mailbox, what I witnessed because Ken had left to go through the house declaring his joy to whoever else happened to be home, shouting it had been "a fucking great show" as if there were tarantulas below that had swollen into the size of dogs.

After I finished that meat, I ran scalding water over the greasy plate and stacked it on end where all of us kept our carelessly cleaned dishes, concealing a crime so small it was barely shameful, so easily admitted that I might as well have confessed, though any of the other five guys who lived there could have stolen that cheap, gristly meat. Or, like I had done, cleaned up that ruined fruit after Ken left the house, scrubbing the doorstep, my back to the street so I could imagine I was being re-evaluated by a stranger.

9

Professor Agnew invited the class to his house for the final night, and he smiled and shook everyone's hands as if no one had turned in shibboleth for his or her final paper. His wife served desserts and coffee. She'd made all of the pastries by hand.

I managed a B in English Novel and better than that in my other three courses. My father didn't mention house fires over Christmas. My mother asked if the boys I lived with had turned out to be nice. I said sure, and she didn't ask me to elaborate. I knew my parents were pleased with my grades when they paid for my bus ride back to school. Neither of them had ever gone to college, and here I was getting nearly all As in a school even more advanced.

Ken and Lando had both graduated. Al, because he lived near Ken in Cleveland, told us that Ken was trying to enhance some vague disability to dodge the draft. Lando, our landlord psych professor told us, was 4-F because he had the blood pressure of an imminent stroke victim. The professor stopped in the first night back in January to ask if we knew anyone who was interested in renting because now there were two vacancies.

At five o'clock, every weekday, I watched *Perry Mason* reruns with three of my housemates. At 5:30 we each chose a character as the real killer and put a dollar in as a wager. Perry's client, for sure, was never guilty. To keep things fair, we chose in a different order each show, though it turned out not to be a disadvantage to choose last because our prediction success wasn't much above the mathematical probability. But it kept us all waiting for that moment, just after 5:50, when bulky Raymond Burr would somehow coerce a public confession in the courtroom from the real killer. When Perry was defending someone, jury duty was easy. Nobody ever had to vote.

$4 on a $1 investment. The weeks when I won twice, I could buy beer. The weeks I didn't win, I drank water instead of orange juice. Once, when I won three afternoons in a row, Al bought a newspaper to check the TV listing to see if I was watching *Perry Mason* on a different channel earlier in the day when everybody else was in class.

At six o'clock we stayed tuned for Cronkite because war news was almost always the lead story. During the first semester, there had been promises of light at the end of the tunnel and assurances we were winning the hearts and minds of the Vietnamese, but on January 31st we discovered that Tet was a Vietnamese national holiday, another way of measuring the beginning of the year, and North Vietnam had chosen their New Year's Day to launch a major offensive that seemed to be succeeding.

"We're all fucked," Al said, and no one disagreed. There would be troop number escalations. Our draft deferments would disappear. Al had won the *Perry Mason* lottery that day, but he was looking as glum as the rest of us. When a reporter mentioned it was now the Year of the Monkey, nobody even mustered *Who cares?*

I had school to distract me. I started to research for my thesis on Ambrose Bierce, whose cynicism struck me as an attitude everyone should have. Besides all of Bierce's stories and his *Devil's Dictionary*, I read late Mark Twain, *Puddn'head Wilson* and *The Mysterious Stranger*, for another dose of bleak humor. I followed that with a dozen scholarly books and a host of articles, making sure I wasn't following an idea-highway paved years before. I was going to be reclassified 1-A on July 1st, but I could finish class work before then because I wasn't on assistantship or fellowship.

On March 31st, everyone in the house watched Lyndon Johnson's speech from the Oval Office. He started with troop limits and the line he'd drawn at the 20th Parallel, so familiar a list of policies I was ready to leave until the television returned to normal programming. But then Johnson, looked the camera in the eye and announced that he was no longer a candidate for the Democratic nomination for president. All of us cheered. Deferments for first year graduate students were a thing of the past, but suddenly there seemed to be hope.

10

Two nights after Johnson's speech we called our landlord to tell him we had an outbreak of flying termites upstairs. When he showed up, I pointed out the closest swarm, a cloud that had materialized from the floorboards in the hall. "Flying ants," he said.

"Termites do this," I said, reaching back to 10th grade biology. "They grow wings and migrate." I was counting on his anxiety about the property he'd invested in to clear up this crisis.

In my old room a throw rug of flying termites rose and fell along one wall in a way that made me nauseous. "I carry a gun for this sort of problem," he said. "It's never let me down. Couple of shots of bug juice will do the trick. Of course, you'll probably want to sleep downstairs for tonight."

True to his word, he sprayed in the old tradition of the way DDT billowed from trucks when I was a boy, and those flying bugs, whether termites or ants, didn't return.

The next morning, in History of the English Language, I asked Mary Waller how her preliminary oral exam had gone the day before. "I failed," she said straight out. "Both parts. The thesis defense and the reading list."

I felt a hot flash in my chest. Her thesis was on Faulkner. I imagined her spouting two hours of received opinion, or worse, choking on her words, maybe crying in humiliation. *Shibboleth*—the word hovered in front of me like the ghost of testing's future. Mary Waller was on fellowship. She was an academic star who'd received an A in Development of the English Novel. "I have until August," she said. "You get a second chance and then you're dropped from the program."

I started to tabulate how many large gulps of the *Penguin Summary of British Literature* I'd swallowed in the past two weeks, accumulating platitudes about writers I'd never read.

"Don't you have Dr. Kessler like I do for the British Literature part? You thought Agnew was tough in English Novel? Kessler is way tougher, so get ready."

I drank a glass of cheap wine before I walked the mile to campus, imagining that the alcohol would make me relax and be more like myself, a personality, someone capable of discussing literature without falling back on ideas that everybody knew. All it did was come out of me in sweat, the day so warm in early April that students I immediately envied were lounging outside in town and everywhere on campus while I hiked up a flight of stairs and into the men's room where I mopped myself with paper towels for ten minutes.

I was solid with Ambrose Bierce. This was my project. I quoted *The Devil's Dictionary*. I talked about Bierce's Civil War experience and the uniformly bleak stories that came from it, including "The Occurrence at Owl Creek Bridge," with which Rod Serling had piqued my interest when he aired it on *The Twilight Zone* while I was in high school. After an hour we shifted to the reading list, beginning, I was pleased to discover, with American Literature.

But with half an hour to go, coming into the conversation exactly with the chimes from the campus library clock, the British Literature expert broke in, steering me toward Lawrence, Woolf, and Joyce, writers about whom I knew only the basics. "What did the thunder say?" Dr. Kessler said at last, as if a storm had rolled in with the heat wave.

"The thunder?" I said, buying time.

"Yes."

There was nothing for it but to say, "I have no idea." My answer seemed to satisfy him, as if he'd rather listen to an admission of ignorance than a string of superficial remarks.

"You find out before the final orals," he said, and moved backward in time to the Victorians. Twenty minutes later all three professors shook my hand as if I'd wowed them. What, I thought, had Mary Waller said to achieve failure?

12

I practically ran back to the house, the sweat of joy soaking through my shirt, my tie pulled loose from my throat so I could unbutton the collar of my shirt. I stopped to buy four six packs I carried in two brown paper bags. I could afford to celebrate with my house mates, and they were happy to toast my success for free. I could drink water for two weeks or trust my luck with Perry Mason, but before the killer was revealed, a news bulletin broke in about Martin Luther King, Jr., who'd been shot and killed in Memphis. We picked up our dollar bills because everyone knew Mason wasn't coming back.

The news shifted back and forth from Cronkite to the Cincinnati news team. At first both suggested the likelihood of unrest in black neighborhoods. Before long, both began showing films of what that meant when it materialized.

The banana episode rose in my throat. The mailman might not realize Ken had graduated. Bulk mail still arrived once or twice a week in his name. The mailman might be pleased that no more mail came from the girlfriend, imagining her with someone who wasn't as big an asshole. Regardless, everyone in our house was guilty by association.

Two hours after the first announcement there were voices in the street. "Fuck whoever's out there," Al said, but I got up to look. The crowd wasn't large by television standards—maybe twenty, all older boys or men, all black. I looked for the mailman in the crowd, but couldn't pick him out.

As I watched through the front window, I sipped a beer from my second six pack, the other two gone to my house mates. What looked to be a bag of trash hurtled into the tiny front yard, and one of the men held a cigarette lighter to it until it ignited. It alternately smoldered and flared about fifteen feet from the house. I imagined it full of junk mail, the fire starter as our mailman.

While I was wondering whether that small fire was enough, whether outrage needed a larger blaze, our landlord walked in the back door, down the hall, and shouldered past me to the front window. He carried what looked to my untrained eye to be a shotgun, and he stared so intently through the window that I half expected him to break it open with the butt of the gun like any number of cowboys I'd watched in movie theaters.

I was relieved, minutes later, when the small group of name callers moved on and the fire went out. "I'll stay and keep an eye out," our landlord said. "You go back to what you were doing." I was still holding my beer. Nearly twenty empty cans were strewn around the common room where my house mates were watching a report on a large fire in Cleveland, the Hough District, and nursing their last beers. None of them had bothered to come to the front window.

"You should be watching this," Al said. "God damned Hough. You should see it for real." The announcer, by now, was repeating himself, saying "unrest" and "shock" and "rage" while standing among firemen and police, telling us what we already knew.

Every inner city seemed to be saying the same thing—broken windows and overturned cars and looting and fires. Because of where we lived—Cincinnati. Because the country recognized the names—New York, Baltimore, Detroit. And right then, Cleveland, shouting, like all of them, something that translated to "God damn fuck it all," already sounding familiar from the flames.

THE PAGODA SIGHTLINES

From: *Vanishings* (Stephen F. Austin, 2013)

"Troops Home Alive Now" is printed in white letters on the grainy cement surface of the pagoda. For anyone who has seen photographs of the National Guard firing at the students on May 4, 1970, at Kent State University, this structure is unmistakable. It's January 1993, however, so right away I think this message on the pagoda was scrawled during the Gulf War. And then, reconsidering, I start listing other choices, including the current one of Somalia.

For Northeast Ohio, in January, it's a remarkably warm day. If the wind would let up, I could be comfortable without a coat. Freakishly, it's almost as warm as it was on May 4. I've brought along a map with arrows which show the paths taken by different units of the Guard that day. It's been over 22 years, after all, and the point of my visit is to reconfirm memory for my novel-in-progress. Now, I find I don't need it, that even with the physical changes—the practice field where the Guard first knelt and pointed their weapons is gone, for instance, a gym annex spreading into the space on my right—I'm as sure of these locations as I am of where baseball players will align themselves when they trot out of the dugout to play defense.

This trip is part of a personal, delayed debriefing. In the summer of 1970, less than six weeks after the killings, I returned to school and took courses in Victorian Literature and The Romantic Era. One was taught by a near lunatic who berated the government every afternoon and accused each member of the class of being an FBI agent. The other was taught by a man who believed you could understand the nuances of Coleridge and

Wordsworth by studying posthumous psychological biographies. I never missed one session of either class, and I regularly attended, in August, the Scranton Commission hearings, listening to officials defend themselves and a woman from town say she feared for her safety each time someone with hair over his collar approached her on the street.

I played golf every Monday and Thursday afternoon on the university course. Its most distinctive feature was the railroad track which ran the length of the eighth fairway, forming a unique and difficult rough from which to play. In 1970, I occasionally slammed my short irons through the gravel of the track bed, scattering stones and scarring my garage-sale clubs in order to save a penalty shot, and twice I huddled under trees during thunderstorms in mid-round, disregarding the possible penalties of another sort of hazard. The second time I waited out the rain, lightning struck a lone tree much like my oak one fairway from where I was as sheltered as all the world's foolish. Never again, I had the chance to say, and I never went back to Taylor Hall, the pagoda, or the parking lot site of slaughter during that summer or the twenty-two years which followed. "When you're good and ready, you'll go," my father would say, and here I am at last.

I look down the hill at the parking lot where most of the victims were standing. From the pagoda, you can use the sidewalk to the parking lot as a sightline. I take a stance like a rifleman; I step to my right and forward and extend my arm, crouching, like the Guardsman with a pistol your eye goes to in the firing sequence photographs, and then I tell myself "enough" and start walking away from petty fantasy as if I'd considered purchasing it at a porn shop.

I swing down to the Victory Bell, the campus rallying point in the spring of 1970. Someone rang it just before noon on May 4, attracting perhaps 200 activists and a thousand passive spectators. "Pigs off campus" was the most common chant, meaning the National Guard, and even that wasn't sustained very long until the troops started their much-chronicled sweep.

I stand on it to take pictures—fixing what someone would see if he were using it for footing in 1970. 1253, I think is embossed just below the bell, but I run my hand over it and perhaps the 1 was a 7 originally, the numbers worn like a grave marker date. I think about pulling the handle, letting loose a peal or two, and I get as far as lifting it, the first stroke like beginning to pump for water, and then I stop, reach inside instead and discover the clapper is shaped like an anvil. When I tap it slightly against the bell, I'm certain the sound carries far enough for the nearest person to mark me down as the sort of tourist who would pick flowers in a conservatory. Or the kind of man who would pretend he was in the National Guard.

It's time to climb the hill back to the pagoda; it's time to retreat the way students did inside the tear gas, walking as slowly as they could to prevent panic from setting in among the crowd. I crest the hill and start down the other side, stop beside the large steel sculpture where someone might lean to watch the skirmish. The sculpture, when I look at it closely, says 67-DRUMM. In 1970, it seemed as if it were always here. I'd begun taking classes in 1969, so for me, at least, it had.

Even now I'm not certain it was meant to be representational. Certainly, the National Guard didn't search for significance, finding expressionistic birdhouses or a looming symbol for chaos. But I notice, from here, that the tree behind the pagoda is dramatically bent away from the direction the Guard fired, and then I remember the pagoda itself was a student project, that it had been completed just in time to appear in photograph after photograph taken on May 4. I'm beginning to see nature as symbolic, construction as metaphoric; I'm turning so literary and dreamy I understand it's time to march down the hill into the parking lot beside Prentice Hall and put my 1970 point of view back under my feet.

I'm right about that, because as soon as I turn around and face the pagoda, everything in front of me seems to loom and threaten. Taylor Hall, for instance, seems ominous and crypt-like, and from the parking lot, I remember at once how far it seemed from the Guard to where I'm standing. I'm trying to think like a character, but I'm so close to this subject, it's difficult. I could have written this novel long ago, after all, and now I'm thinking, even as a man in his mid-40's who should know better, that it's safe this far from rifles. The tree I've come to, already curved by the prevailing wind in 1970, is over 300 feet from the pagoda—I've paced it off. It's foolish trust, I know, but in 1970 I thought you could stand behind somebody and be safe—like someone, otherwise unarmed, with a hostage, believing the trained snipers will refrain from shooting.

Anyone who's read a book about Kent State has seen one of those maps numbered to show where the victims fell: #'s 1-4, the dead; #'s 5-13, the wounded. On some of those maps are printed the distances each of the victims were from the Guard when they were shot. Those numbers should remind even the inflexible that the dead students were, loosely speaking, a football field's length away from the Guardsmen who fired.

Try this experiment. Stand in one end zone and give someone a hefty rock to carry to the opposite end of the field. Have that person stand under the goal post and heave that rock your way. See if you even flinch, if that rock gets within fifty feet of you. Find twenty people then and give them all rocks; move forward to the fifteen-yard line, about as far from them as the nearest dead student was to the Guard. See if you're worried about any of those missiles as they arc through the air.

Not a very exact simulation, of course, since it disregards emotion and fatigue and a dozen other mitigating circumstances, but I am thinking like this even as I try to be objective, surprising myself by so suddenly stepping into the past.

I've learned, since then, about one tribe in the Amazon Basin which imagines the future behind their backs. The past, therefore, is always in front of them, discernible and clear. I would say they have a tradition based on good fortune. I would tell them to keep looking because the future can grow tired of waiting and approach you from the front wearing gas masks and firing rifles while you believe all the threats on your life are still stalking you from behind.

For a while, in the 1970s and early 1980s, each time I applied for a new job somebody would see the Kent State dates on my resume and say "Were you there?" My standard answer, after a while, was "I was around," which, for most people, including myself, seemed evasive, unsatisfactory, and dishonest.

I was never willing to feel sorry for anyone who used the atrocities of the past to elicit sympathy in the present. I told myself again and again that if I ever brought up Kent State with a stranger I'd be like those jerks who say their great-grandfathers were mistreated and the world owes them something now. I thought it made people feel worthless to be helped, that there's a natural selection in this world and nothing to do but stay elusive as long as possible to keep anger and self-pity down like the first tentative bites of a hangover breakfast.

Even now, stepping onto the grass beside the parking lot, I think I was inadvertently telling a general truth. I wasn't anywhere that day but "around"; regardless, nearly all of the questioners knew what they expected to hear, and my unwillingness to specify was one way to keep near strangers from concluding I could illuminate or reinforce the second-hand platitudes they swallowed each time the headache of uncertainty settled in behind their eyes.

And when I take my position beside a tree halfway back in the lot, I'm standing where the narrator of my novel-to-be is loitering when the Guardsmen fire. He doesn't drop and cover. He turns sideways behind this tree, looking back over his shoulder like all of those movie gunfighters who press themselves against the hollows in buildings, seeking safety. Now, when I shift my weight and rotate, I see at once that this tree provides as much protection as blankets pulled over your head when you hear intruders outside your door.

I notice a security phone, something they didn't have in 1970—who could I have called? I notice, for some reason, the three tiers of opaque glass in the center of Prentice Hall's rows of clear windows. The bathrooms, of course, and I know those windows are difficult to see through because the glass is layered and dimpled to prevent light from flowing through in any sort of coherent way. Who will I ask in order to give that glass its proper name?

On the third floor, to the left of the privacy glass, 101 DALMATIONS is strung across a window in paper letters. On the window next door are paper letters which spell REVOLUTION—MALCOLM X. Underneath that message are three additional X's. Just to make sure, I think, but below that window, on the second floor, someone has printed, inside a traditional heart, MELISS + CAT, and, finally, below that, one window says MERRY CHRISTMAS in green and red letters. Immediately, I wonder whether it's the window of the Resident Assistant, whether she's been encouraged by the administration to paste up a message which might somehow be infectious.

Within a hundred yards of where I'm standing are two verifiable illustrations of the decision-making of administrators. The gym annex which covers part of the Guard's May 4 route was constructed on schedule despite student protests "to delay"; the "official" May 4 Memorial which sits on the crest of the hill beside Taylor Hall had its construction delayed for years despite student protests "to proceed."

Such stories bind us with their reminders of shared frustrations, and, I tell myself, in writing this, of shared self-righteousness. For nearly twenty years, I discarded every mailing from Kent State University, regardless of its point of view. I'm putting all this behind me, I said, employing my best Pontius Pilate voice. Such a posture, I've come to understand, comes from fear, whether your excuses follow from having a weapon in your hand or from being an accidental witness.

Whatever has been barking in my ears for the last hour has finally shut up. There is a silence speaking to me now from the pavement of the parking lot. It could be the second or two immediately after the last shot was fired, an expectation forming so quickly in the air it could have roiled up like the tumbling gases and swirling debris of an enormous explosion.

I recognize in myself the sort of feeling that forms the expressions I've seen lately on the faces of televised veterans at World War II sites. Fifty years since this; fifty years since that. And I feel uneasy and embarrassed for such a comparison, as if I were being confronted by my two uncles, both of them veterans of World War II, who said to me in 1970: "What the hell do you think you were doing?"

A couple of times a year now I play golf with one of those uncles. He pays for the cart and occasionally gives me tips about the subtleties of side-hill lies or wet sand in traps near the green. He may or may not remember that he added, in 1970, "They should have shot you too while they had the chance" to his short speech to me about how disappointed he was to hear me complain about the government.

The exhilaration of anger, I might say now, knowing the difficulty of separating hypothesis from observation. In his marvelous book *The Periodic Table*, Primo Levi writes about a lipstick manufacturer who offers to pay Levi well for alloxan, a compound with nearly perfect coloring properties. Since alloxan is principally uric acid and chicken dung is 50% uric acid, Levi gathers a large batch from a local farm and begins the work of extraction.

Whatever he does to oxidize the acid fails. Levi is left with the very things which would drive most of us away: smell and filth and the humiliation of struggling with fecal matter. "The shit remained shit," he writes, "and the alloxan and its resonant name remained a resonant name." I know the truth of that struggle, I think now. I might as well be attempting surgery on my metaphoric oak tree, seeing if both trunks can survive apart.

Inside Taylor Hall, which houses the school of architecture, I look for someone to answer a few questions. I need to know whether or not the interior of the building was configured the same way in 1970 because I want a character in my novel to enter and leave, and I have to know what he would notice as he passed. I talk with four secretaries and receptionists. None of them have worked here more than five years. Finally, I reach the chairman's office. His secretary tells me he could help me because he's been here for a long time. The professor smiles. Through the windows I can see into the parking lot, the side where my character is standing when the shots are fired. "I'm researching for a novel," I say.

"May 4?" he says.

"Yes."

"I've been here twelve years," he says, "not long enough to help you out."

I nod, but since I can see those opaque dormitory windows from where I'm standing and he is the architecture expert, I ask him one more question.

"Frosted burlap," he says at once. "Or frosted hammer." He smiles again, and I extend my hand and say "thanks."

I've done enough for now, I decide, but I've brought a camera and need to take pictures, believing in the off chance of the lens finding something I'm not seeing, that later, when the photos are developed, I'll look at each one and say "There" or "There" like somebody with a time traveler's hindsight.

I feel like a tourist, ashamed, in a way, of myself, or like some tabloid journalist looking for an exploitation angle, but I snap my way through a 24-shot roll before I allow myself to look at things which weren't there in 1970.

The first memorial sits at the base of a tree in a grass cut out in the parking lot. "In Living Memory of," it says, the names of the dead in alphabetical order carved into what could only be described as a tombstone. Dedicated in 1971; rededicated in 1975—despite its simplicity and sentiment, there is something about its size and shape and unremarked location that speaks of official disapproval.

Already I am annoyed, but then I go up the grade on the other side of Taylor to where one part of the Guard stood its ground without firing. C Company—they are the soldiers who you see guarding the body of Jeff Miller shortly after the shooting stopped. The men who fired—A Company and G Troop—retreated almost at once to the burned-out ROTC building from where they'd begun their march into history. The new memorial is built into the hillside here, and I think at once of the Vietnam Memorial, although these slabs of marble are spaced differently, and there are no names on the wall.

Bruno Ast—Architect, I read, *Dedicated May 4, 1990.* Twenty years of wrangling and foot dragging. Something like the negotiations for the end of the Vietnam War. I remember the squabble about the shape of the negotiating table, the merits of rectangle, square, triangle, and circle. A generation of college students has come and gone before this memorial was realized.

Four slabs of marble surge in size from nearest to farthest from the center. Whatever they are supposed to represent to the visitor—the four dead, most likely—I think of walls to hide behind in case of salvos.

And to my left, there's a pedestal with a glass front and a handle on a fold down door. It's like a dispenser for newspapers, but I open it without inserting any coins. Inside, there's nothing, though I think there is supposed to be a candle, one of those perpetual mourning symbols. Vandals, carelessness—or perhaps I'm reading more into this than intended. Maybe there is only supposed to be a stack of fliers describing the memorial, something to tuck into a purse or a back pocket to read in the car while you're driving back to Pennsylvania.

Eventually, I discover the location of the inscribed names. Here the wounded are listed as well as the dead. "Respectfully remembered," it says, and I read the less familiar names, recalling that Dean Kahler was permanently paralyzed, that, as far as I knew, the other eight recovered. Planted on one side of the plaque is holly, on the other, rhododendron—something that keeps a sense of green year-round.

Nearly all of us bleach stains of one sort or another from our lives.

We're lucky if they turn undetectable to the casual looks the world ordinarily sends our way. But what we see matters less than how we feel about it. This matters. And that. And the accuracy with which we carry it to those who might listen.

Right now, I remember one student who exclaimed "How extraordinary, and yet we have survived," saying it so clearly and so soon afterwards, the Guard swirling backwards, still lethal, that I would never write his stilted words into the voice of any character. Who, under those conditions, would ever utter such a sentence? I might have searched him for signs of circuitry or evidence the aliens had indeed arrived.

For a few moments, I let myself lock the fingers of my hands together behind my head and stare through the bare trees toward where the ROTC building lay gutted in 1970. A few years before that day I would walk with my hands interlocked in this position, trying, after every race, to let as much air back into my lungs as possible after sprinting a quarter of a mile for my high school track team. The coach had told me it was the quickest way to recover, and I'd never questioned whether or not he was right.

I haven't come to record anything about the memorial for, after all, it can't be in the novel, which ends in December 1970. But suddenly I open my hands and start jotting these things down—the shape of the stones, how they look from this angle and that and then, how angry I am. I anticipated sorrow or wistfulness or even the sentimentality of nostalgia—but here I am wanting to start taking down names, recognizing the held-breath way I react to rage.

The fusillade lasted eleven seconds. I stopped breathing long enough to sear the scene into memory like a brand. And I had time to add evaluation, judgment, and attitude before I needed to inhale again, restarting my life entranced by the simple disrespect I had for certainty.

If you've seen any photographs of the crowd of students who gathered shortly after the shootings, you'll see that the National Guard, in the aftermath, finally had an honest-to-god mob to contend with. "They can't kill us all before we reach them" was the logic shoving that crowd from behind. Abbreviated and repeated, the chant was "Fuck it, let's go," and I could have sprinted the distance without turning breathless, without thinking of the necessity of locking my hands behind my head to recover.

Now, here I am too breathless with asthma to sustain a sprint down the hill and across the commons to where the Guard stood near the burned-out ROTC. From the other side of Taylor, twice as close to the Guard as I am here, I still couldn't make it before my lungs talked back and refused. Which would have been my good fortune, because on May 4 it would have been like Gallipoli if the crowd had surged forward. It would have been the slaughter of trench warfare, the technology of the human wave against the indifference of guns.

Not only has my memory stayed intact, so have my emotions. It is reassuring and unsettling, though now, busily writing, I look down and see, at my feet, the words INQUIRE LEARN RESPECT engraved in the marble floor, and I know, for certain, there is no reason to reload the camera. I'm not going to forget any of this.

THE WOMAN IN WHITE

From: *Vanishings* (Stephen F. Austin, 2013)

The woman in white blocked the aisle with her grocery cart. She stood beside it, fixed on the disposable diaper display. My daughter stopped to heft three sizes of paper towels, comparing them slowly so I could stare while the woman in white seemed to be memorizing the specific details of the toddler size. "Don't be obvious," Shannon said, "you're in the city now," but the woman in white hadn't moved, by the time Shannon warned me, for thirty seconds.

She wore white plastic bags over her hands and her shoes. Her white dress was tucked in at the ankles and wrists and ended in a high collar where the white stripes of cloth wove themselves around her face and hair like the burial stripping worn by every escapee from the mummy's tomb.

Shannon selected the generic brand of paper towels and u-turned her cart instead of following the aisle. The woman in white, after we'd looped past dog food and cereal in the adjoining aisle, and then passed the other end of paper products where toilet paper was on sale, was still considering diapers. "You'll see her again," Shannon said. "She walks the streets, from here to my block, as long as it's nice out. She stares the same way at Clem when I walk him."

"Does he know?"

"I think so, but he never barks."

"He ought to. She could use a white dog."

"A Shepherd's too big for her."

"Why?"

"Because why?"

"You just 'popped in' didn't you? Without Mom? From Cleveland, as if Buffalo's on the way home instead of adding almost 200 miles to your trip? Because why?"

I shrugged. My daughter had come to Buffalo to design scenery for a playhouse, and after two months, had resigned herself to painting scenery someone else had designed. "That's why they call it an internship," I'd said earlier, keeping to myself all the subjects I wanted to talk about—her safety, her health, her choice of acquaintances, the fitness of her dog who needed, I was certain, to stay alive and well and strong because sooner or later he would be required to save her.

"Exactly," Shannon said. The woman in white had disappeared, and I thought of the generic product display we'd passed earlier, the shelves stocked with cans and boxes wrapped in white paper marred only by the black lettering that named what was enclosed.

We walked the six blocks back to Shannon's apartment in what was, according to Butch, her landlord, a transitional neighborhood. It was sunny and calm, nothing like the weather Buffalo is supposed to have, and five of the six blocks, even the landlord would have to admit, had completed their transition to decay.

I watched Shannon as she walked, for once, without her dog on the end of its chain leash. She carried the twenty-pound bag of dog food and watched the sidewalk half a block ahead for problems I wouldn't notice until I could hear them breathing. Five months after graduating a semester early from college she was suddenly poor, painting for wages she could earn at McDonald's.

A block from her apartment all of the brown-bagging men and small clusters of boys Shannon's age who writhed in place to thumping rap music disappeared, replaced by dark-skinned women and small children, and then, in the middle of the block, by nothing but women, both brown and white.

The women with children looked younger than Shannon. I felt grandfatherly where women Shannon's age had children in school. In that neighborhood, nearly thirty years older than Shannon, I was great-grandfather material, someone whose father could be called in for one of those five-generation pictures you see in the Sunday "family living" section.

"Goddamn fuck it all," a woman sweeping her driveway just ahead of us yelled.

"That's the street troll. She swears all day," Shannon whispered.

The woman seemed to hate the dirt, because she wasn't looking our way and nobody else had been outside for the last two houses. Shannon followed my look and said, "Her daughter and granddaughter are in the house. That's who she swears at."

"Fucking whore," the woman screamed. "Fucking tramp."

"That's for the granddaughter. She's eighteen. They tried to rent the downstairs. To get away from her."

"Your house is across the street."

"Exactly."

"Fucking bitch," the woman screamed.

"That's for the daughter."

"Does she know you?" I said, smiling.

"Yes," Shannon said, "but so far she's kept her opinion to herself."

"Where do men live?"

"You think it's bad, Dad, but it's not," she said.

She answered so matter-of-factly I let it drop. The first week she'd lived here, nearly three months before, her latest boyfriend had called to tell her he'd moved to New Jersey and wasn't saying exactly where. Shannon, as she unlocked the door, set off a scramble of claws on the hardwood over our heads.

Shannon's dog, an enormous white Shepherd she'd named after the one pictured on the front of a novel she'd loved, put its paws on her shoulders when she opened the door. It looked my way, searching its memory for people worth giving a damn about, and it didn't get down until Shannon let her face be licked and turned her shoulders.

"You need that twenty-pounder for ballast," I said.

"You sound like Khalil, the guy who lived in the back when I moved in."

"Khalil?"

"You know, Pakistan or someplace. Short and skinny and aiming to please. He volunteered right off to walk Clem for me. The dog almost

120

outweighs him, and Khalil breaks into a trot. A few strides and Clem takes off running, only he veers hard left and Khalil flops right over him, breaking his fall with his free hand while Clem shakes loose anyway and bolts between two cars, crosses to where the street troll is sweeping puddles and recrosses without looking to stand in front of me on the porch with the leash in his teeth as if I'd tossed it like a stick."

Clem cocked his head and watched Shannon put the groceries away, keeping an eye on the dog food sack. "Khalil got lucky," she said. "He only sprained his wrist, and Clem was alive and well after crossing twice in traffic."

"You run ninety pounds of dog, you should make sure it believes in a world of straight lines," I said, and Clem turned and nuzzled into my crotch as if he'd heard a magic word.

"See? I'm safer by myself."

"In an empty house?"

"I've known three men here since Brian took off."

"Known?"

"We're not in the Bible, Dad. One is Butch the landlord, gone. One is Khalil, the dog walker, gone. And the third is Keith, the actor, presently on tour."

"So there really are only women?"

"The landlord is off fixing up more transitional neighborhood houses. After a binge Butch does it to dry out, I think—six weeks ago he drank himself into a diabetic coma. He does each house once, apparently, and then the tenants are on their own."

"God comes to Buffalo."

"Not really, Dad. Before he drank himself nearly to death, he wouldn't even shovel the driveway. I rode my bicycle for two weeks until a thaw let me get my car out. Come on, let's get Clem out for some exercise and you can treat me to some Mighty Tacos."

As soon as Shannon took two steps toward the door, Clem pressed against her, emitting a raspy whine that threatened to escalate to a growl. He nuzzled into her stomach, his snout nearly a fist. "The vet says he has separation anxiety," Shannon said, taking a step backwards to keep her balance. "He thinks I'm leaving him."

"Psychiatry for dogs," I said. "Have you found a translator for his dreams?" I opened the door as if I were about to reveal the tricks of Houdini, but Clem stayed glued to Shannon. "He doesn't care if *you* leave," she said, reaching, at last, for the leash.

"Every dog has separation anxiety," I said. "You could have asked me and saved the money."

The street troll was gone, but three houses down a woman was slowly pacing back and forth across a yard, walking so slowly and methodically I thought she was holding an invisible metal detector. Clem stiffened and then relaxed, and Shannon said. "Nobody knows what's she's looking for, but she never finds anything. I've never even seen her bend down."

Clem turned off the sidewalk and stuck his face into a bowl of water set just into the grass. Shannon waited a couple of seconds, then yanked him away, but the woman didn't pause or look our way.

"You know that dog I told you about, the one buried in front of the house? That woman was looking for it after the storm, and she was calling and stopping in front of each house, calling as if the dog were inside, and all along the dog was jammed under a couple of feet of packed snow and nobody knew until two days before it thawed enough for me to get my car out. Its head poked out first. A little terrier, black—you'd think you'd notice it, but nothing. It was like a fossil or something. It looked like it would start breathing if only it could get warm."

"And she went crazy?"

"Oh no. She was already crazy. That's the only time anybody around here has seen her leave her property."

"I live off these things," Shannon said two minutes later as I slid five dollars across a greasy counter for three Mighty Tacos and a Pepsi. "They're cheap and filling and local."

We shared our three Mighty Tacos as we walked. I held each one of them to her mouth and she took bites of spiced, fatty beef and kept walking. At first Clem turned as if he expected his share, but then he gave up and went back to sniffing old wrappers and ancient shit in the tiny weed patches between the sidewalk and the curb, pausing six inches from the face of a gray-bearded black man lying on an army blanket.

"'Nother step, sister, and I'm a gonna kill that dog." The man sat up on the blanket, leaving it to Shannon and me to decide whether or not he had a weapon or was skilled with his hands. A torn poster flapped against his feet, a jazz benefit, the sad faces of small children wrapping around one shoe. "Gonna kill it, sweetheart," he said then, "send it straight up to the righteous God."

Clem strained his chain, pawing the sidewalk as if he meant to slide the poster off the shoe and read it for himself. Behind the man on the blanket a truck pulled into the loading zone, and when the driver shoved open the door, it swung so close to the man's head I foresaw hand-to-hand combat, the dog setting into both men because it was too hard to choose which most deserved to be attacked.

"Sorry," I said, stepping between Shannon and the blanket, nudging her forward.

"Men think Clem's a weapon," Shannon said a moment later. "They think they're looking down the barrel of a gun."

"Good."

"Yeah, right."

For once the sidewalk in front of us was clear of distractions for us and for Clem. Nearly twenty-five years ago, before Shannon began school, we'd lived through three consecutive Western New York winters filled with "blizzards of the decade." "When you were little," I said, "a dog that was buried by a snow plow was found alive."

Shannon let the leash lengthen and relax. "You don't have to make up a story so I feel better," she said.

"It's true. You were three. Anyway, you don't have to worry. You couldn't plow Clem in."

"You could hit him with a car, though, because he bolts into the street. And then you could just keep driving."

A block later Clem lunged against the chain, trying to accelerate. "He knows where he is," Shannon said. "This ball park's the only open space for a mile. People run their dogs here after work. You don't want to be sliding into any bases or dive for a sinking liner on the weekends." She glanced at the players as if she had a rooting interest. "If you care, that's Butch in right field."

"The landlord? I thought he was near death?"

123

"The resiliency of men. Dogs remember more."

I looked at her, trying to gauge her depression, but she stopped and we watched the high arc of an opposite field pop up. Butch the right fielder took only two steps and extended his glove for the routine catch. The teams traded places, but she didn't add anything to the miracle of his recovery.

"What was the dog's name?"

"The one in the snow? It was a cocker spaniel. That's what I remember. I guess it lived like some people do when they drown in cold water. Everything slows down so much you don't need as much oxygen to keep yourself running."

"It's still sad," Shannon said. "I bet that dog was afraid of everything after that. I bet it never wanted to go outside."

I wondered if this was my daughter's way of inviting me to ask her to return home, that she was ready to admit a big dog and her bravado weren't enough to get her through eight more months among the crazy and the poor. "He wouldn't be the only one," I said, and when she stared off across the field instead of looking my way or answering, I suddenly couldn't bear to wait until Butch's turn to overswing at the high toss of the slow pitch. I was so sure she was miserable I asked her for Clem's leash to give myself something to do.

When we were almost back to the apartment, I watched the woman inspecting her yard. She moved, I thought this time, in tiny ovals as if she walked according to the Peterson Method.

"I didn't tell you Khalil was a repo man for a furniture rental company."

"So he didn't move, he just got killed?"

"Not quite. The second time he got beat up he quit and left town."

I thought of Khalil the Pakistani knocking on the doors as if delivering pizzas—the unpaid-for stereo blasting, the no-down-payment television blinking a basketball game soundlessly into a room full of men who have spent the monthly charge on liquor and drugs. All I could hear was "motherfucker" and "dothead" and the skittering of backtracking shoes.

"That leaves the actor."

"Keith's ok. We have fun." The woman had written her way to the edge of her property and was reversing herself, using the slant of the left-handed. "But he doesn't eat meat"

"A roots and berries man."

"Not exactly. He doesn't eat fruit."

"You live with a rabbit?"

"What's wrong with vegetables and bread? He'll live forever, and anyway, he's in repertory and they never stay in one place too long. He's been in Cincinnati and Chattanooga and Richmond since his Buffalo stint, so saying I 'live with him' is a wild shot."

Just ahead, the street troll stalked out with her broom to attack the afternoon dirt. "Fucking whore," she yelled, and when her first stroke skittered a small stone against a parked car, Clem pivoted and reared as if he'd just paid for a new paint job, yanking me off the curb. I caught myself two steps onto the asphalt and smiled at the street troll. "Clem doesn't know his strength."

"A dog that doesn't know it's strong will hurt somebody good," the woman said. "You her father?"

"Yeah."

"Oughta shoot your half that dog."

I felt Shannon nudge me from behind and started walking, tugging at the chain. "Gun jammed," I said.

The woman spit into the street. "Fuck it did," she said.

"Fine," I said like a foreign tourist, and she looked away and spit again into the street.

"Too long with a lot makes you forget."

"We're not rich," Shannon said. "He just wants me safe."

"Ought to put your mind to something else then."

"The dog helps me sleep," I said, hearing all of the obvious logic of sound argument shatter on the sidewalk. The woman skidded her broom slowly from side to side as if she were deciding whether or not she was finished. And then she waited for us to pass and swept where we had walked as if she spied every trace of our footsteps.

After we crossed to Shannon's apartment, I said, "The street troll's a reader. She's quoting *Puddn'head Wilson*."

"Fuck she is," Shannon said, and we plunged up the stairs in silence.

We watched a rerun of *Fantastic Voyage*, the actors reduced to miniscule size to break up an inoperable blood clot by riding the blood stream to the part of the brain where it was located. The brain belonged to somebody essential to world harmony, but Shannon was bored with the special effects from my college days until Raquel Welch left the tiny submarine and was attacked by antibodies. They surrounded her, trying to absorb her struggling body." They don't know," Shannon said.

"Of course not," I agreed. "They hate everything they don't recognize."

Shannon watched Raquel Welch escape, but when the next commercials came on, she said, "If they made that movie now they'd give her a bikini to strip down to when the little ship overheats."

I looked away from a man standing in drifted snow surrounded by deep-grooved tires. Somebody had paid to have this commercial run through April, I thought, and here we were in weather that asked for car windows to be rolled down and radios turned up.

Shannon stared at Clem as if he were doing something besides chewing on a balled sweat sock. "Or less," I said, and then I thought we'd reached a moment when both of us might say, "This sucks." Instead, I said, "So many crazies in one place."

"Every place has street people and loony women, Dad."

"But you can try to keep bad choices to a minimum."

"By making none," she said, as if she were finishing my sentence.

I thought of hugging her and kept my hands to myself, ashamed of my fear-ridden options. The dog nosed between us and shifted sideways to face me. "I'll take the dog out," I said. "You're making dinner."

"What would you do without Clem," Shannon said. "I'm watching this until they escape in the teardrop."

"You've seen it before. Why didn't you say something?"

"I haven't seen it, Dad. The plot summary's in a book you gave me when I was in middle school."

I looked at her bookshelf, but I couldn't read the titles from across the room. The wall above them was nearly covered by two of her enormous paintings, both of them the purple and yellow of a nasty bruise, tiny people swirling apart into grainy spaces that looked as if they were invaded by the smog of serious inversions. In one painting a cat watched impassively from the bottom, right hand corner; in the other, a cat watched from the top center.

Letting Clem lead, I chose the direction opposite to the one we'd taken earlier, hoping the next blocks seemed safer. Two women were sitting on the steps of a house, three kids playing in the yard in front of them, enough pleasantness to make me euphoric. "Look at that dog," one said. "It's big enough to fuck somebody."

I didn't want to look down, afraid to find out the dog was aroused. I was only a block from Shannon's, and these two mothers were either drunk or stoned, giggling to each other as if they thought Clem might be seduced. I wanted to go back past the house of the woman who swept the rain, but she'd been outside an hour ago, so she wouldn't reappear so soon.

If Clem was excited, he'd get over it when he got back inside. The stairs. The door. The three rooms so familiar he'd just lie down on the carpet until he heard the key in the lock downstairs or the knob being tested, one sound or the other deciding whether he'd stand silently at the upstairs door or start the deep barking which promised pain.

I'd lived in a house like Shannon's at exactly the same age as she was now. Twenty-two, a first-year graduate student, and the Tet Offensive had spooked me into studying and watching televised news as if it broadcast the meaning of life. I lived upstairs, one room rather than the three she had, and the student in the adjoining room took it upon himself to put a banana in the shared mailbox for the black mailman who, he thought, delivered letters from his girlfriend too late in the afternoon.

Three days in a row, and each day the banana was gone. "Monkey-man thinks it's a tip," that student said, and the third day coincided with the assassination of Martin Luther King, making me consider, for the first time that year, the meaning of "transitional neighborhood." There were two houses between us and the next cross street. On the other side, every resident was black, and when many of them began to mill in the street a half hour after the announcement, their voices loud and their gestures louder, I took inventory in my room, figuring what I could carry out the back window onto the porch roof, what might survive being tossed onto the back lawn. And I took a vow of silence about every petty thought and stupid idea I'd ever been tempted to voice in this lifetime.

I turned the corner, the giggling following behind us, and saw the woman in white coming our way. She had a white scarf wrapped around her face up to a pair of white-framed sunglasses, but Clem didn't even seem to see her. He plowed into her thigh as if white were outside the visible spectrum for dogs.

"Oh," she said, and Clem stumbled sideways, kept his head down as if he were embarrassed to walk into something that wasn't there.

Forty-five minutes later, Shannon handed me a beer and leaned against the counter in her kitchen. As if the weekend had a Mexican theme and we could eat every meal standing up, she'd made chicken quesadillas and had them sitting where she could reach for one without moving. "Clem smashed into the woman in white," I said.

"Smashed into?"

"Just walked right into her. I didn't think dogs did things like that."

"They don't. He must have tried to lick her or something."

"Or he's going blind."

Shannon waved her hand at the quesadillas as an invitation. "Mom told me she was invited to go fire-walking."

"You're right," I said. "There's crazy people everywhere. Mom's friend even pays to be goofy."

"It's therapeutic," Shannon said. "Wouldn't you pay money to have your confidence restored?"

"Guaranteed to last?"

"Of course not."

"You know what you get for a couple of hundred dollars? Physics you can get for free. Stick your hand in the oven," I said. "It's as hot as hell in there, but you won't get burned, not for a while at least."

"Air doesn't trap heat as fast as metal," Shannon said, as if she'd been boning up on firewalkers.

"You bet. You touch those coils and you'll prove that in a hurry."

"So?"

"Firewalkers take science and dress it up as religion. You and I could

128

walk across all the charcoal grills in your neighborhood without a burn to show for it. All we need to do is keep moving."

"I think you have this wrong, Dad."

I swallowed a quesadilla in two bites. "In the morning, we'll go out for a real breakfast before I leave," I said, and Shannon dumped her second piece back on the plate.

"I'm so tired I'm going to puke," she said, and Clem, delirious with staring at the Mexican dinner, didn't follow her to her room. "And I know how to shake cereal from a box and pour milk," she hollered down the hall before she slammed the door.

Hours later, in the dark, I woke to Clem's breathing by my face. As soon as I moved, his paws were on my chest. "What?" I said, but I knew Shannon had locked her door. I sat up, at three a.m., shoved Clem aside, and he nudged me as if I couldn't remember I was to find the leash for taking him out, what he expected from the first person to get out of bed, whether it was dark or light.

And then, when I stood, he skittered to the window instead of the door, staring with the anxious look of a huge dog that had gone mute but expected my small, silly ears to have picked up the threats of the angry or the crazy who had been a block away and were now just outside.

That night after King's murder, the banana-wielding racist had gone door-to-door, telling all six residents to shut off all the lights in the house we rented, and I'd complied, watching from my window as I sat beside my miserable pile of essential possessions until I understood that our black neighbors had more restraint, in the face of profound loss, than that student had shown for the late arrival of personal mail.

The only person to loom out of the backyard's darkness was our landlord bursting through the hedges that lined the edge of the lot. I watched him circle the house, looking up at our darkened windows. When he came around for a second inspection, I saw that he was carrying a rifle, and I moved away from the window to wait out the evening as something other than a shadow to shoot at.

Clem whimpered, his face just below the windowsill, and I remembered the one leering face which had peeked in Shannon's bedroom window when she was ten years old, how it had turned out to be child's art lifted and stuck flat by a storm, and though I wanted to knock on her door now to remind her that most danger was imagined, I was suddenly terrified.

My wife had walked by the open bedroom door and discovered Shannon standing with her pajamas pulled up to her knees. "She wasn't moving," my wife told me later, handing me the paper she'd peeled off the window. "She was just staring at the shadowed window where this crayoned face was stuck."

"If I would have been home, she would have had the door closed," I'd said. "And then what?"

"She would have yelled."

"No, she wouldn't have."

"Why not?"

"Because I might have been the one who opened her door."

That long-ago night RICKY G 3RD GRADE was printed in crayon on the back of the picture, and now I was ready to let Clem piss on the carpet if he wanted because I was afraid to open the door of my daughter's apartment. Roiling up my throat was the taste of all the fatty parts of the Mighty Tacos and the dinner Shannon had made, as if everything I'd eaten that day was reduced to cheap, gristly meat. How long before whatever reasonable thoughts I was capable of would not return? When the powder of the panic at noise and voices covered me so thoroughly I would feel as if I would begin to uncontrollably cough as soon as I took my next breath?

Suddenly, every window looked as if it readily opened inward, as if anyone could bring his inventory of violence inside. And then I thought that if I walked outside I would climb the side steps and work my way across the narrow ledge to Shannon's window, becoming the terrible face which would drive her back home or release that dog from its anxiety before I mouthed the horrible bark of "Hey," one syllable of confrontation followed by the next instead of raising my voice from outside the bleak, brown panels of her oak-stained door.

After Arson

From: *Vanishings* (Stephen F. Austin, 2013)

The soft thud above me might have been the cat, but I knew it was my son placing the barbells on the carpet. Derek worked at the weights in a way that made me worry it was hopeless. On the first night he tried to lift, he struggled to push just the empty bar over his head.

Without walking upstairs to check, I knew there were two small doughnuts, two and one half pounds each, he pressed ten times. He had asked for a bench; he had rummaged through the medicine chest for talcum powder, equating his efforts with the delicate needs of a billiards expert.

Those workouts sustained his faith in growth. Only one boy in his class was smaller. Derek understood heredity, and he was frustrated by the disparity between our heights.

I reminded him about favorable odds and time. He finished three sets and started down the steps to check for results in a mirror by the side door. When he saw I was watching, he turned his back to the glass. "No more 'Wimp,'" he said. "Or 'beanpole.' I'll ring the bell this summer when the carnival comes to the Rotary field."

I told him there was a secret to the carnival's test of strength, that the game he'd asked me to try three summers in a row was rigged. "The wire that the weight's on is slack," I said. "No matter how hard you swing the hammer, the weight won't rise all the way to the bell."

Derek shook his head and recounted the number of bells rung by older boys and fathers, unlike me, who were willing to test themselves. "The carnival guy always takes the slack out for a swing or two," I explained. "He makes sure somebody rings the bell occasionally, or else nobody else will play after a while."

Derek thought for a second. "You're just embarrassed," he finally replied.

At the end of one of those nights when I returned home late, my wife was waiting for me with an expression of crisis stitched onto her face. Liz was otherwise unmarked, so I expected to hear about my mother's heart or splints applied to Derek or one of our other two children.

This time I was wrong. It was Derek, all right, but instead of a doctor, a policeman. What does a boy just turned eleven have to do to be detained for questioning? In a small town like ours, not much, but this was serious, Liz insisted, a fire in a public restroom, the near-catastrophic spread of flames through a theater.

Or something close to that. Paper towels had been lit. They had flared, according to what Liz had been told, threatening the brittle wooden walls of the converted barn, but Derek and the theater were still standing. Nevertheless, a confrontation was waiting for me in the theater office, and I was expected to drive back across town to meet it.

Derek claims, Liz said, that he had been only an accidental witness, standing in the restroom when another boy had tried to prove himself with matches. After I asked why I was needed then, Liz shrugged.

When I arrived, Derek was sitting across a table from a policeman who simply nodded when I entered. I figured him at once for a tyrant or a fool. SELINSGROVE SEALS was printed in white, block letters on the front of the red cap Derek wore. I checked off a series of hard-edged possible responses to the stupidity of what I anticipated was about to happen.

"Tell me what happened while your father listens," the policeman said.

There were long pauses in the rehearsal, Derek explained. His part, as well as the other boy's, was small, and they had time to fill. When he watched the other boy light the towels, it had seemed like a performance, something he was expected to watch. He had not even helped throw water when the towel roll opened up across the floor, flames traveling like thick thread. Even when it was over, it still seemed like the other boy's role, and Derek hadn't said anything to anybody because nothing looked to him like it was damaged.

Except, I thought, now Derek was accused because he expected everyone to be truthful and didn't understand the word-against-word dilemma of investigation. I looked to the policeman to see how he was interpreting, but instead of saying anything, he nodded again and left the room.

Sometimes I am surprised by things. Sometimes there are moments when the world is pliable enough for hope. When the policeman returned, he was pleasant and articulate. Derek was believed. The other boy had lied so badly he could do nothing, eventually, but confess.

"It's because you had a coat and tie on," Liz said when we got home. "Being dressed like that at 10:30 at night impresses the police." Derek twirled his hat on one finger, blurring the stylized blue seal below the white letters. A couple of revolutions and it flew off into the centerpiece of dried flowers.

"Everything is going soft on this planet," the policeman had said while Derek was retrieving his jacket. "You need to keep a watchdog now just to keep from sinking into the world."

"We have a cat," I had said, and he had looked quizzically at me. He had laughed, too, although a beat was missed. The hat with the aggressive blue seal displaced the flower arrangement. "He's still in the play," I said. "The other boy is being replaced."

"On such short notice?"

Derek reached out to pull the hat free. He began to twirl it again.

"It doesn't take DeNiro. Somebody can learn it in a few days."

This time the hat landed by my feet. I picked it up in a way that kept Derek from asking for it back.

At breakfast, before his brother and sister come downstairs, Derek explained the urgency of his recurring dream. It was my fault, Liz reminded me, that he has it.

He is running from the pods. All of us have changed, invaded by aliens. Beginning with the remake seen more than two years before and ending with the original watched last month, Derek has sat through both versions of *Invasion of the Body Snatchers*.

After watching the remake, he'd gone to sleep, as usual, with his Darth Vader punching bag—one of those tall, weighted balloons that sways and bounces and always returns to upright—standing beside his bed. An hour later he'd woken to the certainty of an attack by the pods. A life-size one stood near his face.

"Am I changed?" he had screamed. "Am I changed?"

I had tried to reason with him. I had turned on the light to show him Vader's plastic face.

"You're pretending," he had said. "You're a pod man. The real you is in the garbage."

Vader had to be deflated. A night light had been found in a drawer. "Eight years old," Liz had said, "and you've given him a changeling complex."

The pods had returned several times a year since then, and his horror stories, when I tried to extract them, broke off in him like ticks. I imagined holding some kind of medicinal flame to each of them. I imagined his watching the original film when he is eleven will show him it is time to stop worrying. Instead, I listened, this time, to his revelation that everyone who is not real has a tiny red mark behind his ears. After I poured the orange juice, I allowed him to check near my hair line.

"Every time," he said, "I am the only one left who isn't changed." When I asked him what he saw behind my ears, he shrugged and returned to his cereal.

That night we watched a television program that showed clips of famous televised magic. Near the end a magician made the Statue of Liberty disappear. The statue weighs 225 tons, we learned, seeing an audience follow the action in person.

The magician prattled on about freedom and immigrants and his mother, an enormous curtain tellingly closed behind him. "I remember this one," I said, "but I didn't watch."

A set of commercials came on. "He can't do it," Derek said. "It's just a trick."

After the commercials, when the curtain finally opened, the statue was gone. Searchlights played over the empty space; the live audience was astonished. And then the magician closed the curtain again and began to preach about the importance of freedom, running on so long I told Derek he was moving the audience, not the statue. "They think they're looking at the same space, but he's turned them," I said. "Now he's stalling while he turns them back."

Derek leaned forward and stared. When the statue reappeared, he sat up and said, "You're wrong. It's a fake statue. He's changed it just like the body snatchers."

"It's him, Dad," Derek said a few weeks later, pointing at the newspaper. I was watching a Pittsburgh Pirate relief pitcher walk the winning run into scoring position.

He placed the paper on my lap and showed me the picture on the front page. I glanced down at one of those faces you know but don't know. "Who?" I said.

"The policeman at the playhouse."

"Oh." I thought of how reflexively I waved at such people, hoping a gesture was enough. A lefthander trudged into the nearly hopeless situation. The heart of the lineup would surely drive in the run that would put the Pirate losing streak at five.

"He got killed. Somebody shot him four times."

"Around here?" For a moment, just before I picked up the newspaper and began to read, I thought of how many times someone had said this, looking around the vulnerable spots in his house as if insulation could keep out every kind of weather.

The killer, the paper said, had been seeking revenge. He had stepped out of the darkness and fired four times through the patrol car window.

It turned out he was mistaken. The policeman he had meant to kill was sitting in another car at the beginning of the speed trap. They had switched cars. It was boring, after all, to do nothing but read numbers. Thirty minutes had passed since the killer had been given a speeding ticket—time enough to go home, load a rifle, and return. Perhaps the road, two lanes along the river, had reminded him of a frontier. There was a Country & Western bar a short distance away. After he fired the shots, the killer walked to it and ordered a beer and smoked a cigarette, according to a patron, by taking cowboy-film drags.

So the arrest had been simple. There was even an eyewitness. Parked in front of the patrol car was a pick-up truck whose driver was being cited for littering. Sitting under the dome light, the policeman had been writing the citation when the avenger fired. The litterer had looked out into the face of a man who had just fired a rifle into the body of a policeman. They had stared at each other until the man on foot had crossed the road, tossed the rifle onto the seat of his jeep, and walked off toward the tavern.

Later, everyone in the bar claimed they knew he was the killer because he had been the only one who had not rushed to the door when a man shouted from outside that someone had been shot.

"He didn't take no mess from nobody," a friend explained when he was interviewed. "He didn't 'low nothin' to fool with his head."

There were short biographies of both victim and killer. There were comments from teachers and relatives. The killer's friend ran on for half a column. "Bad news went down when you messed with him," he said at the close.

After a spring of record rain, nothing for over a week but heat, the black flies prospered. In our part of Pennsylvania there was a characteristic fanning of the face in warm weather. A stranger riding through town would wonder at the mannerism. If he stopped to inquire, he quickly discovered its source and either was assimilated or covered by welts.

For fifteen minutes, I had been brushing the gnats away and watching the lot in front of the college auditorium fill with police cars. Five hundred uniformed mourners had been promised. An equal number of civilians.

The black flies broke into small clouds and covered the crowd. Derek walked across the grass toward me. He looked strange in pants—school had been out for a week. His expression was equally out of place. A first funeral should be some vague great-uncle who seemed to have been born old.

We sat far to the side. There were, perhaps, a dozen people we knew there. None of them were policemen. The service was a Catholic one. Several priests stood on the stage, but only one was elaborately dressed. He would say the important things.

The program, I realized, was exactly like a church service. At least until the homily, which was filled with allegories for hope and faith. Derek looked straight ahead. He might have been afraid to turn, believing someone would lecture him immediately about behavior. However, when I didn't read the responses or sing the hymns, he was silent, too.

When the policemen who chose to take communion filed through the aisles, all of them cupped their hands in front of them. Some lessons stay. No one was self-conscious.

An hour of that, prayer and praise. A large picture was mounted above the closed casket. Even from thirty rows back I could tell it was an enlargement of the photograph in the newspaper.

The priest concluded by telling the story of a little girl's fantasy of heaven. She claimed, when asked, that everyone had the same expression of happiness.

It was that perfect smile, she said, the one that animals have in my picture books. Derek appeared to be listening closely.

And then the five hundred policemen exited. They were forming, I was sure, an elongated corridor of grief through which the coffin and the family would pass.

POTATO CHIPS

From: *Vanishings* (Stephen F. Austin, 2013)

Except for potato chips, my mother never bought anything at the grocery store that wasn't on sale.

One week she'd come home with six boxes of Kellogg's Corn Flakes and four boxes of elbow macaroni, all but one of each stashed together on the shelf in the hallway guest closet. Butter, milk, and cheese came to our refrigerator in marked-down oversized packages and cartons. The meat for our dinners was determined by ten cents off on a pound of pork chops, five cents off on hamburger, fifteen cents off on cube steak or frozen fish.

She clipped every newspaper coupon for staples. Our toilet paper varied from sale to sale, twenty-four rolls of Charmin nearly smothering of eight bars of Ivory soap beside a pile of threadbare towels in the bathroom closet. And downstairs, in the damp root cellar beneath our front porch, were shelves arranged by sales on canned peaches, apricots, grapefruit sections, tuna, French-cut green beans, and creamed corn. One can of Dole pineapple sections, the remnant of an earlier eight-can binge, would sit forlornly beside six bright new cans of A&P house brand pineapple.

But there was only one brand of potato chips that satisfied my mother—Quinlan's—and I was as glad for that as I was unhappy to discover it was Puffed Rice and not Cocoa Puffs that was on sale when she set down a bag full of five discounted boxes.

Before I turned ten, she'd occasionally test Wise and Bachman's and

Lay's, deciding there were too many dark ones (Wise), too many broken pieces (Bachman's) or too many that lacked sufficient salt (Lay's). When she rejected all of them "once and for all," I was happy because I loved Quinlan's as much as she did. They were thin and light and wonderfully greasy, deep fried in palm oil years before anyone but people my mother called "the fussy" worried about cholesterol. Above all, they were so heavily salted that after a few minutes of gorging, I could feel my lips puckering into ridges I'd have to lick in order to keep them from cracking.

If all the problematic ingredients, trans fat included, were printed on those bags, we didn't read them. Of course she admitted potato chips weren't good for anybody, but this tiny luxury was such a pleasure, and she seldom humored herself in any other way, that she claimed it wouldn't hurt to have one little sin. For my mother, chips were like cigarettes, something to be indulged no matter their long-term consequences, all of which were uncertain. After all, she said, there were plenty of healthy looking eighty-year-old smokers around, weren't there?

When my homework was done, my mother and I would open a fresh twenty-ounce bag and sit by side on the couch to watch dramas on television, most often the plays that were on *Studio One*. The shows were live, something she thought special even though the original scripts often ended with my mother saying, "I don't get it, Gary. Did you get it?" because the stories finished with at least a bit of ambivalence.

And if we missed *Studio One*, my mother busy with housework or exhausted from working in my father's bakery, we had chips to eat while we watched quiz shows like *$64,000 Question* or *Twenty-One*, answering just enough of the easy questions to make us believe we could win the big prize if we studied up.

Those shows were just getting started when my father left for work. My sister, even though she was older, went to bed at ten o'clock because she didn't want to stay up late to waste her time with television. "You can catch up tomorrow night," my mother would say to me, tearing open a brand new bag or taking the clip off a half-eaten one.

In fact, my father and my sister didn't even eat potato chips, content with the Macintosh apples marked down one week or the seed-infested, stringy tangerines that seemed to be perpetually on sale.

Good. I didn't mind sharing ice cream that arrived in two-gallon cartons that didn't fit in the upstairs refrigerator freezer and only came in chocolate or vanilla. I didn't care if my sister drank more than I did from the fourth consecutive family-size can of Hawaiian Punch.

But I was happy my mother hoarded those chips, stuffing the half-eaten bags behind empty casserole dishes or inside the baking pan that was only used for Thanksgiving turkeys or Easter hams. I sometimes had to spend fifteen minutes to find the bag, and I'd have to memorize exactly how it was placed and how tightly rolled up it was before I took the largest handful I could without making a detectable difference. There was never a bag so nearly empty I couldn't take some. If my mother and I were that close to the bottom, we'd finish them and lick our fingers to add one last delight before she threw away the package.

Even as we stuffed ourselves, my mother told me we were eating in moderation. There was even denial because we could eat only one bag per week. Going shopping was done on Wednesdays, as measured and regular as other household chores—laundry (Monday), ironing (Tuesday) house cleaning (Thursday). We always had to make do until the following Wednesday, and that routine made us feel, for an hour, two nights a week, as if we were celebrating salt-filled holidays.

But soon we had the bag emptied by Friday night because the year I turned thirteen we started watching *The Untouchables* on Thursday night and *The Twilight Zone* on Fridays. My mother thought Robert Stack was rugged and handsome, and even if there was no end of criminals for Eliot Ness to bring to justice, she always knew how things turned out. Likewise, for *The Twilight Zone*, which delighted her by pulling a surprise near the end, but one that wasn't confusing.

The problem was how far from the next Wednesday we were without any chips in the house. She wasn't going to buy a second bag. Not ever. If we wanted to have chips for *Peter Gunn* or *Mr. Lucky*, private detective shows she said she watched because "You love them so much," she was going to have to make them herself. She already owned a deep fryer she used for chicken and breaded shrimp, and now she purchased a vegetable slicer that turned a potato into a wonderful plate of incredibly thin slices. She dropped those potatoes into the bubbling grease, and we stayed in the kitchen while they cooked, the room smelling like the kitchens of restaurants my father called "greasy spoons."

My mother watched the stove because there was a chance all that hot grease would ignite, but mostly she paid attention to make sure she got the potatoes just right. A light tan, just enough to turn them crisp and no more. "As good as Quinlan's," she would say, laying them out to drain on old newspaper like she did for bacon strips on Sundays, and then she'd shake salt onto them until they were coated. There'd be enough for a bowl full, fewer than we'd eat from a bag, but they were so rich and salty we didn't care. *Peter Gunn* only lasted for half an hour, so there was hardly any time left for the plot to wrap up without chips to swallow. And having them every third week—another self-imposed schedule she honored—meant we could imagine self-discipline even as we managed to add a third night of chips more than once a month.

When I was sixteen, my mother went for a physical because Pennsylvania had a new law that required one for driver's license renewal. She'd been suffering from headaches for years, and when the doctor took her blood pressure, he was so alarmed by the numbers, he had her admitted to a hospital. A stroke, he said, was imminent. It was a miracle she was still on her feet.

Her hospital stay lasted only two days. There was prescribed medicine that kicked in, the numbers dropping to the ordinary range of high before they released her. She joked about her "scores" with friends so they could marvel, and before too long she was down to high/normal. The biggest problem was that right there, on the top of the list of dietary things to do, was "No salt."

Dinners were easy. The rest of us could add salt while my mother watched. She seldom bought processed food, and she made her own soup. But now there were no chips in the bag with six boxes of Farina that I would add chocolate syrup to in order to gag down during the second month of eating it for breakfast.

For a month, I checked all of her hiding places, and each one stayed empty. The deep fryer stood spotless and forlorn. By the second month I bought my own bag of Quinlan's. I had a driver's license by then. I worked from 10:30 to 5:30 on Friday nights in my father's bakery for $1.25 an hour, and I could afford to indulge myself.

By the second month I smuggled potato chips into the house and kept them in my room. By now I'd given up watching television, and I ate them while I listened to rock music for hours on my tiny clock radio. Three or four times. Because shortly thereafter my mother brought home a bag of chips with the groceries. "For you," she said, "because I know how much you love them."

"I'll just have a few," she said. "Doctor's orders."

They weren't hidden anymore. Held together by plastic clips, the opened bags sat on a shelf beside whatever cereal was stocked for a few months. I stuffed myself on Wednesday nights when my mother was out of the house for choir practice, and I didn't complain when I could tell she'd cheated on her diet.

And so it went until I went off to college. She waited for my vacations to bring home a bag. She didn't say anything about her blood pressure, and I could tell, when I tasted dinner, that the food was already salted. But by the end of my sophomore year in college my father had closed the bakery, in part because of declining business, but also because my mother wasn't able to stand on her feet all day to sell what he baked.

When I was married and bought my own chips, no longer loyal to Quinlan's, she would sit in my kitchen to talk, reaching inside the bag I had from time to time, always saying "Just a few." I never heard my father object, and when I began to buy new brands that were rippled or kettle cooked, she never commented except once, when she said, "I think Quinlan's might be out of business."

When I visited her house, there were always chips. "I knew you were coming," she'd say. There were a variety of brands now, all of them on sale, the price marked down with a sticker on the bag, but she said she still only bought them one at a time. She was taking four kinds of medicine for her blood pressure and her heart. As always, before my father carved, she picked the salted skin off one side of the Thanksgiving turkey and handed part of it to me before she devoured the rest. "It's almost as good as chips," she said, and I agreed, coming back into the kitchen during dinner to pick off whatever crispy strips of skin remained.

When, in her 50s, she was out of breath from modest exercise and in her 60s, out of breath from walking to the mail box and back, she kept eating chips because "why stop now?" Twenty-five years younger, I was already slowing down. Before my fortieth birthday, I made myself begin to wait two weeks between bags of chips I stopped automatically salting food. It seemed like a healthy diet to only buy two bags of chips a month and to only eat deep fried food at restaurants.

My mother never had the stroke that once seemed imminent, but she had congestive heart failure and her organs began to shut down, her kidneys the first to go for good a few days before she died in her sleep at home shortly after having my father walk a letter to me to the mailbox that said, near its end, "I've never felt so nauseous," a sentence I read after I returned from her funeral because that letter arrived two days after she died.

And now? Twenty years later I compare brands of potato chips for the percentage of fat per serving. For the past five years I've refused the kinds that contain trans fat and have given up my favorite brand for one that seems less dangerous. And I exercise regularly, believing in the penance of sweating profusely four times per week.

Like a man who limits himself to five cigarettes a day as a way of minimizing his chances for serious illness, I've stuck to my diet of one bag every two weeks.

With exceptions.

For those, I use her excuse of thrift. This week there are two bags of chips on the kitchen counter because the sale was "Buy one, get one free." "40% less fat than regular chips," the bag says, rationalizing those two bags into the fat-equivalent of one for me. The day I bought them I emptied half a bag with a turkey sandwich—no mayo, no oil—rationalizing again.

Except for those television shows accompanied by potato chips, I never sat with my mother to be entertained. Such behavior was the same as "doing nothing," and when those few shows were over and the potato chips gone, there was work to be done. My mother was quick to criticize the laziness of others, mine so much included that I was embarrassed to be caught watching television at other times by myself.

None of my three children seem to crave potato chips, so I don't have my mother's excuse of buying for their visits. Instead, they buy chips for me when I visit, and by now I understand that they want me to indulge myself because it somehow softens my own workaholic nature.

When I feed my face in their living rooms and on their decks, it's easy to remember that my mother was at her warmest when she gave in to the small pleasure of potato chips. And there's always the self-satisfaction of pushing the bag away at last, showing that I can make myself stop while I lick my fingers one at a time, relishing the joy of salt and grease.

BRAINS

From: *Vanishings* (Stephen F. Austin, 2013)

My mother said fish was brain food. She breaded it and fried it and told me to finish whatever she put on my plate, and for a while I expected my IQ to rise, maintaining the same belief in that promise as I had in the carrots she fed me to cure my nearsightedness.

Long after I lost my faith in both of those home remedies, right about the time I got my first pair of glasses, my father put two pans on the kitchen stove one Saturday morning and slid slimy-looking meat into them from two different packages. He saw me turn my head and barked, "Don't be so squeamish."

As usual, I wasn't wearing my glasses, so all I had to do was take two steps back to turn the meat into fog. Whatever filled those pans where Crisco was melting into puddles beneath it was comfortably blurred. "What is it?" I asked like I knew I was supposed to.

"Veal kidneys," he said, pointing to one pan. "Calves brains," he said, pointing to the other. "Wait until you try some," he added, but I was stuck on the word "brains," and he read my face. "You don't know what's good," he said. "You want the real smart food, here's your chance."

When he relented, asking me to try one or the other, I chose the kidneys. They didn't promised to make me better in any way, but they didn't seem much different than the hearts and livers of chickens and turkeys, meat, even as a nine-year-old, that I loved.

The kidneys, once the smell of urine faded as they finished cooking, were rich and greasy and delicious. My father was pleased. He ate all of the brains himself.

2

Despite not eating brains, I did well in school. Later that year, near the end of fourth grade, my teachers suggested I skip a grade, and a "readiness evaluator" tested me for an hour, asking, early on, for the quick recall of body parts, current events, and trivia. I loved showing off what I'd read. For science, I mentioned Ptolemy, the sun as God's spotlight; I sequenced Copernicus, the church, and Galileo. He smiled and read me puzzles like the one about Bill meeting his mother-in-law's only daughter's husband's son. What relation, he questioned, is this person to Bill? His son, I blurted, not bothering with the proffered pencil, and I thought he'd be astonished because I could calculate, in seconds, the equal number of quarters, dimes and nickels (twenty-four) to get nine dollars and sixty cents. I knew how many nines (twenty) I had to pass counting from 1 to 100, and how to slosh water back and forth from a five-quart container to one that holds three quarts in order to finish with exactly four. I thought the expert loved my top-scale score, would show me off to every teacher in the district, but my parents voted *no* and *no* before he spoke.

In our yard that winter I built, after a snowstorm, a model of the solar system, rolling and shaping the huge ball of Jupiter, the extraordinary mound of the sun. I worked the planets to scale, measured circumference and the distance from sphere to sphere to sphere. I needed the neighbor's yard for Pluto, and when the frost planets seemed plain, I gave them their moons to scale, snow berries and packed pebbles of ice. At the end of the street I snowballed another star. I stood, according to my imagined scale, a hundred million miles from it, thought of my house, and readied myself for ignition because surely, in all that snow, some life had formed and evolved to visit me.

3

That summer, when I had to spend afternoons at my father's bakery because my mother had started working there to help make ends meet, the woman who owned Peluso's, a nearby bar, introduced me to her son. "This is my boy Raymond," she said, as if she expected us to become friends and play together. He was nearly twice my size, and I guessed that he was about twice my age. His face was round, and his eyes seemed glazed. When he spoke, he sounded the way my father's records did when I changed the speed from 78 to 33, but Mrs. Peluso acted as if she understood every word.

"He loves his lime pop," she said, pointing to the bottle he held in his hand. "I keep some in the cooler with the beer."

Raymond slurred a few more words, pointing at one of the display cases where trays of cookies were laid out. "Such a sweet tooth," Mrs. Peluso said while my mother retrieved one of the vanilla sugar cookies and handed it to her.

Raymond seemed agitated. He growled out another phrase or two, and Mrs. Peluso stepped toward the door, tugging him away from the case with a sort of leash that was attached to a harness he wore around his chest and back. "He'd eat it and ask for more if I let him," she said, and then she led him into the street like a dog.

"Down Syndrome," my mother said as soon as the door closed. "It's her cross to bear."

"He can't even talk," I said.

"Yes, he can. You heard him. A mother lives long enough with that, she learns what it means." My mother closed the display case and leaned on the counter as if she needed to get closer to where I sat by the space heater that wasn't turned on until November. "You know," she said, "he's not the only one. It's not rare."

I looked out the front window as if I expected Mrs. Peluso to be listening, but the street was empty. "I never saw anybody like that," I said. "Where are they?"

"They're put away mostly. There are places for that."

"Where?"

"Where bad luck lives," she said. "Where, God willing, you'll never be."

4

In health class, eighth grade, we learned the descending categories for results on the Stanford-Binet IQ Test that all of us had taken in first and fourth grade.

You couldn't do worse, if you made a mark, than idiot. I thought of Raymond, who still loved lime soda and slurred his private language at the end of a leash near my father's bakery. That year there were imbeciles bused in and out of half-days in the resource rooms, and like other eighth graders, I told "little moron" jokes:

> *The little moron was playing with matches and burned the house down. "Your daddy's going to kill you when he gets home," his mother said. But the little moron laughed and laughed because he knew his daddy was asleep on the couch.*

My friends and I laughed and laughed at everything the little moron did. *Why would he take his ruler to bed? He wanted to see how long he slept.* And we wanted, joke by joke, to bring the dead metaphors to life—time, butter, and fire flying out his busy window.

"That will do," Miss Hutchinson, our health teacher said, sick of those jokes one afternoon.

"Three generations of imbeciles are enough," the Chief Justice of the Supreme Court said in 1927, supporting the Eugenics Record Office, which wanted to sterilize everyone deemed unfit. Harry Laughlin, Superintendant, hoped, in two generations, to eliminate what he considered the submerged tenth of our population. He meant the blind, the deaf, the orphans and the homeless. He meant the poor and the stupid, and the Supreme Court backed him up, finding an example in the "clear and present danger" embedded in the family tree of the Bucks, who were illegitimate and poor; who were Emma, Carrie, and finally Vivian, who made more than enough of those morons and was declared deficient at seven months after someone gave this expert testimony: "There is a look about the baby that is not quite normal, but what it is I can't quite tell."

None of the Bucks, it turned out, was a moron like the one who took his ladder to church for High Mass, but like Emma and Carrie, Vivian was sterilized, too, for good measure.

5

In college, an English major, I took a course called "Swift and Pope." One afternoon the professor, to give us context, delivered a lecture on The Great Chain of Being, how angels move above us while brutes make do below. Edward Tyson, the professor said, was a comparative anat-

148

omist in the later 17th century, and he believed that he'd verified the thinking approved by the church. He studied a chimpanzee, expecting a link that placed it close behind man. One thing it liked, happily, was wearing clothes, a good sign for the brute one floor below mankind's apartment. And the first night out at the bar, it drank itself to all fours, then altogether down, comfortable with vice. Drinking is fine, Tyson reasoned, but knuckle-walking had to stop before that chimp could model for the Great Chain Encyclopedia. Tyson needed that chimp to walk upright, something snug between the large apes and us for the arpeggio of the Great Chain. But in one of Tyson's old plates, the chimp uses a walking stick; in another, it ambles away, holding a rope stretched overhead like a commuter's hand rail. And as for the pants? In hours, they reeked, were changed, then stunk again.

At the time, the professor went on, those chimps were as exotic as the humans from Africa, who were placed one step above them and several steps below the British in the writings of Charles White, biologist, who championed, a century later, the Great Chain of the Upright by defining intelligence through the shapes of jaws and foreheads. The American Savage was next in his chain, the Oriental its neighbor. Charles White worked his way, by facial features, to Europe, and, by extrapolation, to the Greek ideal in antiquity. And as for intelligence? In the Golden Age of assigned place, the white man bound to God, form followed function.

During the next class we were asked to recall Pope's heroic couplets, passages chosen from "Essay on Man." The Great Chain of Being jangled and clanked while we remembered how the bored superior beings "Show'd a Newton as we show an ape," another theory taken to heart, the professor explaining how Immanuel Kant, in the Charles White years, believed Jupiter was the planet of sufficient size to support all of God's higher beings, the ones who were links between us and the angels.

6

One summer afternoon five years after I graduated from college, my cousin and I sat our year-old sons on her living room carpet, and I counted the handicaps in her first-born until I felt her stare and had to turn away. An accident, she said her doctor had told her. Too little air. Unfortunate.

I nodded like someone saving his job in an office of lies. My son pulled himself up on a chair and staggered until he fell. Her son crawled as if he'd lighted on the huge, invisible web of God. "My sister's boy has a problem, too," she murmured. "Both of us are moving closer to cities so this never happens again."

Too little air in Pennsylvania where we lived. Too little air in Georgia where her sister lived. Too little air in the living room where we stared from one boy to the other, so quiet, so long, we might have been practicing conservation, as if that room had been sealed by a landslide and we were finding the essential, slow rhythms of survival.

7

Without knowing what I offered, that son of mine, a few years later, sampled the veal kidneys I occasionally made for breakfast before I walked to the nearby high school to teach. He asked for more. I told him what he'd eaten, but it didn't slow him down. He was four years-old and wouldn't have been able to point out where his kidneys were located if some pre-school expert had asked in order to determine his school readiness.

For that whole school year he asked me to wake him on the days I cooked kidneys. One morning I asked him if he'd try brains, and he looked horrified. I told him the story of his grandfather, and he said, "Grand Pap eats brains" as if he was revealing a secret kept for centuries.

8

By the time my daughter and another son had been born, I learned that some mornings chimpanzees are known to skip breakfast and hike in a group to where the Aspilia grows. They gibber in a way that shows reluctance, chatter in a manner that sounds as if they're complaining, but all of them gulp the plant's bitter leaves, each cleaning a branch like children frightened by the taste of medicine.

Aspilia, it turns out, is a purgative in the rain forest, a home remedy to fend off parasites and fungi. The chimpanzees have been filmed by scientists, who have also learned that the oil of the Aspilia destroys the malignant cells of certain tumors. Likewise, we can be instructed by the pharmacy of the primates if we watch the sick chimp who drags herself to the foul bush of Vernonia to chew its leaves and swallow its juice. We can witness her next day recovery, how she grooms herself again and forages for food.

It turns out that in the natural selection of medicinal plants, the ignorant and stupid will swallow poisonous leaves, end their faulty genes with an incorrect prescription. Pay attention, survivors lecture, to pattern, color, texture, scent. Eat these stems during the rainy season. Take two of these petals for climate change. And here are the aids for fertility, their counterparts for prevention. There are howling monkeys who follow a diet that helps produce daughters or sons, who eat acidic or alkaline to shift conception odds for the x or the y of sperm. And if we observe the howlers who feel betrayed or trapped by conception, we discover that they grind the leaves for induced abortion, take care of themselves without consulting doctors, lawyers, politicians or priests.

Remarkable. And when I did research on my own, I learned that Tyson's clothed chimp never got drunk again, but some animals lack discipline. For example, elephants, when introduced to beer, go back to it when given a chance, chugging twenty at a time.

9

Ten years after we watched our first-born sons on that living room carpet, my cousin told me about Fragile X Syndrome, how her son made progress through care and love. Her husband was tossing a ball to our eleven year-olds, casually and carefully by turns. Two steps closer, two steps back, handicapping the distance and the arc of the ball. My son, later, listed all of Fragile X's unlucky signs of awful coordination and speech, the long face and big floppy ears of the donkey.

I was told that my cousin's son knew the name of every bird at the feeder near the back patio, and I agreed to say, "What's that?" each time one settled. He shouted, "House wren," waved his hands, bit his fingers, and screamed "House wren" for the next and the next, laughing and laughing at my ignorance. And whether it was the same bird, three different ones from the same species, or he was bluffing like a parrot, I asked again, looking to where my son was throwing horseshoes for the first time, already bored with ringer and leaner, the simple language for play.

10

When my cousins hosted a party for their parents' fiftieth wedding anniversary, I had a chance to spend a few hours with their three Fragile X sons, all, by then, in their late teens. My older son was in college; the boy who had shared that carpet with him worked clean-up at McDonald's.

The two brothers from Georgia bumped butts and squealed, "Hammer time!"

"Can't touch this!" I shouted back, giving solidarity a shot.

"Hammer time!" they shouted, ecstatic, slamming again before they tumbled to the carpet of the reception hall.

Their mother gave me a smile that was part grimace. "They each have a Walkman," she said. "It kept them busy on the drive from Georgia. They listen to the same thing over and over."

"It looks as if they love M. C. Hammer," I said.

"They're sedated," she said, and when I couldn't think of anything to say in answer to that, she added, "Just this once. Just for today. I can't have them spoiling this."

Later that afternoon, she told me about the tests I could have my daughter take to find out whether she was a carrier. "For your peace of mind," she said. "So you know for sure."

11

Someone has claimed the dinosaurs forgot everything but the drugs of flowering plants in the centuries they first flourished. Those lizards gorged and got high; they overdosed and died in an apocalypse of the giants. We've laughed and laughed at their idiot ways, more foolishness in the great chain of brutes who rattle the links of their life spans—the sestina of dog years, the sonnet of the hamster, the haiku of the may fly.

And we believe so much in the epic of our lives, the photographs, the slides, and the long pauses for our stories that enlarge the past until our memories are edited to accept the anthropic principle, how the purpose of everything has been to lead to our ascendency.

My uncle keeps a chart of ancestors that he shares with my mother, the men's occupations in parentheses beneath their life-spanned names. *Tailor, tailor, tailor,* it says, fading like an echo through the nineteenth century and stopping, 1782, in Germany, five generations fixed in one village before the coming to America.

The great chain of a construct. All but one of them died from lung disease; I use an inhaler for cats, pine trees, and the dust from his redundant flow charts, checking for myself in my mother's weaknesses and my sons in mine. When the meal is served, my cousins, the mothers of imbeciles, watch their husbands tend their boys' plates, buttering corn before they carefully cut ham to prevent their teenage sons from choking.

Thirty years after that health class and fifteen years after watching those babies with my cousin, I could repeat the rosary of heredity, say Fragile X, the syndrome that claimed my cousins, their three imbecile boys, one generation enough, in this case, to confirm a chromosome passed down like a family job. If that flaw had been handed down through my uncle, I'd beaten the odds by being something other than stupid. And my sister was a carrier unverified because she had no children.

Vivian Buck? She managed to make the honor roll in grade school the year before she died. My sons? Both of them were gifted enough to take, like their father, skip-a-grade intelligence tests.

12

A few weeks ago, in a city I was visiting in order to talk with college students about stories I've written, there was a fair going on. My student escorts, happy to show me local color before we were due at the college, pointed out the longest line at any of the food booths. "Guess what's sold there," one of the young women said.

We were in Southern Indiana. I figured maybe beef or pork slathered in some sort of special sauce. "Close," she said, pausing for effect before saying, "Brain sandwiches."

"Really?" was all I could come up with.

"Pigs' brains this year," she said, "because mad cow scares off customers." She was twenty-one, and she and her friend had sampled those brains as freshmen. "They say it's a week's worth of cholesterol on a bun," she said, "but yet there's a whole wheat option for those who think healthy. And plenty of onions," reminding me how my father eventually added those to the brains I'd refused fifty years ago.

Loitering among a crowd of Hoosiers who were swallowing something like a heart attack, I thought of how my father had tried to teach me the body, how each soft part of animals could be eaten for pleasure while we imagined it healing its namesake within us.

13

There's the Internet now, information readily accessible, and Fragile X has become more widely known. I never had my daughter tested, but my cousins finally told me it was their mother's side of the family that carried the gene, that it was their brother who had beaten the odds.

Their father is dead now, and for the first time since that 50th anniversary, we all gather together for the funeral. The three boys are men now, nearly thirty like my sons. The two boys from Georgia have been placed in a home by their mother; the one from Pennsylvania, no longer working, lives at home.

Hammer Time has been over for years, the parachute pants a staple for laughter, Hammer himself in public financial difficulty. But neither boy has a Walkman today, and their sister (gifted, it's turned out) sits between them.

My cousins' mother knows the news about blood lines. They've trusted her heart not to break. Until she dies there is little chance we'll all be together again. She smiles grimly. "He went peacefully," she says about her husband's death. "In his sleep, the way we'd all like to go."

After the funeral, the extended family assembles in one huge, rented room to face the camera of each parent. The light is weak and varied near the north window. The children of younger relatives are sullen or self-conscious or bored with the afternoon's focus on the past. My two sons and my daughter, none of them touched by Fragile X, pull themselves up straight. "Ok," I say, "ok," finding the three imbeciles who are gripped on the shoulders, two-handed, by grandmother, mother, and carrier sister, each of those wild boys smiling and still, momentarily, for my flash.

Hard Candy

The summer my older son was about to turn three, I took him to the library of the college that had just given me one year's grace to find another position. Such things were supposed to be confidential, but the librarian knew I would not return in September or, at the latest, be gone the following June. "I'm sorry to hear the news," she said, and smiled at Derek, who followed me through fiction and poetry as if he were on a leash.

Though the library was empty except for the three of us, Derek whispered when we emerged from the stacks near the two small artificial palm trees that flanked the entrance to the periodical room. "May I touch today?" Derek said, and I said "Sure," whispering myself and glancing back to see that the librarian seemed charmed.

Derek petted the fronds and held them for me to touch, and a minute later, when my son had behaved better, I guessed, than any other faculty child in the librarian's memory, she offered Derek a piece of candy.

I nodded, lost in imagining a shelf of my future books in this library and a thousand others. The candy looked to be lemon flavored. A sourball. I smiled when Derek said, "Thank you" and popped it into his mouth. The librarian turned back to the rhythm of processing books returned by students eager to be rid of them as the semester ended. "It's good," Derek whispered, pointing at his mouth. And then, before he had crossed the lobby to where I was standing, Derek suddenly stopped and stiffened, turning mute and flushed.

I raced to where Derek was standing and pounded on his back at once, resorting to what my father had taught me at a Boy Scout meeting years before the Heimlich maneuver was printed with illustrations for a kitchen wall chart.

Nothing. Not a sound but my open palm slapping my son's back, the tone turning deeper when I closed my hand into a fist and thumped.

"Turn him upside down," the librarian shouted, and the advice made such enormous good sense that I grabbed Derek's legs, lifting and flipping him. With one arm, I hugged my son's legs against my chest and pounded again on his back, using my fist, Derek's face slapping against my thighs until, after the third thump, the lemon candy spurted out onto the blue carpet between my black shoes.

The librarian and I looked long and hard at that candy and each other, neither of us speaking until she said, "I didn't think." I memorized the size and shape of the moist hardball for ten seconds before I led my son into the late spring afternoon without saying another word to the woman who had nearly killed him.

I strapped Derek into his car seat. He kicked his feet and looked past me toward the deserted parking lot. I tested the metal clasp. Though it held, something felt odd about it, and I unlocked it and hooked it a second time, tugging the strap twice. "There," I said, touching the clasp again, examining the seatbelt strap as it crossed Derek's body, pulling it away from his throat.

CROSSWORDS

From: *Vanishings* (Stephen F. Austin, 2013)

My mother loved crossword puzzles, spending hours, sometimes, until she managed to work out the answers to clues like "bright colored aquarium fish" and "English composer, Frederick." "Danio," she'd finally fill in, and "Delius," and for a day or two she'd leave the large Sunday newspaper puzzle face up on the end table by the couch like a trophy.

But she refused to do the crosswords in puzzle books, not because they were too hard or too easy, but because the solutions were printed in the back of those books. Anyone seeing her filled in puzzles would never be certain she hadn't peeked. The puzzles, according to her, were cheapened by those filled-in grids because, she said, "You never know if somebody cheated."

Because those answers were there, anyone could work the puzzles in those books, my mother insisted, even the ones marked "expert." All they had to do was flip to the back and sneak a quick look. And it didn't matter if they only glanced at one word in the upper right hand corner, covering the answers with their hand and inching down to reveal just that one word. Nothing was satisfying after that.

If they're out there, I've never seen a puzzle book with no answers in the back, but I thought of my mother as I sat on a plane last week working the crossword in the United Airlines magazine. That magazine has the solution printed on another page, cheating so accessible I knew that my mother would rather sink into boredom or anxiety than do that crossword.

Of course, it would have been a different story if she believed the next passenger could open to the flawlessly completed puzzle and discover that the solution wasn't printed elsewhere in the magazine. She would have begun the puzzle at once if there could be belief that she'd managed every letter exactly. In ink. Without a cross out or an overstrike. As if she could solve it perfectly, letter by letter.

Suddenly, I admit, I wanted to tear out the answer page before I began, stuff it into the wrapper for the tiny pretzels that come with the complimentary drink. And I didn't want to make one error as I worked that puzzle in ink. There I was, my mother's son carrying on her attitude as if it were securely lodged in my DNA.

Someone might sensibly point out that without the answers I'd never know if my solution was correct. My response? I'd know because the letters all intersected perfectly, even the final clue that asked for an archaic spelling. And if I became stuck with two or three letters unfilled, I'd keep that puzzle in front of me, still believing, until the seat belt sign went off at the gate, that the improbable variant spelling might come to me.

My mother sometimes opened a dictionary to words beginning with *pl*, combing through pages to discover a seven-letter word for which she had only those two beginning letters. In the dictionary by my computer there are twelve pages of words beginning with *pl*. What joy she must have had finding the word eight pages in at *plo* after fruitlessly reading through the *plas*, the *ples*, and the *plis*.

It was a way of living. You fill in every space without being able to verify your answers. Like a variation on faith—if you could check, what was the point of the struggle? If the answers were available, life was cheapened.

And the day after she died, twenty years ago now, there was a newspaper folded to the crossword puzzle lying face up on the end table by the couch. I knew, before I checked, that it was the puzzle from the day before, one she'd completed, filling in every last letter, for certain, before the solution arrived the following day.

THE PHYSICS OF DESIRE

From: *The Darkness Call* (Pleaides Press, 2018)

The spacecraft Planck is the coldest known object
in space, including dust and gas.

PICTURES

My father, hands on his walker, stays seated in his chair with the fab-
ric-covered arms so sweat-soiled the pattern has been erased. The small,
decades-old television shows darkness. He says, "You try" as if I might
resurrect the guests he says he watches until he sleeps. This morning, the
second week of weather too warm even for July, his lawn is infested with
a widespread eczema of flowering weeds. Every window in his house
with no air conditioning is closed and locked.

VOYAGER

As always, I am working at faith. Stars, I've just read, must be three billion years old in order for complex life to evolve on one of their planets,
and even then, need the luck of the Goldilocks Effect, the neither too
hot nor too cold porridge of atmosphere stirred with water and age.

Years beyond gravity, Voyager II, launched in 1977, carries a golden
record with sounds and images that are meant to represent us to residents of distant planets. It speeds that news toward aliens we have imagined since Ezekiel, the four-faced, four-winged creatures he witnessed
setting early standards for extraterrestrial invaders.

THE TIME THROAT

Along the Susquehanna River, last week, a man I'd once worked with chattered me through thistle and milkweed to where the water widened and turned shallow enough to surface what looked to be a bridge of stones. A month earlier, the water running higher, an evangelist concentrating on where his feet were placed could have seemed a temporary Christ, but my former colleague meant me to believe in a red carpet for aliens who are speeding to us via a time tunnel, one that will open next to the stones he and other believers had laid.

UFOLOGY 1

A hundred years ago, photographs of cardboard cutouts of fairies copied from a children's book were taken by two young girls, Elise Wright and Frances Griffiths. They were circulated through the celebrity of Arthur Conan Doyle as proof of the reality of fairies. A century later, the heavens are clouded by visitors from other galaxies. Abductions, now, are so common only the friends and relatives of the snatched are excited. In each story, the kidnapped undergo a physical exam. In every saga, their possessions are taken—a watch, a cell phone, a wallet. The items are hoarded by the aliens as if they were relics to be worshipped like a shroud, holy splinters, or the bits and pieces of saints and martyrs.

PLANCK IN SPACE

The spaceship Planck has been traveling for years on a mission to measure what remains of the Big Bang's transformational light. By now it is the coldest object in space, near absolute zero, its name making me look up Max Planck, the physicist, his theorem I memorized in high school. I find a comment attributed to Planck's teacher in 1880: "Physics is finished, young man. It's a dead end street." Now, when I try to decipher Planck's Constant, the way to measure the tiniest spark of energy, calculated to 10^{-34} given off by the minutest bits of matter, I feel helpless.

Relics

Our Italian tour guide, last summer, cited the wealth of the Catholic church, how it has supported the reassuring propaganda of religious art. For centuries here, she said, just the one choice, and led us into our third cathedral of the day, where, she said, we would see parts of St. Catherine, a virgin, dead, like Christ, at thirty-three, but blessed, during her lifetime, with the stigmata.

Ufology 2

In October 1955, in Kentucky, when the unearthly light wavered across the McGehee's harvested field, the little green invaders were armed. They laid a perimeter around the farmhouse, and unprovoked, fired their alien bullets, but luckily the McGehees owned four shotguns and didn't hesitate to use them, saving themselves and presumably, us, the green midgets retreating to blast off for a planet where household defense has been outlawed, some peace-loving place easily conquered, its inhabitants nothing like the honest, sober, and religious McGehees, who swore on their personal, family Bibles every fantastic word was true.

The Time Throat

The universe, my former colleague said, is scattered through with throats, and one of those mouths, miraculously, empties here. For work, years ago, he taught two languages; for faith, he spoke as if he were certain that I was worthy of secrets. "Like a worm hole?" I said, looking at the sky above the Susquehanna as if a funnel cloud of calm might descend.

Ufology 3

In Roswell, New Mexico, in the UFO museum, there are models of thin-faced, enormous-eyed aliens like the ones who supposedly crashed there in 1947. In photos, a host of shadows and glare alongside the testimonies of sober pilots and recent Presidents—Jimmy Carter claiming the space ship was big and bright and moon-sized, Ronald Reagan's plane buzzed by a speeding white light. In the busy UFO gift shop, an alien ceramic teenager; an alien head lamp; alien bobble heads, large and small; all of them with the same emaciated, black-eyed face.

VOYAGER

Carl Sagan added his lover's pulse and breath to Voyager's golden record, recording the brainwaves of Ann Druyan, who concentrated on what it's like to fall in love: Kisses and laughter. Footsteps. Heartbeats. She trusted the aliens to understand human passion after they cracked the mysterious code for the physiology of desire.

PICTURES

As if, after death, her body could be photo shopped, my father, for twenty-five years, has prepared to reunite with the version of my mother he touched before my birth, believing that he, in turn, will be seen by her as young and fit.

RELICS

St. Catherine wrote of experiencing a "mystical marriage with Jesus." She claimed to receive Communion directly from Christ and chose to abstain from eating because fasting led to holiness. Her frequent, prolonged refusals of food likely led to her death.

PLANCK IN SPACE

Millions of miles from here, the spaceship Planck is equipped to show the origin of ourselves with instruments so perfect they could, from Earth, detect the heat of a rabbit upon the moon.

UFOLOGY 4

"Life exists on other planets and we will find it within twenty years," the scientist Andrei Finkelstein said last year. He explained that ten percent of known planets circling suns in the galaxy resemble Earth, so many chances for life on such planets that it was impossible not to believe the aliens thrived. Furthermore, he said, the aliens are most likely to resemble humans with two arms, two legs and a head. Finkelstein made the remarks at the opening of the international symposium called "The Search for Extraterrestrial Intelligence" in St. Petersburg.

VOYAGER

By the time Voyager left the solar system, Sagan was years dead. Druyan, unhooking her lace-trimmed bra or sliding off a slip, might have recollected how Sagan imagined the lingerie of another planet, how the era of intimate contact would begin when her recorded desire, at last, approached the distant, intelligent discoverers.

THE TIME THROAT

"Worm hole is such an uninformative name," my former colleague said, so dismissive that I kept to myself what I'd recently read, that there was a theory, now, that employed worm holes of "Planck length," a distance of about 10^{-20} the diameter of a proton. Thus, the writer had said, "extremely small."

PLANCK IN SPACE

If everything goes as planned, the instruments on board the spaceship Planck will draw up a map of the Cosmos as it appeared thirteen billion years ago, as close to the moment of "first light" as is possible. That first light is also known as "relic radiation."

PICTURES

My father shows me a photograph labeled "McConnell's Mills, 1939," my mother in a bathing suit, thin and pretty, smiling. He turns to "1940, North Park," my mother holding a tennis racket, a sagging net behind her. In another, dressed in the same short-skirted tennis outfit, she is seated at a picnic table holding a slice of watermelon with both hands.

RELICS

In the Basilica of San Domenico, the guide said St. Catherine was so important there was a rivalry between cities for her remains. Her body, she said, is elsewhere now, but the head and thumb are here before you, her face still well-preserved through the compassionate grace of God. We shuffled past the sarcophagus roped off from the eager who might be tempted to touch. St. Catherine's thumb was displayed close by. Her head was shown so far away I had to squint to see it clearly.

Stephen Hawking has warned humans to beware of alien contact in a recent Discovery Channel series titled, "Into the Universe with Stephen Hawking." The episode with his caution imagines a scenario of alien life forms coming to Earth in enormous spaceships, on the hunt for resources after draining their planet dry. Hawking says that "If aliens visit us, the outcome would be the same as when Columbus landed in America, which didn't turn out well for the Native Americans." He says that humans should cease efforts to contact alien life, such as the 2008 NASA experiment that sent the Beatles song "Across the Universe" into space.

PICTURES

In its own box, what looks to be the original from the studio, a framed photograph of my mother in her wedding dress, November 27, 1941. The war is ten days away. My father says, "I want you to know where I keep these."

PLANCK

The spaceship Planck will detect what remains of that original light when only temperature existed, tracking theory to the bright beginning of everything. I imagine the rabbit on the moon, the probe that could dive bomb it like some inter-terrestrial falcon a merciless exhibit for the Natural History of First Things, the solid sky plunged into light that lasts, we're told, forever, so close, now, to God or absence, we watch the chilled instruments for the precise moment of miracle.

RELICS

In Siena, while we filed by the boxed thumb of St. Catherine, we watched one of our tour companions, the woman who photographed each meal she ate, slip Euros through a slot to light a candle, and we averted our eyes as she knelt to pray after dipping her fingers into an ornate basin and moving her dripping hand through the sign of the cross.

THE TIME THROAT

"My daughters are grown now," my former colleague said. "They are believers. Like me, they expect to be the first humans seen." When I stayed quiet, he said, "Haven't you always wished to know every secret?" so rapt with anticipation I listened as if he'd had those daughters hide nearby to begin the song of Sirens, the summer air above the river shimmering for cosmic sailors lured by their ravenous need for worship.

PICTURES

"It's the faces on that thing that keep me company," my father says, holding the photograph album, but looking at the blank television screen while I twist dials and push buttons as if I might bring it back to life. "I just need to see them. I don't need the sound to come back."

VOYAGER

Now that science has stripped nearly everything bare of awe and threatens to make us soulless, our mind's electricity must be deciphered when that disc is played, proving that others dream beyond themselves, that somebody else longs to be entered for love or pleasure. Voyager II, in late 2012, is nearly 10 billion miles from the sun. It will be 40,000 years before it approaches another planetary system. An eternity from us, someone will go home, centuries from now, and undress to embrace, joyous with learning those life-forms that rely upon only two legs share the ecstasy of love.

CATCHING

From: *The Darkness Call* (Pleaides Press, 2018)

MISS KLEIN EXPLAINS CONTAGIOUS

Twice a week, during third grade public health, Miss Klein filled the room with fear while we sat in perfect rows marked by small spots in the wax, the ones that revealed restlessness, that shamed if they showed like lace-edged slip hems. The contagious, she said, leave filth that hides on buses and streetcars and seats at the movies. Believe me, you'll never know who's been there and given you the itch and fester.

The contagious never cover their mouths when they sneeze. They wipe their noses on their sleeves where crusts collect like scabs that bleed. The contagious borrow combs and touch fountains with their mouths. They gobble food they've dropped to floors. Not setting rings of paper, they squat on public toilets, never scrub with water that's been run to scalding hot. What's worse, she said, the contagious shout words you mustn't say. They ruin their yards with bottles, cans, and tires. The contagious are everywhere, common as flies. Splattering stains, the contagious spread like lies. Look around. You'll see what I mean. Eyes open, class. Keep yourselves clean. Everything that makes children sick is catching.

CHILDREN'S TELEVISION

In Portugal, once, the script of a children's soap opera called for symptoms of a mysterious disease. Soon there were hundreds of children sick with those symptoms. Episode by episode, the epidemic deepened.

Each symptom was completed like homework. Mothers feared their daughters would be permanently pock marked; they followed their sons' geometrical proof of cough and rash and fever, afraid of its solution. All of them watched until the script declared an end to epidemic. But after every child recovered, after school reopened, someone hinted that a child, next season, would be crushed inside an accident's car.

MY MOTHER LISTS THE THINGS THAT ARE CATCHING

Measles. Mumps. Chicken pox.
The flu. The common cold. Strep throat.
Whooping cough. Smallpox. Tuberculosis.
Head lice. Ringworm. Impetigo.
Poison ivy. Poison sumac. Poison oak.
Comic books. Television. Rock and roll.
Lying. Stealing. Cursing. Idle hands.

TULIPOMANIA

In the early seventeenth century, in the Netherlands, tulips, newly arrived from Turkey, charmed everyone. Tulips loved Holland's soil. New breeds were developed. Flowers with vivid colors and dramatic lines and patterns that resembled flames were coveted. The price of bulbs that promised the drama of color went up. Gardens flourished. There were mornings when people awoke to the glory of extraordinary color and needed more tulips.

The best of the hybrid bulbs were named after famous people: Admiral Liefkin, Admiral Van der Eyck, and most expensive and rare, the Semper Augustus, all of them coveted like fantastic, fashionable clothes.

The rich had to own the best of those bulbs. It showed bad taste to be without a collection of bulbs. Speculators in tulip bulbs made huge profits. People bought bulbs on credit, eager to be rich.

At last the price of a single bulb rose to as much as the equivalent of two million dollars, until, in 1637, the bubble burst, and the deepest believers were ruined.

Third grade, and yet, so far, I hadn't missed a day of school. I knew what contagious was. I'd had chicken pox and measles at four and five because my older sister had brought those sicknesses home before I'd started school even though she washed her hands in the bathroom and never wiped her nose on her sleeve like I did.

I kept bundled up all winter, wearing boots, a hat with ear flaps, and a scarf my mother choked me with from December through February. But the contagious, my mother reminded me, were sure to get me if I didn't stop breathing through my mouth.

"You look like somebody who will catch everything that's going around," she said.

Or "You look like you're catching flies."

Or "You look retarded."

I was a mouth breather because it felt better. My mouth brought in more air. My nose seemed to be clogged up all the time, and yet nobody in my family said a word about allergies and their consequences. My father had taught me that allergies were for sissies. Dust, pine trees, grass seed, cats—all of those items were so common there had to be something weak in me if I had problems. If I kept my mouth shut, I'd be fine.

I watched movies where somebody was gagged and imagined dying that way, unable to get air through my untouched nose. Other kids held their breath underwater to see who could do it the longest, but I didn't need water to pretend to drown. All I had to do was "lip seal" for a few minutes and I'd feel like I needed to surface.

The doctor said I should put a straw between my lips and keep it there. He didn't say anything about school, when that straw would earn me permanent humiliation. For a few days I kept the straw in place around the house, at least when my parents or my sister might see me. The rest of the time it was in my pocket collecting a film of filth where I'd moistened it with my mouth while I sucked in great gulps of air.

But my mother was right. I had serial sore throats, going off to school scratchy and raw. "Just shut your mouth and keep it shut," my mother said. And I did. For five minutes. For ten. And every time she was close enough to see me.

CHAIN LETTERS

Chain letters return like strains of flu, popping up periodically with promises of wealth. One of them, the "send-a-dime" began in Denver, 1935, as the pyramid of replies was expanded by the yeast of greed. Evidence? The postal volume in Denver rose by more than 100,000 items per day. In some cities, "chain-headquarters" opened like flea markets. And within days everyone had a letter to sell, and there was no one left to buy.

THE YEAR BEFORE SALK

Miss Klein said polio didn't go away like chicken pox or the measles. You caught it from filth, and you wore braces and used crutches forever. Or worse, you were stuck in an iron lung like the ones she showed us on the screen she tugged down from near the ceiling. There were kids our age who were never going to do anything but lie inside machines that helped them breathe. "Let this be a lesson," Miss Klein said. "Don't ever forget to keep clean."

We brought in a dime every Friday during third grade and slid it into a slot inside a card featuring a smiling child on crutches. Miss Klein kept our cards inside her desk. I loved seeing my card fill up. When there were ten dimes, we started again. "You wash your hands, all of you, Miss Klein said after we slotted our dimes. "God knows who handled those coins. How filthy he was and what you could catch."

When I swam in a lake that summer, my mother ran a hot bath and stuck me in it, telling me to soak for a while. "That's not a swimming pool where germs are killed. I hope you kept that mouth of yours shut in that water," she said. "Just imagine what other kids have done in there. And animals. And everything under the sun."

I still didn't wash my hands or blow my nose every time it began to run, but now I was terrified of lake water. Nearly every one of my friends swam in lakes, yet none of them caught polio that summer. But when fourth grade began, there was Richard Hartman, two years younger, wearing leg braces and using crutches, looking exactly like the children in the ads for the March of Dimes that raised money for polio research.

Mrs. Gardiner had new March of Dimes cards for each of us. Jerry

Mushik laughed when I washed my hands after I'd inserted my dime. He put his on his tongue and closed his mouth. Richard Hartman didn't seem to be getting any better. The dimes weren't going to help him, my mother said. It's too late for that. Jerry Mushik licked his dime for three straight weeks. In the cloakroom he forced two boys to lick their dimes, and none of them got sick.

DANCE MANIA

In the thick history of hysteria, Frau Troffea, in 1518, suddenly lifts her arms as if she's hanging sheets on a line to dry in Strasbourg, France. Hallelujah, she could be singing, but then her feet skid into the swerve of dance, limbs chattering out of sync with any tune her neighbors know. There, in the sixteenth century, spectators gather like they do for the first dance at a wedding, but she carries on for days, tranced by some phantom partner who leads until one of those onlookers joins, then another, so many more in this weeks-long fit of dancing, that outdoor ballroom fills four hundred strong, moshers for the inaudible, the song on repeat, the pit keyed to a frenzy of thrashing, each dancer with room enough for solitary violence. Nothing can end this except exhaustion or, for many, death, that manic choreography famous for casualties who endured to the heart's collapse.

LAUGH TRACK

During the years before the laugh track, when the Russians had mastered the atomic bomb, and Pittsburgh, where we lived, was a first-launch target, comedies, in black and white, blinked through the snow on our Dumont's screen. My mother would say "Shhhh" to hush me mute, whatever was funny sealed behind my lips, not to be opened until the commercials came on because I was there to watch and listen, not act the fool.

Some nights the sirens that would signal world's end sounded in tests. Some nights the television paused to remind us to seek shelter when its shows ended for real. But now there were programs, suddenly, where each line was hilarious, laughter rising and falling as often as breath. It sounded like people my mother knew, the chuckles of men in suits, the titters of women who wore dresses and stockings to shop for butter and milk.

My mother began to laugh along. She had company now, but I kept my mouth shut because there was never the laughter of boys, somebody under twelve happy to act the fool. Television was really funny these days, she told me, the sounds returning so often we recognized the laughs as if they came from our neighbors. At home, in living rooms, there were people like us in shorts and T-shirts, underwear and robes, who agreed about humor.

And then, a few of those laughs disappeared as if their owners had sickened or died, replaced in the front row by foreigners. My mother said she could hear the accents of those who spoke Spanish when they wanted her not to hear. Or worse, the snickers of Russians, as if there was laughter coming through those earphones at the U.N. during the daily talk of World War III.

From commercial to commercial, my mother went silent again, listening for strangers, people she said I should fear, who would find us funny when we tried to run, believing the head start we'd had was the only way to save ourselves.

THE LAUGHTER EPIDEMIC

In 1962, following a schoolboy's joke,
thousands of people in Tanganyika
laughed nonstop for months

Like chicken pox, one joke passed from child to child, the contagious entering their houses to spread the rash of laughter. Villages, within days, housed hilarity. Boys whispered into their fathers' ears, their teeth bared from grinning. Mothers, hugged by daughters, were tickled to cackling. Comedian zero, that jokester, laughed and shook. "A fit," the teacher thought, smiling, as the class snickered at history like generals, each incident a punch line. When school, hysterical, was closed, the children howled as they scattered onto homeward paths, the sound of joy, by now, so widespread, even the surrounding jungle seemed hilarious.

THE DEVIL'S CHILDREN

"The sins of your fathers," Mrs. Shaffer said, "belong to you," and she listed the ways from drunk to unfaithful while our Sunday school class constructed heaven and hell, silently attaching the future for all of us onto the church's new bulletin boards. Melanie Troxell, whose father was gone, cut narrow spaces into heaven's gate, forming a grate so we could see inside where white wings we drew floated against a cloudless blue sky. We shaped a purple robe for God and a loose, white cloak for Jesus, their faces turned away because we dared not look upon them. "The whirling of those white wings," Mrs. Shaffer said, "looks like it was created by the sweet, benevolent breath of God."

All of us designed the black wings for hell. Dick Wertz, his father arrested, scissored scarlet triangles for eternal flames and left the green door to hell wide open for the paired hands we made by tracing ours. We forecast weather for hell, heavy rain, every drop vanishing above the flames because not one would ever reach us when God saw into our sinful hearts that year before boys and girls were separated for Sunday School, before we began to learn the secret sins of lust and envy, using the sin of falsehood to deny how we abused ourselves and blasphemed, counting the commandments we broke each day although Mrs. Shaffer made us sit, one by one, beside the dark, detailed face of Satan she drew, learning, each Sunday, how it felt to be the devil's children.

Three Condemnations of Hair

Near the end of the eleventh century, the pope decreed that men with long hair should be excommunicated and no prayers offered for their hell-bound souls after death.

In 1705, in Russia, Peter the Great condemned the beard, levying a tax on the bearded rather than threatening them with hell.

In 1838 the king of Bavaria forbade the mustache, saying those who had one would be arrested and shaved. When all of the mustaches disappeared, no one needed to be arrested.

Self-Contagious

At last, during fourth grade, the worst sore throat I'd ever had kept me home from school. "Now you're like everybody else," my mother said. When it worsened, the doctor made a house call and diagnosed an advanced case of strep throat. He warned that my throat might have been neglected too long. I had a heart murmur and could, if things turned worse, come down with rheumatic fever. My mother, looking terrified, hovered nearby. I knew I could give myself something worse, that I was self-contagious.

POSSESSION

In the 17th century, in Loudun, Mother Superior Jeanne des Agnes claimed the spirit of Urbain Grandier, the parish priest, visited her at night to seduce her. Soon other nuns reported spectral foreplay, moaning in ecstasy at night, convulsing and speaking in tongues during the day. Exorcism followed, but the nuns remained possessed by the demons Asmodeus and Zabulon who had entered the convent with a bouquet of roses thrown over the wall by Grandier. When the trial went public, crowds of thousands came to watch. A third demon that possessed those nuns was named—Isacarron, the devil of debauchery.

Out of the nuns' mouths flowed public blasphemy. From the files of the exorcist came the contract from Asmodeus, signed in blood by Grandier, a host of demons, and Satan himself. That contract has been saved for centuries, so that long after Grandier was burned at the stake, those nuns recanting and regaining their holiness, we can witness Satan's pitchforked signature and the decorative names of the demons.

That contract, historians are sure, is in the handwriting of Mother Superior Jeanne des Agnes, who claimed sorrow for her lies.

THE WAR OF THE WORLDS

In 1938, on Halloween eve, Orson Welles and the Mercury Theater Company broadcast a play based on H. G. Wells' *The War of the Worlds*. A still-famous panic followed. Martians had landed in New Jersey. People rushed to their cars and packed the roads. They hid in their cellars. They loaded guns. The Martians, who "glistened like wet leather," invaded New York City before Earth's bacteria killed them.

Interviewed after the panic, Orson Welles said he thought the story "so improbable," he was afraid people would be bored. He was surprised that even once in a lifetime a hoax like that could work.

In 1944, *The War of the Worlds* aired again in Santiago, Chile, six years and publicity doing nothing to prevent more heart attacks and injuries from an epidemic of panic.

In 1949, in Quito, someone reread that play, and the duped, when they discovered how they'd been fooled, burned the radio station. In that invasion, twenty people died, the revenge-driven earthlings watching the panicked tumble from upstairs windows, which was what invaders deserved, the fire each time, ask questions later.

THE CRUSADES

One Sunday, just before we were moved to the next "higher" class, Mrs. Shaffer said the Crusades were the pinnacle of holiness. "Imagine," she said, "a host of armies fighting for Christ." She told us about Peter the Hermit, who was the hero who preached so well Christians everywhere joined up to rescue the Holy Land from the heathens.

"There were many crusades," she said, "because the struggle never ends." She explained that for hundreds of years, every Christian wanted to march to Jerusalem, so many volunteers there was always a next Crusade. "And listen," she finally said, "in 1213, there were 30,000 children who marched. Imagine that, boys and girls. Imagine them being willing to be martyrs for Christ."

A MONTH OF CRUSADERS, 2010

March 29th—Moscow, two women detonate on the Metro, 40 dead

March 31st—Kislyar, two bombers, 12 dead

March 31st—Khyber, Pakistan, one car bomber, 6 dead

April 4th—Baghdad, three car bombers, 42 dead

April 9th—Ingushetia, Russia, one woman detonates, 2 dead

April 12th—Mosul, Iraq, one car bomber, 3 dead

April 19th—Peshawar, Pakistan, one bomber, 26 dead

April 23rd—Baghdad one car bomber, 11 dead

April 26th—Sana'a, Yemen, one bomber, 1 dead

April 28th—Baghdad, two car bombers, 5 dead

THE MARTYR IN OUR TOWN

This week, 2011: July 27th, Iraq, 10 dead. July 30th, Afghanistan, 4 dead. All of the martyrs seem as far away as famine. In small towns like the one where I live in no one expects a martyr who would scout the public places where we gather in great numbers. Who would enter our malls and note the busiest stores; who would scan the food court's longest lines. Who would, on Fridays, watch football at the high school. Who would, on Saturdays, sit through a blockbuster film? Who would, on Sundays, attend church, sitting with families on wooden pews.

In his small apartment he studies prophecies and commandments. He reads only the holy translations. At last, when winter justifies his knee-length coat, he thickens his waist with dynamite, develops a nails and ball-bearings paunch. He enters the one restaurant where every diner has three forks, two spoons, and wine on ice, ticking as he gives his reservation name. He decides that the tables nearby are perfect with use, steps forward as the hostess offers a complimentary hanger for his heavy coat. All this, he prays, will spread, go airborne, a pandemic contagion. She employs the word "sir" just as he triggers himself, ascending.

DURING THE FARM SHOW PARADE

From: *The Darkness Call* (Pleaides Press, 2018)

In the next town over, early in the parade, the recently acquitted drive their red truck slowly, the Ford F-150 as polished as the fire trucks and the horns of the high school band. From both windows, they throw Tootsie Rolls and hard candy wrapped in cellophane to scrambling children, then wave like the mayor and the Farm Show Princess who follow the Civil War re-enactors and their hoop-skirted wives.

An hour ago, because the acquitted said they would carry a sign and a poster, a volunteer had approved their red pickup as a float, slotting it between the Cub Scouts and the Gym Starz in their sparkling tights. Now, all of us along the parade route read the sign that says, "Our trial wasted $17,000 of your money," beside a poster of the District Attorney stuffed into a garbage can.

I'm here with my granddaughters, ages six and nine, because I picked a local parade to entertain them. The parade is small, the route short. They live in Los Angeles, have access to the annual Rose Bowl Parade, but here there are farm animals up close and children their age walking by and waving in Brownie uniforms and dance outfits. Both girls are paying attention.

The acquitted, I think, might have passed the victim's family. I concentrate on their mouths to read their words. I watch their gestures for tells.

I'd read the newspaper's daily reports on the trial. Like my neighbors, I'd expected a guilty verdict even though many of the witnesses seemed unreliable. Every adult here must remember the recent testimony about the seventeen-year-old fatal beating that was finally being prosecuted.

The kegs of beer in the field of a local farm. The large crowd and their heavy drinking. The young man who would be killed coming on to the girlfriend of one of the acquitted, his hand on her bare arm.

All of us likely remember the descriptions of the beating. A half-sister to one of the acquitted saying the victim was "assaulted hard core while people watched." Another witness claiming the victim took a few licks, but "just a little knock around, nobody falling down or like that."

For sure, all of us must remember the farm's owner repeating the advice she claimed to have given the acquitted that day: "You want to kill somebody, you move that body off my property."

Which some claimed they did in the bed of that Ford F-150. Which some asserted they did not. Regardless, every one of those witnesses agreed, that young man's body ended up lying along a seldom used country road. The acquitted, meanwhile, lived as suspects for seventeen years.

My granddaughters love the rabbits in their cages and the tethered calf led by a girl who looks to be about ten years old. I grip their hands to keep them from lunging for the candy, but neither one tugs to free herself, as if the murmur that rises around us as the truck passes is a warning to be wary.

After the acquitted pass, a nearby woman unwraps one of their butterscotch candies. She sucks on it, her mouth working as if she is delivering a curse. I think of how likely it is that some of the spectators are armed. Whether the news of the acquitteds' float has reached a relative or close friend of the murdered man.

Hearts

From: *The Darkness Call* (Pleaides Press, 2018)

1

In space, the hearts of astronauts become rounder. According to the scientists who have studied this phenomenon, the hearts of those who spend long periods of time in space were transformed into a shape that averaged nearly 10% more spherical after six months.

2

In Minnesota, recently, the hearts of moose have so often faltered too soon, they've suffered a cluster of early mortality so profound that they have been wired and followed from a distance by veterinarians. When interviewed, one of them explained that when a moose heart stops beating, it sends a text message to their phones that says, "I'm dead at x and y coordinates," directing them so quickly to the downed, they have a better chance to decipher the clumsy heart.

3

My sister, who has examined the human heart in the commonplace of gravity, has prepared herself for surgery on her own faulty heart. The doctor is a friend, the anesthetist a colleague. A volunteer for study, she has already been monitored a dozen ways, details of her heart and the outcomes of her surgery to become averages or anomalies.

4

One afternoon, during eighth grade, I stood with my classmates around the cow's heart Miss Hutchings unwrapped on her desk. Inside and out, she said, we need to know ourselves, halving that heart to show us auricles, ventricles, valves, the wall well-built or else. Her fingers found where arteries begin. She pressed the ends of veins. She said we were learning the circulatory system the proper way, observing first hand.

5

That cow's heart Miss Hutchings displayed looked nothing like the ones that had been suggested on Valentine's Day, during cartoons, and in art classes, beginning in first grade with Mrs. McIntyre having us draw a sweeping arc from near the top of our red, folded construction paper down to the very bottom. "Now cut, children," she said, "very carefully along that line and then unfold." And though some of them were V-shaped and others looked more like balls, in a minute all of us had the suggestion of a bright red heart to write, "I love you" upon and carry home to our mothers.

6

Previous studies have shown that astronauts are exposed to a range of health issues when taking prolonged trips into space, including losses in bone density and muscle mass and vision anomalies, but now it's been shown that there is more to be concerned about than those problems. The rounder the heart becomes, the weaker it gets. A rounded heart is a heart at risk.

7

Once, riding in her car while I was visiting Maine, I listened to my host tell a story about hitting a moose on the stretch of highway we were traveling. A family had pulled up behind her on the shoulder, the father asking, "You got a use for that moose?" I smiled, thinking that was the punch line, but there was more. A moment later she described the haunch of moose she'd bartered from that family. "That moose was all mine, by rights," she said, "but the father dressed it out, so it was a fair trade." Even though it was raining heavily, she accelerated, our speed feeling like an exclamation point, the air inside the car so rich with story, change easily entered me.

Because I love to eat organ meat, I asked her whether she'd received part of the heart and liver. "Not the heart," she said. "Not that."

8

And last week, in Pennsylvania, when my vocabulary for encouragement stumbled and stalled, I offered my sister the weak consolation of listening to her analyze the pros and cons of heart surgery. The muscle, she said, can regain what's been lost. Just in case, I've updated my will. Three hours, on average, this operation takes, she went on, though by then I was fixed on the sort of planning that included a will revision, the summary she provided about how post-operative rehab is organized failing to adhere to the moist walls of my memory.

9

Both of us had listened for years to our father's reports on his aging heart. About the tempo at first, the pacemaker fresh under his skin after he'd fainted at the wheel and drifted, through luck, into a field as level as his crab-grassed lawn. Sixty, he'd say, as if he was in training. The first time he exposed its shape near his shoulder I imagined his body penetrated by some circular alien who would, inevitably, invade his blood.

10

After our class had inspected the cow's heart, Miss Hutchings unwrapped the hearts of chickens and turkeys, the hearts of swine and sheep. She arranged them by size on the thick, brown paper sack, leaving a space, we knew, for ours. Richard Heckman, whose father's heart had halted, examined his hands. Anne Cole, whose father had revived to cut hair at the mall, stepped back, turning away from the entry to the steer's aorta, the four chambers we were required to know.

11

A long-held belief of many traditional cultures is that eating the organs from a healthy animal supports the organs of the eater. For example, eating the brains of a healthy animal improves clear thinking, and eating animal kidneys will cure people suffering from urinary disease. That logic means that the best way of treating a person with a weak heart is to feed the person the heart of a healthy animal. There are countless reports about the success of these types of traditional practices. None of them have been verified by scientific testing.

12

"Feel this," my father said, guiding my hand to the simple Braille of his new pacemaker. "Sixty," he said, "over and over like a clock." I told him about the billion heartbeats of the mammal, how the shrew had three years to live at 800 beats per minute, and the cat had twelve at 200. "We have thirty years," I said, "because we use up100,000 beats per day, but we get more because of science and medicine and help from how slowly we mature." When I told him this, my father was well over eighty, closing in on three billion, and I was past two billion.

13

Some statistics I didn't tell my father:
The human heart usually weights about ten ounces, but the heart of the blue whale often weighs about 1300 pounds. It averages about 8-10 beats per minute that can be heard two miles away. On the other hand, the tiny hearts of hummingbirds are the largest proportionate to their minuscule body weight. Their heart rate runs to over 1000 beats per minute when they're active, but it slows when they sleep to less than 100, a necessity, or they would starve to death before morning.

14

According to the Alaska Department of Fish and Game, the average weight of a moose heart is three pounds. "It's like holding a football," the spokesman adds.

15

"The heart doesn't work as hard in space, which can cause a loss of muscle mass," says the lead scientist for ultrasound at NASA and senior author of the study of astronauts' hearts. Though the astronauts' hearts returned to their normal, more oval shape, shortly after their return to Earth, what's left to learn is whether there are serious, long-term consequences, something that can't be known for years.

16

"You know these things when you teach in a medical school," she says. "I've known for quite some time my heart cannot heal itself." She talks as if I, too, have always known she's had what she calls a "persistent disability," something "nagging whose voice has gotten louder." As if that voice could carry hundreds of miles, revealing her heart's distress. She says the surgery is a choice that's been made by her body.

She is thin. Skeletal comes to mind, and all I can think to say is, "It's good you have the inside information on your surgeon."

"I'm thankful that I know these people," she says. "I trust them."

17

Until I was twelve years old, I looked forward to the ritual of tiny candy hearts being shared at the Valentine's Day parties we had in grade school. *Love You Much,* it said in blue letters on the pink candy. *Be Mine* was repeated in red letters on pale blue hearts. From fourth to sixth grade, I looked at Susanna Frank or Nancy Harris or Kathy McMichaels each time I swallowed one, sending sign language their way.

18

The ultrasound pictures of the long-term-in-space astronauts' hearts are stunning. The hearts look as if they've been molded like clay, becoming so nearly circular they appear to be incapable of working. It doesn't surprise me to learn that astronauts often get lightheaded and faint upon standing when they return to earth because of a sudden drop in blood pressure. I think of my father, hospitalized at last, admitting he had, despite the pacemaker, fainted twice when standing, the third time after bending to place his ball on a tee at a public golf course. Despite my father's protests, his friend had called an ambulance. Within a week he underwent his second heart repair, this time triple bypass surgery.

19

The day after we looked at animal hearts, Miss Hutchings asked us to take our pulses. Using the stethoscopes she'd brought to class, we listened to each other, boy to boy, girl to girl, because of the chance we'd touch. The images of those butcher hearts faded while I dreamed of pressing my ear to the rhythmic hearts of Susan Rolfe and Janelle Frank, whose breasts, so far, had brushed me a few times while dancing. And then Miss Hutchings recited the quart total of our blood, the distance it must travel, leaving and returning. We learned all of the names for the necessary routes it followed, ending with capillaries so close to the surface I understood, though she didn't say it, we could nearly reach them with our lips and tongues, rushing the blood to each of the sensitive sources for joy.

20

The sugar Valentine's candy I once loved in grade school are called "conversation hearts" in the ads for them on the Internet. They come in two vague sizes—small and large—but both kinds still feature the familiar messages from my childhood: *Marry Me, Sweet Talk, Darling,* all of the speaking hearts in pastel colors, three pounds for $15.76.

21

Now there are variations on that candy's simple design:
    Heart-shaped Twizzlers
    Heart-shaped lollipops
    Heart-shaped sucker rings that fit on a finger
    Heart-shaped candy strung into bracelets
    And colorful, decorated heart-shaped boxes in multiple sizes that contain those heart-shaped candies, the packaging suggesting a truncated Russian doll.

22

A woman named Mercy Brown was once exhumed for public autopsy. The people in the town in which she had lived believed that a current local cluster of consumption might be worsened by those who had died from that disease, but it could be bettered by burning the uncorrupted heart of the victim. Not only might there be an end to an epidemic, there was a chance, people said, that her brother Edwin might be cured of his tuberculosis by eating the ashes of her heart. Mercy's father had to watch his daughter raised from the grave after being months buried. He had to endure the burning of her heart. Edwin, at last, swallowed the ashes, but he died, regardless, in two months, leaving his father to live alone and remember his daughter being twice buried. This happened in Vermont, in 1892. Mercy Brown was also thought by many to be a vampire.

23

The rounding of the heart could mean trouble for people who want to embark on long-term missions to Mars. Astronauts currently spend up to six months at the orbiting International Space Station, which is staffed by rotating crews. Missions to Mars would take about 18 months and may offer no return trip.

24

As if she wants me to be convinced her upcoming operation is routine, my sister tells me our cousin has undergone his third operation, that he has flown from Virginia to a Texas hospital for the latest surgery. So thin, she says, his pants want to fall down, his shirts hang like curtains, reminding me how, every late August, my mother held up what he'd outgrown, what I'd grow into, dressing me for school and church for a year, two if we were lucky, teaching the lesson of the threadbare, the ill-fitting and the out of style, learning what was good enough. He's still standing on his own two feet, my sister says, wearing her hand me down language, adding he's in our prayers and he's a fighter like a litany, like I should say amen or sing the Doxology before a recessional hymn of hope. My sister, who learned to sew her own clothes, who wore homemade, but new, who needed to perfect the careful cut and stitch because she was older than every female cousin, declares "Our time will come" like some minister for fatalism. She's at the window of the spare room where I've slept, saying the weather, so sunny and mild, is heavenly while I try to ignore the sewing machine, the half-finished skirt and the thick file of patterns collected in the good light I have to tear my eyes from.

25

IS IT SAFE TO EAT A FRESH RAW MOOSE HEART?

Someone has already posted that question in an Internet forum about large game animals. He received half a dozen responses:

"I wouldn't. Chances are you will be just fine afterward, but eating that heart raw isn't very smart. As a rule of thumb you shouldn't eat anything raw from a game animal, especially an internal organ like the heart."

"No, it's not safe to eat the raw flesh of a moose or a deer or any wild animal, you can get heartworm."

"Apparently you forgot why we let large game animals hang after we gut them and then let the carcass chill to near 32 degrees. It's to kill the intramuscular parasites."

26

Now it is understood that in order to keep the heart healthy in space, astronauts must know the amount and type of exercise they need to perform to guarantee their safety on prolonged spaceflights. It's been suggested that exercise regimens developed for astronauts could also help people on Earth who have physical limitations also maintain good heart health. Those models could also give doctors a better understanding of common cardiovascular conditions for ground-based patients.

27

During the last years of his life, approaching ninety, our father wore sweaters even in summer, so cold, so often, he kept the windows shut in his un-air-conditioned house. He would probe for his pulse, reporting, "Still there." After that small, brief joke, he'd wait five minutes, sometimes ten, before listening to his wrist again, head bowed, leaning forward, as if he needed to coax a heartbeat with prayer.

28

When I attended my 50th high school class reunion recently, there was a large poster that was labeled "In Memoriam." It listed those from my class who had died, a bit reminiscent of the Vietnam Memorial, complete with a few small, impulse tributes of programs and table favors laid beneath it. Susan Rolfe and Janelle Frank, I discovered, had each been dead for more than twenty years. Except for our war dead, causes weren't listed, but like all the others, their hearts had stopped.

29

In the midst of writing this essay, I take a heart age test and learn my heart is a year younger than my age but I have a 22% higher risk than average to have problems in the next ten years. I remind myself that I've lowballed all of my answers, that this is a worst case scenario, but there's no denying my mother's heart failure when she was younger than I am, my father's bypass and pacemaker, my sister's impending open heart surgery.

30

A few answers to the raw moose heart question were more condescending:
"There is an Animal Planet RV show about humans getting animal parasites. You stand a good chance of being their next guest star."
"If you want to take the chance, it's your body."

31

Everything points to a glass or two of red wine being heart-helpful, but I drink only white wine and then only rarely, preferring beer. There is evidence that hearty laughter is good for the heart, but I seldom laugh out loud. I blame it on my family history, all those dour, judgmental Germans drinking beer and frowning until they tumbled with heart attacks and strokes.

32

There seems little question that eating organ meats has fallen out of favor among people I know. I tell them that liver, kidney, and heart are some of the most nutrient-rich foods you can eat, but there aren't any takers. At the grocery store, when I look for veal or lamb kidneys, there are none, and when I settle for a package of chicken hearts, the clerk goes "Eeew!" and acts as if she'll pass it through without ringing it up just to avoid touching it.

33

Even when, in the assisted living home, my father stopped watching television, when he slept twelve hours a day and napped three times, his fingers went to his wrist as he woke, repeating, "Still there," Even when he gave in to the wheelchair. Even when half his weight vanished although he ate, like always, everything that was served. Even when his sentences turned shorter, the ends lost like addresses, phone numbers, and the names of the dead, his fingers returned to his wrist to read the braille for "still there," while I waited, despite reason, holding my breath for his up-to-the-minute news.

34

Although raw moose heart is uniformly cautioned against, there are several methods posted on the Internet for how to prepare moose heart for cooking, most of the directions similar to this:

> When the heart is still fresh, soak it in a bucket of cold sea water or fresh water to flush out the blood. Rinse well. Trim the fat and the tops of the valves off well so that the final product is mostly red and the top is relatively level, with clear access to the chambers of the heart. At this point, the heart can be kept in the freezer if wrapped well in Saran wrap and butcher paper, however it is best when eaten fresh.
>
> The recipe calls for:
> 1 moose heart
> ½ loaf of your favorite white bread
> About 4 stalks of celery, chopped into small pieces
> 1 onion, chopped
> 2 cloves garlic, minced
> 2 Tbsp parsley leaves
> 2 tsp rosemary
> 2 tsp oregano
> 1 tsp sage
> Olive oil
> 3 Tbsp butter
> Salt and pepper to taste
> Water, red wine and soy sauce to taste

35

This morning, the day of my sister's surgery, a waitress spread whipped cream into a thick, valentine heart across my son's banana-walnut pancakes. Because, she said, a circle would never make you think it's a heart, so unashamed of sentiment, her heavy body turned delicate in the sweetened air.

36

All this afternoon I regret the impossibility of omniscience. And yet I am thankful. At last, from across the room, my wife's phone sings its song of incoming text. And though the news, this time, is good, in the altered atmosphere, I believe our dependable, dangerous hearts are becoming spheres.

Things that Fall from the Sky

From: *The Darkness Call* (Pleaides Press, 2018)

Rocks

From a freeway overpass in Central Pennsylvania, four teenage boys fling rocks at traffic passing beneath them along Route 80. One misses hitting anything but the highway. One nearly the size of a bowling ball bounces off the cab of a semi. At last, one strikes the windshield of a car heading east. When the car immediately slows, pulls off the highways, and parks, the boys hurry to their car and drive off.

Space Junk

In 1962, a twenty-one pound metal object plummeted from the sky and landed at the intersection of two streets in Manitowoc, Wisconsin. Eventually, it was confirmed to be the remnant of Sputnik IV, becoming the first example of a significant piece of space junk surviving re-entry after falling out of orbit. When first noticed, it was imbedded three inches deep in the asphalt street.

Powder

In 1969, in South Carolina, a white cloud spewed from the new Borden plant near the small town of Chester. It rose and drifted and hovered above the town, eventually beginning to fall. The day became white and sweet like the air above a rolling pin thinning cookie dough. Children stood beside their mothers, their hands clutching toys they would not part with. The weather seemed to cut the neighborhood into the shapes of families. The cloud was soluble on tongues. It surrounded each face. Already there were footprints on sidewalks, the anticipation of brooms. Some of those dusted by that shower took vows. As if time was ending, there were declarations of love and promises to do better. But not for long. The powder turned out to be Borden's nondairy creamer. The company offered reassurance. Though later, when the whitened bathed, some of them stroked the film that had formed along their cheeks, their fingertips dizzy with the wonder of children touching the rouged faces of the dead.

NUCLEAR BOMBS

The United States government calls nuclear bombs that go astray "Broken Arrows." Four such broken arrows fell from the sky on January 17, 1966 when two US Air Force planes collided over southern Spain. A B-52G bomber was struck by the KC-135 tanker plane sent to perform routine air-to-air refueling and broke apart. Three of the bomber's H-bombs landed in or around Palomares; the fourth landed about five miles offshore in the Mediterranean. There was no nuclear blast, but plutonium was scattered over a wide area.

ROCKS

Sharon Budd, a middle school teacher from Ohio, is a passenger in the car the boys hit. She is struck full in the face. In her husband Randy's 911 call, he says, "This is bad. Something came right through the windshield." He is unhurt. So is the driver, his nineteen-year-old daughter. "There's a rock that came in," he goes on. "She's grasping for her life. My God, half her brain is gone. Oh, my God." His daughter can be heard screaming during the 911 call.

SPACE JUNK

Nearly every day during the winter when my younger son was thirteen, he searched the sky for the first sign of space junk that was forecast soon to tumble out of orbit. "What if it lands here?" he asked more than once, and each time I told him that was so close to impossible there was no sense even thinking about it. "But not 100% impossible, right?" he said, and he began to research the size and weight of what was about to fall, how much of it might survive re-entry. He relayed the following details to me:

> The name of the object is Salyut 7, the last of nine space stations the Soviet Union launched from 1971 to 1982. It blasted off on April 19, 1982, and has stayed aloft for nearly nine years. Six different resident crews have spent time aboard during its operational life. It is about 52 feet long and 13.6 feet across at its widest point. It weighs about 22 tons. A spaceship called Cosmos 1686 is still docked to the station. It weighs just as much as the space station, and all 44 tons of it is about to plummet toward Earth.

SEEDS

A father calls his wife and children outside to witness the eastern sky turning dim with clouds the color of blood. They stand transfixed, staring skyward until rain falls like a swarm of sand. They live in Italy. The year is 1897. What falls are seeds, all of them from Judas trees, none of which grow anywhere near them. The light after the shower is so yellow it seems to have traveled from a jaundiced star. The father kneels to run his hands over those seeds, reading the Braille of what might be said by a solid rain.

NUCLEAR BOMBS

The bombs that fell near Palomares from the destroyed plane weren't armed, so there was no nuclear explosion. Parachutes attached to the bombs were supposed to bear them gently down to earth, preventing any contamination, but two of the parachutes failed to open, and those bombs blew apart on impact, scattering highly toxic, radioactive plutonium dust, a major hazard to anyone who might inhale it. And there was the issue of finding the one that fell offshore.

ROCKS

Randy Budd says his wife had just finished speaking with their eldest son before the vehicle was struck by the rock. After hanging up the phone, his wife asked their son to send her a selfie from his station in Fort Bliss, Texas, which he did. "I really miss you," he texted. Shortly after, the windshield exploded. Randy adds, "I didn't know where her head was."

SPACE JUNK

My son asked to sleep downstairs in the room where his older brother had lived before going off to college. From time to time I caught him walking with his eyes focused on the sky. "Will we be able to see it coming?" he asked, and when I said, "Not likely," he had me go outside with him with binoculars. He worried that most of the late January and early February days were cloudy. By then he understood that the space station and its attached ship would break apart and mostly disintegrate before it reached Earth, but still he worried. "So many pieces makes it worse," he said. The whole thing plunged back to Earth on February 7, 1991, breaking up over Argentina. Some debris was discovered scattered over a town called Capitán Bermúdez. There were no reported injuries.

SMALL STONES

When I was in first grade I was proud of being able to throw stones across the wide street in front of the house where we rented three upstairs rooms. I stood on the wall that ran up from the sidewalk and waited for cars to drive by in the far lane, tossing small rocks over them as they passed. Standing on the wall gave me the advantage of height. The stones, hardly more than pebbles, looked to my six-year-old eyes as if they were arcing down from the sky. Eventually, one fell short and landed on the windshield of a blue car. When the car pulled into the alley beside the house and the driver stepped out, I ran inside, up the stairs and into the room I shared with my older sister. Within a minute a man was speaking with my mother about the small crack the stone had made.

The crack, it turned out, was tiny and so far into the corner of the glass that unless it spread, the driver wouldn't ask for money. All I had to do was apologize, forcing the words out between sobs.

NUCLEAR BOMBS

Nobody on the ground in Palomares was killed by the falling bombs. 700 US airmen and scientists were employed to search for bombs and clean up. Three inches of topsoil was removed, sealed in 4,810 barrels and shipped to a storage facility in the United States. Twenty ships, including minesweepers and submersibles, were deployed by the US Navy to find the missing bomb that was in the Mediterranean. The cost of the sea search was over $10 million. Four months later, the missing bomb was finally hoisted on board a US warship from a depth of 2,850 ft. How much plutonium is still near Palomares is unknown.

ROCKS

The teenage rock throwers' names are brothers Dylan and Brett Lahr, Tyler Porter, and Keefer McGee. McGee was driving his Mitsubishi Eclipse when they stopped on the overpass near Route 80's Milton Exit. When the car below them slowed, they fled to the house where the brothers lived. They tried to watch a movie, but dying to know how much damage they'd caused, they got in the Lahr's gold Honda Accord and drove past the scene to see what was happening. When they saw a police car, they returned to the house. They went back yet again and saw more police cruisers. The police took notice of the Honda's license plate.

DOCUMENTS

In 1973 a set of papers fell from a distance higher than a nearby 300-foot radio transmission tower. It looked, to the witness, as if a briefcase had opened, a latch sprung loose among the clouds. A hoax was suspected, but a few lines about the event eventually appeared in a newspaper. The documents, it was reported, were full of graphs and formulas that explained "normalized extinction" and the Davis-Greenstein mechanism of astrophysics.

NUCLEAR BOMBS

My first air raid drill was in second grade. Everyone in the grade school was herded downstairs to the basement and told to stand against a wall away from any windows. Close your eyes, the teacher said, don't open them until I tell you. After that, we had those twice a year. We had fire drills once a month. In third grade we dropped beneath our desks and covered our heads with our hands. "All clear," the teacher said both times. The school was six miles from Pittsburgh. She told us that the city and its steel mills were prime targets. "Pittsburgh is very important," the teacher said, something I always remembered when the nearby fire station tested its air raid siren. "Could we see the bomb falling?" I asked her, and she answered, "Don't you worry about that." Every time I was home alone when the sirens wailed, my father sleeping, my mother at work, I watched the sky believing this was the time the warning was for real.

Rocks

At the hospital, the teacher's forehead and skull cap was removed to allow for swelling in her brain. She had lost an eye and the other was severely damaged. In a short period of time, she underwent five surgeries, first to save her life, then to reconstruct her face, and, at last, to provide her with an artificial skull cap. In the first newspaper report after the boys were arrested, one of them denies throwing any rocks as if abstinence is a synonym for innocence.

Frogs, Toads, Fish

Not rare, these things falling from the sky. In fact, they are so common that a standard reason is provided by scientists—whirlwinds suck up water and carry what's in it until everything falls from the sky.

Nuclear Bombs

A B-52 was flying over North Carolina on January 24, 1961, when it suffered what was reported as a "failure of the right wing." The plane broke apart, and two atom bombs plummeted toward the ground near Goldsboro. The parachute opened on one; it didn't on the other. "The impact of the aircraft breakup initiated the fusing sequence for both bombs," the investigators of the incident reported, an admission that both weapons came very close to detonating. The bomb whose parachute opened landed intact. Fortunately, the pins that provided power from a generator to the weapon had been yanked, preventing it from going off. The bomb with the unopened parachute landed in a free fall. The impact of the crash put it in the "armed" setting, but another part of the bomb needed to initiate an explosion was damaged, and it did not explode. Secretary of Defense Robert McNamara said, "By the slightest margin of chance, literally the failure of two wires to cross, a nuclear explosion was averted."

ROCKS

When I search for other incidents of rocks thrown from overpasses onto passing cars and trucks, there are dozens of stories. The one closest to where I live and where Sharon Budd was struck happened shortly after. A man was driving his Kenworth truck on state Route 924 within a few miles of the Budd incident when a rock crashed through his windshield. However, it missed striking him. When I move to recent incidents farther away, I read about a man who was driving home on Interstate 35 near Austin, Texas when a rock came through his windshield and smashed into his face. He is paralyzed on his right side and is unable to talk or write, according to a television report on KEYE. Another station KXAN reports that three other motorists were injured in rock throwing incidents on the same highway within a month of the one that paralyzed that driver.

CONCRETE

One afternoon, just after recess ended, a corner of concrete from just under the roof of my elementary school broke off and fell fifty feet into the playground. Our teacher kept us in our seats. She told us to pay attention to what we were doing, not what was happening outside, but when school ended, everyone I knew veered out of the path to where the school buses waited to take a look at the crash site. We all knew exactly how long it had been since we had stood in the spot where the stone struck the cement. Last week. Yesterday. That morning. Minutes before.

SPACE JUNK

I look for a more recent example of enormous objects falling from orbit and find the story of the 6.5-ton UARS satellite. NASA's space shuttle Discovery deployed the climate satellite in September 1991. The $750 million satellite was decommissioned by NASA in December 2005. When it fell to Earth, the event was reported this way:

> NASA estimates that UARS will come crashing back to Earth
> Friday night (Sept. 23) or Saturday morning (Sept. 24). At the

moment, they're not sure precisely where; pretty much anywhere on the planet between the latitudes of northern Canada and southern South America is a possibility. Researchers further estimate that about 1,170 pounds of UARS' 6.5-ton bulk will survive re-entry. Chances of human casualties are extremely remote; NASA pegs the chance of a piece of UARS debris hitting anybody anywhere in the world at 1 in 3,200.

NUCLEAR BOMBS

According to a Department of Defense document. two months after the close call in Goldsboro, another B-52 was flying in the western United States when the cabin depressurized and the crew ejected, leaving the pilot to steer the bomber away from populated areas. The plane crashed in Yuba City, California, but safety devices prevented the two onboard nuclear weapons from detonating.

ROCKS

When asked by reporters who are covering the Sharon Budd story, Pennsylvania state police can't say how many times someone threw an object that struck a vehicle last year, because its database lumps those incidents in with incidents in which something lands on a highway. What is known is that in 2013, troopers responded to 213 "assault-propulsion of missile" incidents that include both categories. The numbers of such incidents was 229 in 2012, and 282 in 2011. What the reporters also learn is that in Pennsylvania, fences are erected on highway overpasses in urban areas that have sidewalks and are near a school or playgrounds. The Gray Hill Road overpass in the New Columbia area from which the rock was thrown that hit the Budd car doesn't meet that criteria because it's in a rural area, with no sidewalk. The overpass is 22 feet high.

WATER BALLOONS

At the beginning of ninth grade, at the high school band picnic, I followed four other freshmen and one sophomore up the winding outside staircase that led to the top of the water tower at Allegheny County's North Park. The sophomore had given us balloons to fill with water and shown us how to tie them securely. I had two that wobbled in my hands. Some of the other boys balanced two in each hand. "There's always somebody who doesn't know we're up here," the sophomore said. He played French horn. I played trombone, and by the time we reached the 100-foot-high observation deck, I was uneasy with the height and being associated with boys who thought tossing water balloons was cool. Every other boy screamed when a balloon burst close enough to somebody to soak them. I was the only one who didn't lean over the railing to see the damage. Before the last balloons were tossed, I made my way down the stairs and hoped that anyone coming up the 154 metal steps would remember that I wasn't part of the group that tossed the balloons, that anyone soaked would see me halfway down while the next balloon arced toward them.

NUCLEAR BOMBS

The Defense Department has disclosed 32 accidents involving nuclear weapons between 1950 and 1980. There are at least 21 declassified accounts between 1950 and 1968 of aircraft-related incidents in which nuclear weapons were lost, accidentally dropped, jettisoned for safety reasons or on board planes that crashed. The accidents occurred in various U.S. states, Greenland, Spain, Morocco and England, and over the Pacific and Atlantic oceans and the Mediterranean Sea. Another five accidents occurred when planes were taxiing or parked.

MORE POWDER

On July 10, 1976, an explosion at a northern Italian chemical plant released a thick, white cloud. Close by was the town of Seveso, and the powder quickly settled upon it. Soon small animals began to die. Cats. Dogs. It took four days before people felt sick. They were nauseous. They had blurred vision. And things were worse with their children, who broke out in a skin disease known as chloracne. The town wasn't evacuated until weeks later. The white mist that fell on Seveso was dioxin. After a while, the residents returned. Eventually, babies were born disfigured. Liver disease became common.

ROCKS

The police questioned Ron Johnson, who lives only 100 feet from the Gray Hill Road overpass. He mentioned to them that kids had tossed rocks at tractor trailers from the same bridge about seven years ago. "Then they put the signs up, 'No standing on bridge,' and there for a while the cops were coming by on a regular basis checking. But nothing happened, so the cops stopped coming by."

SPACE JUNK

The largest stone meteorite in recorded history struck Earth near Kirin, China in 1976. More than 100 pieces of the original large meteor reached Earth, some of them weighing hundreds of pounds. One weighed 3,902 pounds, the largest ever recovered.

PENNIES

When I was fifteen I watched as a friend sailed a penny out a window from the 25th floor of the University of Pittsburgh's Cathedral of Learning. "If you're high enough," he'd said, "a falling penny will kill somebody." We rushed to look down, but I already knew there was no way he could throw it far enough out to have it hit the ground without bouncing off the outside walls that were built wider at the bottom like a narrow wedding cake. When I said so, he threw another. "We should go higher," he said, but we couldn't get access to any of the seventeen floors above us, the full 535 feet of height. Minutes later, on the street, there was no sign of anyone harmed by the pennies he'd tossed from about 300 feet high.

NUCLEAR BOMBS

A website, nuclearsecrecy.com, allows users to simulate nuclear explosions. It says that one bomb the size of the two that fell on North Carolina in 1961 would emit thermal radiation over a 15-mile radius. Wind conditions, of course, could change that. The website warns that calculating casualties is problematic. Population clusters vary. So does topography.

ROCKS

There have been reports of fatalities from rock throwing incidents, including two drivers killed by rocks as big as soccer balls tossed onto a German highway in 2000. Like the boys who hit the Budd car, all of those rock throwers were teenagers. They were charged with murder.

Space Junk

Twenty-six large asteroids have exploded in the Earth's atmosphere in the first thirteen years of the 21st century, all of the explosions registering the power of at least one kiloton. The frequency of an asteroid striking earth with the power to destroy a large city is calculated at about once per century.

Bodies

One famously landed on a car in San Diego, dropping from a mid-air accident like a fantastically narrow storm. The driver and her child were unharmed, but afterward, she had a habit of glancing up like a weather forecaster. An episode of the television series *Six Feet Under* begins with a scene that recreates this improbable landing.

Rocks

I learn that before the boys threw rocks, they drove through a cornfield to see how much damage they could do, and I remember riding through a corn field in a car as a freshman in college. It was October, not July. "We do this every year," the driver, a townie, said. "We're not hurting anything. It'll just all get cut down in a few weeks anyway." I was anxious the entire time we plowed through the stalks, not because I was worried about being caught, but because it was so hard to see that anything could have been in front of us before that driver could react. The farmer, knowing this vandalism happened every October, could have laid boulders in the field, anticipating the annual car full of teenage jerks.

Space Junk

The largest iron meteorite weighs more than 60 tons. It was discovered in 1920, on a farm in Namibia. It is now a national monument visited by tourists.

More Bodies

It's rare to believe a body is falling from a cloud. It takes height that turns us breathless, a thousand feet or more to make us think "sky." In high school physics class, we learned Newton's Second Law, the one that offers a formula for the acceleration of a falling object: g=32 ft. per second squared. The velocity of the falling object could be calculated by the formula v=g x time. The World Trade Centers were over 1300 feet high. The morning of the terrorist attacks distance and speed throttled our breath while suited bodies plunged like drops of a passing shower. Those bodies were falling about 120 miles per hour when they hit the ground. They have been filmed. They have been watched again and again. How some held hands when they leaped. The sky, that morning, was clear.

Nuclear Bombs

In December 1965, a month before the accident at Palomares, the James Bond film *Thunderball* was released. The story line was eerily similar. Bond's mission was to find atomic bombs that had been lost at sea, and news stories about Palomares made the connection. In real life, it was much harder to first locate, and then recover the bomb from the seabed.

Rocks

Four months after the incident, as part of a plea deal, Keefer McGee agrees to testify against his friends. In court, he says, "We decided to throw rocks at cars, just go out and be bad." He describes how, when they reached the overpass, Dylan and Tyler jumped out armed with rocks they'd gathered earlier. "There was a loud crash when Dylan's stone hit," he says. "We all laughed as we drove away."

More Bodies

The newly completed World Trade Center is 1776 feet tall with its antenna, a 408-foot spire, included. The builders have called the antenna a mast to insure the Trade Center is judged the tallest building in the United States rather than the Willis (formerly Sears) Tower in Chicago. The new Trade Center has fewer floors but has been designated tallest by the Council on Tall Buildings and Urban Habitat. In Chicago, years ago, my friend refused to go up in the Sears Tower, so I went alone. As always when I was close enough to the edge to see down into the city, every instinct told me to stay back, but the safety shield was high enough for even me to relax. Even so, riding down in the elevator felt like rescue.

Nuclear Bombs

University of California-Los Angeles researchers estimate that, respectively, Hiroshima and Nagasaki had populations of about 330,000 and 250,000 when they were bombed in August 1945. By that December, the cities' death tolls included, by conservative estimates, at least 90,000 and 60,000 people. All of the United States nuclear bombs involved in major accidents since then were far more powerful than those.

Rocks

Sharon Budd spent weeks in an induced coma. It took thirteen hours of surgery to reconstruct her face. The surgeon said it was the worst case he'd ever seen. In a later interview, Randy Budd talked about growing up in a rough Ohio neighborhood, learning early to take care of himself. How that affected his feelings about the four boys. "There's some of that in me," he said. "That's one way I have of how, if someone does something wrong to you, to handle it."

More Bodies

People have experimented with postures in the air to acquire maximum velocity. The record free fall speed is 330 mph within ordinary atmosphere. However, claims have been made for falling at beyond the speed of sound from the upper atmosphere. Jumping from the stratosphere in 2012, Felix Baumgartner became the first man to break the speed of sound in freefall. He climbed to 128,100 feet in a helium-filled balloon. Recently, Alan Eustace, a senior vice president at Google, fell from the top of the stratosphere, plummeting nearly 26 vertical miles in the span of about 15 minutes. In doing so, he broke Baumgartner's 2012 record for world's highest-altitude freefall. The official figure on Eustace's maximum altitude was given as 135,890 feet, or 25.74 miles. Baumgartner held on to the overall speed record, however. On his return to Earth, Eustace achieved a top speed of 822 miles per hour, breaking the sound barrier and generating a sonic boom, but shy of Baumgartner's *Guiness Book of Records* approved speed of 833.9 mph.

Rocks

In October, when Sharon Budd steps out of the Geisinger Medical Center for the first time, she wears a pink #BuddStrong T-shirt. Her artificial skull is covered by a pink and white knit cap. Outside the rehab facility, she is filmed ringing a victory bell reserved for patients who overcome long odds. When she first entered the facility, she was so confused she couldn't manage any of the therapy. Three months since the incident, she has no memory of it. I watch the video of the event several times. As she walks, Sharon Budd is braced on both sides by smiling attendants. At the victory bell ceremony, she is still lightly supported. According to her doctor, she is now "nearly independent, walking with a little assistance, able to take care of herself."

Rocks

In November, Sharon Budd's family notices seepage coming from a scar that runs across her forehead. She has to undergo a sixth surgery at Geisinger Medical Center to treat an infection underneath her artificial skull. The cap is removed and has to remain off for four to six weeks. Now she must wear a protective helmet but is able to return home. However, she will need to come back to Geisinger every two weeks for an exam.

Rocks

The two boys who were seventeen at the time want to be tried as juveniles. The lawyers for all the boys want certain evidence to be suppressed when their clients come to trial. Most important, they say, is not to admit as evidence the 911 call made by Mr. Budd. Likewise, pictures of Mrs. Budd should not be permitted to be shown. They are prejudicial, the lawyers claim. These exhibits are too emotionally charged.

PROXIMITY

From: *The Darkness Call* (Pleaides Press, 2018)

When my wife and I arrive in Los Angeles, my daughter says a peacock's blown into her neighborhood from Griffith Park, driven by the record Pacific wind of two days before. "Lucky for that bird," Shannon tells us, "we have all these trees and roofs."

When I ask where it is, she says, "You'll see it. It was still here this morning."

Happy to relax on her balcony after the long flight, I scan every possible roosting place, but the pine trees and the apartment house roofs below yield nothing. The traffic on Los Feliz Boulevard is as incessant as ever. I follow the setting sun around back, and when I slouch in a soft chair on her small patio that is at least sheltered from the traffic noise, a peacock seems more likely to show up.

Sure enough, though I see nothing on the steep, wooded hill that sweeps up behind my daughter's rental house, I hear squawking, so I walk inside to tell her I heard the bird. "That's not the peacock," Shannon says. "That's the woman who lives in one of the apartments below us."

When we hear the squawking again, Shannon explains that by last night (only a day after the peacock's arrival), her neighbor had learned to mimic the peacock's odd call. "She has it almost perfect," my daughter says. "She even squawks over the sound of traffic. You'll see her while you're here. She's sure to come up the stairs from her apartment to visit."

I hear another call, but I keep to myself that it arrives like a sound check for lunacy.

*   *   *

As always, when we visit for a week or more, my wife and I rent an apartment on the other side of Loz Feliz Boulevard, a short walk away from the cramped space Shannon shares with her two young daughters. In the morning, I use the fitness room; nearly every afternoon I walk to the movies or the library. My wife swims in the apartment's outdoor pool every afternoon.

On the second day of this trip, she tells me helicopters hovered overhead while I sat through *End of Watch*, the sort of cop movie she's happy to let me watch alone. "Something was going on," she says, "and not far from here." We don't pay for the apartment's cable service when we come to Los Angeles, and we always leave our computer at home, but before we go to dinner with my daughter, Shannon logs on and learns that Johnny Lewis, an actor who was in the first two seasons of *Sons of Anarchy*, has beaten his landlady to death, killed and dismembered her cat, and either fallen or jumped to his own death from the roof of a Los Feliz house.

Under the heading "Breaking News" are a few additional short sentences: "Investigators believe *Sons of Anarchy* actor Johnny Lewis killed his elderly landlord, Katherine Davis, 81. Lewis was found sprawled in the driveway."

"Did you ever watch that show?" my daughter asks.

"For five minutes once."

My wife notices the Lowry Street address of the crime scene. "That's right behind our apartment," she says. "No wonder the helicopters were over my head."

"Right behind?" I echo.

"Really close. A couple of blocks up."

After dinner we make our way home in the dark, and I tell my wife I want to walk up Lowry to the murder scene. "Why?" she says, and I let it go and follow her inside.

"Something always happens close when you come here," I say. "Remember the fire?"

"That's nothing like a murder. That's some place we could look at later when everything was taken care of."

Once, when my wife visited without me, she arrived the day a fire in Griffith Park spread rapidly, the smoke and ash reaching my daughter's apartment as they ate dinner. The next day they were evacuated to a motel and spent two days bunched together in one room. Six months later, we walked through the park until we reached a place where the path began to twist upward and we could see where the charred trees spread out below us, and where, on the other side of the shallow valley, untouched vegetation let us know just how close the fire had come to making the leap into the neighborhood of expensive homes set into the hillside across the street from my daughter's apartment, the same neighborhood where the landlady's murder had just occurred.

We buy a newspaper, the first time since I'd picked up one when we'd been in town near the 40th anniversary date of the Manson murders. "Near Griffith Park" is how the setting is described in the article about Johnny Lewis killing his landlady. It's the same phrase used three years earlier when my daughter mentioned that the house where the less-pub-licized, second night of Manson murders took place was located directly above her apartment. I was surprised then, but we were leaving the next day, and I forgot about the LaBiancas and their nearby house until now, when a murder with a celebrity alleged killer already generating a brush fire of publicity was just as markedly close.

I ask Shannon to remind me about the exact location of the LaBianca house.

"Right up the hill behind us," Shannon says, and my wife adds that I was told the same thing three years before. I let her impatience go, step outside to reconnoiter.

From my daughter's patio, the forty-three year-old events seem less remote. The distance to the top of the slope looks to be about 100 feet, but the hillside is steep enough to convince me a fall and serious injury would be likely if I chanced a climb. "There's some sort of wall up there," my daughter says when she sees me looking up. "And there are coyotes," she adds, her way of protecting me from foolishness.

"Ok," I say, "I'm not going straight up," but I tell my wife I not only want to walk to the Johnny Lewis murder site, I want to climb the street that leads to the La Bianca house. "We're in the murder neighborhood," I say, and she frowns.

"There's something wrong with you," she says, but she agrees to go to the LaBianca house because everything happened so long ago. Even better, she knows exactly how to get there.

A few minutes later, when a loud squawking reaches us, I say to my daughter, "There goes your neighbor again. Is she crazy?"

Shannon doesn't answer until the squawking comes again. "That's the real peacock," she says.

"All this violence right on top of us," my wife says the next morning as we cross Los Feliz Boulevard on our way to Shannon's apartment. "But at least the homeless guy is gone."

The year before, for five months, a homeless man nested among the trees in the only hillside space without a house set into it on my daughter's street, his clothes strung upon branches like chronic laundry, shopping carts shimmering like chrome-slathered antique cars. Even when we couldn't see anyone, my wife tensed every time we walked by during that visit. Every day during the week we visited, though the squatter's space was three doors down, she told our daughter she should call the police without waiting for the residents right next to that vacant property to call.

As we round a sharp curve, a woman is standing by our daughter's steps. Though her hair is as black as her black blouse and tight black leggings, her face is heavily lined, and she looks to be, like my wife and me, in her sixties. Shannon introduces us, adding that the woman lives "right down there," and I know we're meeting the peacock caller.

She doesn't disappoint. She reports a night of coyotes, how she listened to them for hours, worrying until a half-hour ago, when she saw the peacock resting upon the gray-tiled roof of the house next to my daughter's.

"From way up there," she says, "that beauty could photograph Los Angeles." All of us look up to the empty roof. "It has to be close," the woman says. She is so fixated that I expect her to give us a squawk or two, but she goes down the steps to her apartment without working up a call.

"She used to be a makeup artist," Shannon says.

There's no way my wife and I can climb directly up the steep hillside, so we need to walk a half-mile loop to a street that begins to wind upward to where the houses become progressively more lavish and expensive. We follow the twists of Waverly Drive until we reach the Cardinal Timothy Manning House of Prayer for Priests. which, according to my best estimate, directly overlook's our daughter's house.

"It looks like a resort hotel for monks," I say.

The enormous property is gated, with a perimeter wall that lines the street for such a distance that I go back and step off 350 paces, guessing about 300 yards of frontage. The Spanish style buildings stretch across much of the perfectly kept grounds. The Brothers of the Good Shepherd, who apparently host other priests looking to spend time on retreat, would make a fortune if they sold this property.

"There's no chance of homeless squatters lasting more than a few minutes up here," I say.

"Right," my wife says, "but down where your daughter lives, it took months for the police to chase that guy away."

"Once they got around to it, they emptied that place of his like burglars," I say, but I'm regretting that there's no possible way to walk to the edge of the steep hill and look down on my daughter's house. I imagine an alarm system. I conjure well-trained dogs.

But it's not far to the LaBianca House. Though the street number doesn't match what I'd looked up, it unmistakably matches the photographs I examined on the Internet the day before. While I stare up the driveway from the same angle as a few of the crime scene photographs, my wife tells me that two doors down, across the street, our granddaughter attended a birthday party for a classmate earlier this year.

"Really?" I say, remembering that I'd read, once, that Manson had attended a party in the vicinity as well, that the reason the LaBianca house was chosen was the accident of his familiarity with Waverly and the isolation of the houses there.

Before I'm done marveling at the chain of coincidences, a man approaches walking a tiny, tightly-furred dog that excitedly tugs its leash until it stands right by my feet. When I reach down to give it a quick pat, the man says, "Mr. Muggles likes you."

"Looks that way," I say.

"I walk him for his owner. He's lived up here for quite some time but doesn't get out much anymore."

I can't help but estimate that "quite some time" might very well place that dog owner on this street in the summer of 1969, and the dog walker, as if reading my mind, says, "After the Manson thing, the new owners of that house changed the number of the street address. Some people come up here and get confused."

"I can understand why" is all I can manage, and with a smile, the dog walker guides Mr. Muggles away from us.

"We should be getting back," my wife says. We've agreed to walk our granddaughters and the dog back to our apartment and keep them overnight, giving my daughter a "day of rest" because her marriage has fallen apart, her husband living elsewhere. The way down wears hard on my arthritic and cartilage-missing knees.

A half hour later, reading from my daughter's computer, I tell my wife that Johnny Lewis played a character called "Half-Sack" because he was missing a testicle. "Of course," she says, and I forego the rest of what I've learned about the scenarios of *Sons of Anarchy*. But when I read a story that describes the scene of the murder as an "artist's villa" and lists the site as in the 3600 block of Lowry Street, I say, "You're right about how close that house is to our apartment."

"Then go ahead and take a look tomorrow morning," she says. "You're the one who thinks it's interesting to look at murder sites."

"There's a house Walt Disney lived in up there behind you, too," our daughter says, but I don't react until she adds, "The story has it that the LaBiancas lived there before they moved up to Waverly."

"This is getting creepy," my wife says. She pulls out my daughter's wedding album, and the way she looks at the photos makes me believe she is looking for signs of the marriage's failure that she somehow missed on the day of the ceremony.

With my wife fixated on the photos, I turn to my daughter.

"Remember when Mom got out her wedding dress for you to wear?"

"I wish I could have," she says, "but it wasn't in good enough shape. Mom looked beautiful in it."

Our granddaughters come out of their room with their overnight bags packed, keeping me from blurting out another case of proximity, how in one of the professional photographs taken before, during, and after our wedding, a young girl is attaching paper flowers to the car my wife and I would drive on our honeymoon. She lived next door to my wife's family and was visibly excited to be part of what was happening that August afternoon in 1968.

Thirteen years ago, shortly before my daughter was married, that girl, because she was scheduled to testify against a man accused of a crime, was murdered. The accused man broke into her house and killed her. He lived next door to her in an adjacent, refurbished row house. He'd tunneled through the wall to get to her. He'd dragged her body back through the hole in the wall and dismembered her in his basement.

Just as we all step outside, we hear the distinctive squawk, audible even over the noise of a furious surge of cars on Los Feliz as the light changes.

"The real peacock," my daughter says, though we can't make it out. "What do you think that sound it's making means?" she goes on. "Fear or loneliness?"

The following morning, I take the dog along. It needs to exercise, and it makes me feel like I have a purpose other than rubbernecking. The drawback is the white German shepherd's excitement to be outside, how, when it tugs at the leash, my knees remind me that Lowry is as steep as Waverly, that coming back down with the dog scrambling ahead will be penance for curiosity.

If there's a yard that doesn't display a security sign, I don't see it. Half the signs have extra warnings that promise an armed response, and I take it as a suggestion, this morning, that the response would come from within.

By the time Lowry spirals up to the 3600 block murder site, the houses unmistakably "loom" on the side of the street where the crime took place, each house built for height, I imagine, to guarantee a view.

The short driveways are all steep, the houses fortress-like. A few houses have pulley systems that I guess are for the luxury of delivered groceries and packages.

Nobody is outside near the murder house, but now I'm happy to have the dog on its leash because it makes me look like a resident of the neighborhood, someone who lives close by, someone who belongs there. The driveway at the murder site is pitched so steeply I can see at once how a head-first tumble from the roof or even the balcony could be fatal.

What else I'm certain of is that from an upstairs window in that house, someone could look across Los Feliz Boulevard and see my daughter's apartment.

That evening, when we walk our granddaughters and the dog to their house, Shannon tells us the peacock has been retrieved and returned to Griffith Park. Her neighbor, apparently, hasn't gotten the word, because we all hear her squawk what now sounds like a plaintive, impossible mating call.

On the way back to our apartment, approaching the grove of trees where the homeless man once lived, my wife says she's worried about coyotes. "I've seen them," she says, "even if you never have."

Nearing Los Feliz Boulevard, packed as always with cars and trucks and buses, I begin to limp. It is all I can do to cross the highway before the "walk" sign blinks off, and the traffic lunges forward.

AFTER THE THREE-MOON ERA

From: *The Mayan Syndrome* (Madhat Press, 2023)

The dozen fetuses of the sand shark feed on each other
until only one is left to be born.

1

While eating breakfast, I read that some astronomers now believe Earth once had three moons. The scientists have a short list of hypotheses for two moons vanishing: They might have been sucked into the sun. They might have been shattered by the one moon that survived collision. Regardless, those other moons have vanished like glittering charms on a bracelet sliding off a child's wrist, the night sky empty with places where some arrangement of reflected light might have aligned itself against the darkness.

2

As a gift, decades ago, I had photographs of my father, his three brothers, and sister restored, all of them originally taken when they were twenty-one. My father, beginning in his mid-eighties, pointed out how they had died in reverse order, beginning with his youngest brother. Each time I visited he made me examine that composite as if I had never seen it. "I'm the only one left," he said as he repeated their names, working backwards toward himself. "Who would believe that?"

3

In early spring, when I visit during the year my father turns eighty-nine, he sings hymns aloud, tells me he wakes each morning expecting

211

to be reborn, repeating it three times as if I'm the genie for resurrection. He says he hears the brothers I never had softly talking in the small bedroom where I slept while not one of them was born. They whisper, he says, about the way he refused them, saying "never" in the disciplined sign language of the rhythm method, keeping each of them a jealous spirit.

When he sings "In the Garden," I imagine those brothers, each day, rising to where my childhood window looks out at the rhododendron roof-high, the peace of its curtain, fragments of light that testify like character witnesses for weather. They move their mouths to those hymns that are heavy with sunrise and eternal joy.

The house holds the early darkness and the dry heat of the furnace, and my father repeats the chorus, raising his voice to be heard by those unborn boys who wake him each morning like birds.

4

One of my students tells me she devoured her twin in the womb, a doctor solving that natural crime with the spaced clues of ultrasound. "My mother explained it all to me," she says. "She gave me a copy of the ultrasound photograph that was taken when there were two of us."

She confides that she keeps her shadow twin sealed inside a scrapbook she opens on her birthday, leaving the photo face up in her bedroom. For when, she says, her family sings around her cake. For when their voices swell enough to reach her sister.

5

"The face seemed to warm up suddenly, sparkle returned to the eyes." So wrote a scientist named Robert Cornish in a report to the University of California in 1933. He was working on a way to revive the dead by strapping them to a seesaw and rapidly teeter-totting the corpses in order to circulate their blood.

A long time he and his assistants had spent at this primitive CPR, working the seesaw as if they were attempting to draw water from a long-unprimed pump. At least once, according to Cornish's report, their persistence brought a bit of color to the face of a recent heart-attack victim before it reverted to ashen.

Cornish needed to perfect his technique, but human bodies were hard to come by. He began to work with dogs, personally killing fox terriers, naming each of those freshly dead dogs Lazarus, referencing the optimism of the New Testament story. When some of those dogs breathed again, reviving for an hour or two before dying a second time, he was sure he was on to something.

Better yet, Lazarus IV and V lived for a few months. Newspapers reported the story. There was enough excitement and curiosity about his work that a movie was made that spliced in five minutes of footage of Cornish and his dogs. Lazarus IV and V, however, were blind and brain-damaged, inspiring, according to the newspaper stories, "terror in the ordinary dogs they met."

6***

On my next visit, as an early birthday present, I bring my father a gift, a book that traces the stories behind the composition of more than fifty selected hymns. The words and music for all of the hymns are included, and the book, with its dark, austere cover, has the feel of church about it, as if I should rise from my chair as he opens it, ready to join in singing the processional.

It's been eighteen years since he lost the glasses my mother made him get in order to be able to read any print smaller than headlines. He squints at a few pages, pauses at those which have the hymns printed on them to read the titles that are printed in the large Old English Text font of the Lutheran hymnal he's sung from for more than eighty years. Finally, he closes his eyes, one hand resting across a page, and begins to sing "The Old Rugged Cross."

I take my father to dinner, eating in a restaurant so familiar he can order what he's had three times before without having to read the menu. On the way back to his house he asks me to park on Butler Street for the first time in nearly twenty years. The street is so deserted, there is room for ten cars, but I know to drift up to where a vacant lot sits among the buildings that house bars, a beauty shop, a tattoo parlor, and a long-closed hardware store that still sports its name on the side of the building. He uses his cane to shuffle into the middle of that empty space where the bakery he owned for sixteen years used to stand.

"The bakery's been missing so long, pretty soon no one will know it was here," he says.

"Probably," I say, an easy agreement. It's been almost forty years since the building was torn down a few months after the bakery closed. Shortly afterwards, the cement we're standing on was laid over the vacant space to provide parking for people who rented the rooms above those nearby businesses, though now, when I glance up, I can't see any lights in the upstairs rooms on either side of us and no cars are parked near where we stand.

I half-expect him to begin a hymn, but instead he leans on his cane and says, "The house where I was born is gone, and the house where you were born is gone," sounding so mournful I offer to drive him to both sites, one leveled to make room for a widened highway, the other long ago razed and replaced by a church. With the sound of traffic passing, he seems to hear nothing of what I say.

"Right here," he says, and when he spreads his arms, I guess that he's standing at the memory of workbench, that when he pulls his hands back together and lifts them, the cane dangling from his right hand, he is ready to carry something to the bank of ovens in the nearby remembered room.

After a few seconds he lowers his hands, steadies himself, and asks me to stand closer. He tells me my mother is slicing bread, the cash register behind her, the three of us working together because he is icing a wedding cake just before delivery, spiraling sweetness so thick with sugar and lard around the figures of the bride and groom, no one should eat it, trusting me to balance the three white tiers to the car.

7

After my student tells me about her lost twin, I read that before the use of ultrasound, the diagnosis of the death of a twin or multiple was made through an examination of the placenta after delivery. Now, with the availability of early ultrasounds, the presence of twins or multiple fetuses can be detected during the first trimester. A follow-up ultrasound would reveal the "disappearance" of a twin.

8

The year my father turns eighty-nine, a scientist suggested that the new superconductor was capable of creating a cosmological bomb billions of times more powerful than the atomic bomb. He said the odds were as likely as one chance in ten, at least one chance in fifty, speaking like a bookie about the end of Earth when the superconductor began to operate at full power. The rest of his scare was an explanation of how showers of heavy-mass particles might end us with ultra-dense quark matter, the vocabulary for our vanishing full of unrecognizable nouns.

I wanted to dismiss it, but during the week in which I read that scientist's warning, two friends my age died on successive days, and I woke on the third to a phone call I believed was one more, as if a chain reaction had begun, as likely, it seemed as the seven billion of us becoming fodder for a brand new black hole because those superconductor scientists were poised on the brink of Genesis, hurtling back to where nothing is alive but the gods.

9

Because his house becomes so dusty, especially the master bedroom where I sleep, I have an asthma attack during two consecutive visits. The next time I arrive, I tell him that I have other business the following day, that I have a reservation sixty miles away in order to be closer to my morning appointment.

And that's mostly true. I drive for an hour and stay in a motel along the highway I use to return home. It's one hour cut from the four-hour drive, and I've stayed late enough that the trip wouldn't have ended until after one a.m.

The motel room is clean and free of dust. I watch the late news and sports on the Pittsburgh channel that my father watches each night before he hobbles, bracing himself on furniture and the walls of his hall before lying down in the bed I slept in for thirteen years.

10

In the early 19th century there were scientists who demonstrated how electricity seemed to reanimate a dead body. Executed criminals were often used, their faces twitching, an eye-opening, an arm or a leg jerking when a powerful battery was connected to particular muscles. There was enough publicity about these demonstrations that's it's nearly certain Mary Shelley was aware of them. So Dr. Frankenstein, with the advantages of her fiction, was able to reanimate the dead, standing over the body like a glorious thunderhead, in love with choice.

11

Once a month, from when I was nine until I was sixteen, my father showed slides, projecting them onto the living room wall. He showed the new ones first: landscapes taken from mountaintops; old buildings shot from such a distance that my sister, my mother, and I were barely recognizable standing in front of them; close-ups of flowers he identified, walking up to the image to point out their characteristics with his finger; aging relatives we visited on vacation trips, sleeping in their houses to avoid motel bills. After that he showed old slides, all of them snapped one-by-one into the metal frames required by the projector. There was never a night when some appeared upside down. Or when a slide jammed, the wall going a brilliant white that made everyone blink.

When I was sixteen, my mother bought him a new carousel projector. In order to use it, he had to unsnap a thousand slides from those metal frames.

12

"I never would have thought," my father frequently said after my mother died, meaning that he would outlive her.

"I thought I'd be with Ruthy by now," he repeated once he passed seventy-five, and he described an afterlife that seemed to be so much a physical continuation, I thought he expected to play golf and tend a garden forever, having time to master the sport he'd taken up in his sixties, enjoying fresh vegetables for a billion meals. By the time he was past eighty, I suspected that he worried about finding himself revived as the decrepit man he was becoming.

13

In 1964, when I was a freshman in college, a scientist named James McConnell published the results of his experiments with flatworms.

Flatworms were stupid, difficult to teach, but he'd rehearsed them until the brightest reacted to light, learning its link to a simple shock that McConnell supplied. He pulled aside the best of those slow learners and halved those pupils to see whether their heads or tails, both of which survived, could exceed the coin flip of chance. And later, when they were completely regenerated, he doubled those gifted students again into dozens of nervous worms, ones that quivered as soon as the light flashed to prophesize the imminence of pain. They were learning, it seemed, to anticipate the agony of an artificial sunrise and the relief of darkness. Finally, eager to discover whether learning could be physically passed from one generation to another, he fed those that had mastered the simple association of light with pain to those without such training. The success he began to claim was that what one worm had learned could be transferred to another by a regulated cannibalism.

Here, he declared, was the possibility of outrunning the slow meander of evolution. He saw the future of humanity in the precocious curling of worms, memory a matter of gorging to omniscience. There were people, subsequently, who dreamed of their children feeding upon them, how their fear and love and knowledge would be passed on to their children, keeping them, in one sense, alive.

14

"Pretty soon," my father began to say at eighty-five, "I'll be the only one who remembers the old days." He told me his "growing up" stories over and over until it seemed as if he was feeding me his memory. I was a willing listener. I didn't tell him that this was my version of revival, passing through the memories of future generations.

15

The things my mother wore:

Before we drove to church, white gloves that held a tissue to open the car door to keep them from being smudged. The new pair she kept in a box until the next wedding, Easter, or Christmas Eve. The two pair with three embroidered lines. The one pair with tiny, glittering appliqués.

While I walked into church with her each Sunday, not yet complaining about compulsory attendance, the black veils attached to her hats. The way she could make the veils flutter if she tilted her head and exhaled. How thin the cloth strands were, allowing her space to see the hymnal as she sang each hymn in alto's harmony as if she were in the choir.

In the years before illness took the weight off her body, the girdles she wore with every dress. The sound of elastic being tugged down at the end of each Sunday. How she exhaled behind her closed bedroom door.

16

Vanishing twins may occur in as many as one of every eight multifetus pregnancies and may not even be known in most cases. In one study, only three of twenty-one pairs of twins survived to term, suggesting intense fetal competition for space and nutrition. In some instances, vanishing twins leave no detectable trace at birth. More than one amniotic sac can be seen in early pregnancy. A few weeks later only one.

17

For a few years, the headless woman was a staple at the county fair. Justina, she was named one summer, and the pitch man claimed she'd lost her head in a faraway Egyptian trainwreck. One year her name was Tiffany, who'd been decapitated when her speeding car ran under a truck. The last one I saw in person was Britt, the bikini girl, beheaded by a shark, so lucky, like the others, to die near a doctor who could save her.

Impossible, I said, by that time in junior high school, but just after I spoke, Britt shuddered, letting me know she was suddenly cold. "What she deserves, dressed like that," my mother observed. Britt's alien silhouette was shadowed on the wall behind us, a threat of flexible tubing twisting up like new plumbing from her sliced, scarf-covered throat.

No matter their names, by then I understood that those women's headless bodies were always going to be young and sexy, preserved for study as if research was driven by lust. The old and the heavy were left headless; nobody repaired boys who were reckless, a thing to consider. "Those women aren't angels," my mother cautioned. "Don't you forget that."

Which was fine with me. By that September, I was an eighth-grader who wouldn't admit that all I wanted was a brainless whore who knew only what touched her—my fingertips and tongue, my lips and warm breath. Right then I was wishing that if there were miracles, I'd rather have my body saved than my soul.

18

Some mornings I want to do CPR on the bodies of the exhausted words. *Nithing. Aboulia. Viduous. Squirk.* Their denotations are so distant someone has published them to make a profit from the obsolete and rare.

Yesterday I saw marbles for sale in a museum gift shop. I plunged my hands into the bin and remembered aggies and oxbloods, cat's eyes, steelies, and glimmers, the names I've heard no one use for decades. I loitered nearby, wanting to see if even one child would choose them for souvenirs instead of a toy he could remote control. They might as well have been strands of hair plucked from the saints of our least urgent needs.

I watched while the ancient words of *trespasses* and *hallowed* came back, followed by remembering that my mother kept my first clipped hair and fingernails, that she told me I could have them some day when she was gone, though more than twenty years after her death, those things are as lost as the ancient words for *miserly person, loss of will, empty* and *embrace.*

19

At eighty-nine, my father gives up his cane for a walker. Because he is embarrassed by his weakness, I have to convince him to go to the familiar restaurant. I park by the front door and leave the car running while I help him stand. I unfold the walker and set it up for him, telling him to go inside while I park the car.

When I return, he hasn't moved. During dinner he says, without any prompting, "When you have just one son, there's no room for anything terrible to happen."

20

I mention to the student who absorbed her twin that my daughter sent me ultrasound photos of both of her yet-to-be-born. That I stuck those photos among cards and snapshots and short lists of things-to-do on my refrigerator, not telling her my daughter asked not to know their sex, her two daughters old enough, now, to study their early selves like scholars of pre-birth.

21

Things my mother used:

Two stationary tubs in which she moved the laundry from side to side, rinsing until she lifted each item and guided it into the wringer, the tight space between the rollers squeezing the water from our clothes, preparing them for the light.

The clothesline woven between two steel clothes posts cemented into the backyard. Dozens of wooden clothespins to suspend our laundry above the small lawn through the afternoon from March to November, above the cement cellar floor in winter, where they hung for two or three days like ghosts of ourselves.

Her flat iron. The water she sprinkled to keep its heat from scorching, pressing everything, even our underwear, before she let it retouch our bodies.

22

My daughter has painted a sky of chairs that sparkle like redundant constellations. Her heaven is moonless, the chairs, she says, ascending. The sky bleeds from one side from the wounds she imagines on an adjacent panel, one that waits nearby, brilliant with light. Her two daughters, ages seven and four, dream of painting it blue, a sun shining the chairs invisible.

23

Things my mother did for my father:

Turned on the television. Changed the channel and adjusted the rabbit ears until he could make out the Pittsburgh Pirates or a football game.

Let him read the newspaper at the dinner table, the sports section spread out by his plate while she talked to my sister and me through dinner as if we were a family of three.

Dialed the black, rotary phone in the kitchen. Called him when the person he wanted to speak to answered.

24

When my mother died, my father called no one for months, complaining that "Everyone has forgotten me."

25

On the way to visit my father, I pass the former site of West View Amusement Park, gone more than thirty years into apartments, a grocery store, the fast foods of familiar franchises. I park where the roller coaster turned sharply before it reached the road and West View's business district. When I close my eyes for a minute to imagine the park restored, one passer-by raps on the window to ask if I need help.

26

The science of the three-moon era:

The enormous impact that spawned our moon could have sent other satellites into orbit as well. They likely remained in their orbits for up to 100 million years. Then, gravitational tugs from the planets would have triggered changes in the Earth's orbit, ultimately causing the moons to become unmoored and drift away or crash into the Moon or Earth. The tugs from the other planets are very, very tiny, but they changed the shape of Earth's orbit, which changed the effect that the Sun's gravity has on the moons, which destabilized the lost moons.

27

Things my mother left behind:

Four black veils attached to hats stored in a box under a thick comforter high on the steps to the attic. Five pair of white gloves, two pair in boxes, unused.

Deep in a drawer of lingerie, two girdles untouched for a decade.

A washing machine with a wringer attached. A hundred feet of clothesline. Eighty-seven wooden clothes pins. A flat iron. The glass bottle with a sprinkler's head on top. The bottle clear, the head light green.

There is a haunting poem by W.S. Merwin called "For the Anniversary of my Death." It begins, "Every year without knowing it, I have passed the day/when the last fires will wave to me." Anyone reading those lines surely considers the anniversary of his own extinction.

It's less stressful to research the date and place some species we've never seen died for good—the final great auk on Elday Island, the last Labrador duck outside New York.

Even more exact, the ones exhibited like the lone Carolina parakeet that collapsed on February 21, 1918, at the Cincinnati Zoo. The final dusky seaside sparrow dying on display inside DisneyWorld, June 18, 1987, those one-of-a-kinds living for months or years without seeing a body like their own. The rest of us moving on without them, the world made irrefutably new by one more emptiness.

29

Simultaneously, during the three-moon era:
The crescent moon of anticipation,
The half-moon of mercy,
The full moon of joy.

30

When my wife and I are dressed and healthy, her body temperature registers eight-tenths of a degree colder than my ordinary one of 98.6. She shivers in any weather below seventy degrees. Occasionally, in Central Pennsylvania, she wears gloves in May and September. It's not much good joking about how she's farther from fever, how sweaters become her, how her jackets are stylish and smart. Or, if I feel the need to use a bit of trivia I picked up from the local PBS station during half time of a football game, to bring up the Thomsonians, who believed all sickness was caused by a deficiency in body heat, claiming that every disease could be cured by a medicinal steam bath.

It's something to consider because three months past ninety, my father is wrapped in two late August sweaters, the furnace growling in his delirious house where each plant has wilted like his short-term memory and his stove, for the past year, has been covered by signs that say NO in large letters to lower the probability for fire. My wife and I have driven the 200 miles to Pittsburgh the day after our own discussion of aging, meeting with a woman who specializes in Elder Law, the legalese of wills and trusts for the future distribution of whatever assets we have, the talk turning to assisted living, comas, and long-term vegetative states while air conditioning chilled my wife to putting on the jacket she carries, even in the heart of summer, for overcooled rooms.

Afterwards, walking outside to the surprise of warmth, she didn't remove her jacket. "How could you stand it?" she said.

"She made everything seem hypothetical," I said. "It was like we were talking about somebody else who was going to fall apart and die."

My wife hugged herself in the late afternoon sun. "I mean the cold," she said. "It was absolutely freezing in there."

31

Within one of those annotated lists featuring "famous last words" is the final one spoken by Dr. Joseph Green, a nineteenth-century English surgeon. Upon taking his own pulse, he managed, according to *The New Book of Lists,* to say "Stopped" before he died.

My father, by the end of September, has been moved to a facility for the nearly dead. He has a room with a door that doesn't lock, and the first time my wife and I visit he is wrapped in a flannel shirt and one of those sweaters from August, both buttoned to his throat while the heat hums from three baseboards on a warm fall afternoon.

My wife places her jacket on a chair. My father, nearly deaf, guesses at what we say. "That's good," he comments from time to time, imagining, I'm nearly certain, that we're telling him about how well we're doing or what our children have accomplished. "Nothing much going on here," he says at last, but he has begun to take his pulse every ten minutes or so as if he expects to hear, like that dying British doctor, the moment it will stop.

Finally, I tell him he's been in this building before, that he and I visited years ago because he had made a significant gift to the foundation that operates this facility. "That's good," he says, reaching for his wrist, and I lean close to say, "Let me show you something special" before I wheel him to the elevator that takes us one floor below to where I remember the chapel is located.

He doesn't react to the brief journey. My wife helps me navigate his chair between a set of pews in the chapel, and I wheel him to the window he purchased fifteen years ago, a stained glass mural in memory of my mother who, at that time, was already more than five years dead.

He doesn't recognize anything even when I set him inches from the plaque that states his name and hers. I ask him to read, but despite this prompt, he doesn't seem to understand. My wife, who stands nearby, bends down and reads the words aloud, shouting into his ear.

"How about that?" my father says. "It's for Ruthy."

"Yes," I say, "you paid for it."

"How come I've never seen this?" he says, and I wish I'd brought along the photograph of him standing beside the window the day it was unveiled.

My father stares at the window for a minute, and then, without taking his eyes off it, he begins to reminisce about my long-dead mother. He settles on listing old gifts he bought for her—a set of pearl earrings, a Sunday-dress, and a piano, all of them things that my sister helped him pick out.

He doesn't mention the one time he asked me to help. In late November, for their fifteenth anniversary, the gift of wax fruit he'd somehow set his heart upon. "Each piece will last and last," is how he put it. I was eleven years old and didn't ask him to reconsider his choice. I thought the fruit looked real, the colors blended to look just short of ripe, as if, when he arranged them in the wooden bowl that sat on our kitchen table the following day, they would be perfect.

My father handled the apples and pears; he hefted the peaches, bananas, and bunched purple grapes. He seemed to be weighing them. Finally, he made a small pile of assorted wax fruit on the department store's counter top, estimating, I thought, the size of our kitchen's wooden bowl that was usually full of opened envelopes and advertising circulars that featured store coupons my mother intended to use.

The next afternoon, while my mother was changing clothes after church, he dumped all of the paper out of the bowl and placed the mess on the dining room table. With his right hand, he swept his breakfast sweet roll crumbs into his left and shook them into the wastebasket. He ran hot water into the stained coffee mug he used for a week between washings, a habit, he'd told me once, that he believed was his gift to my mother because reusing it reduced the number of dishes she had to scrub every day.

Finally, he spread that wax fruit out like a set of trophies. The grapes were the last to go into the arrangement, lying on top, the overhead light reflecting off their surfaces. "Isn't this a pretty picture, Gary?" he said when he'd finished. I heard my mother coming down the hall. Before she entered the kitchen, he added, "Just think. They'll look beautiful forever."

32

The vanished twin can die from a poorly implanted placenta, a developmental anomaly that causes major organs to fail or to be completely missing, or there may be a chromosome abnormality incompatible with life.

33

For a year or two, just after that wax fruit anniversary, I was fascinated by pretending to be dead. "Soon enough, your time will come," my mother said, catching me holding my breath in front of the sweep hand for seconds on my bedroom clock radio. "Kid stuff," she said. "You should know better."

After that, I was more careful about my secret pastime, one that moved past simple breath-holding. In a library book, I studied what the mystics did to appear as if they'd stopped their hearts, shutting down the pulse with a block of wood under the armpit, pressure that worked like a tourniquet. I kept the book in my desk at school, but I mastered that technique well enough to simulate a stilled heart. I laid fingers to my wrist as I died, coming back again and again to briefly muffling one part of my autonomic system, dying in my room, or better, among trees in the game lands near our house, lying down where somebody, some day, might discover me. I stared at the path I'd taken to whatever small clearing I'd chosen, imagining hikers who would turn curious or eager or absolutely afraid, everything so still for seconds that I believed in the power of leaving and returning, the comfort of being sprawled like the nearly drowned, doing CPR on the self, taking that first great gasp and bringing my heart's beat back after someone laid fingertips to my wrist, holding them there in wonder.

225

The second time my wife and I visit the nursing home, I notice that my father has no pictures of my mother in his room, which means I have two more pictures of her in my house than he displays. "Do you want a picture of Mom?" I ask, and he shakes his head.

"It won't bring her back," he says, for once not saying "That's good," and when I show him the wedding announcement I've discovered between the pages of a book about the national parks he had sitting out in his living room, he can recite all four paragraphs from the local weekly newspaper. "Thanksgiving 1941," he says. "Dorothy Seitz, maid-of-honor. Ruth Lang, given by her brother Karl. Mildred Van Wegan (nee Lang) attended from Michigan. The Reverend Blair Claney officiated."

How many times had he read that notice in the twenty years since she'd died? "We had the long weekend for our honeymoon," he says. "And a week after that, the war."

It's nearly Halloween by now, and the children of the nursing home staff wear costumes and go from room to room to do an indoor trick or treat. My father, because he can't hear or he doesn't read the facility's weekly newsletters, doesn't understand, so he has no candy on hand. Regardless, he seems fascinated by the princesses and vampires. "Remember *Frankenstein*?" he says. "I saw it in the theater as a boy. Boris Karloff. That was scary for a boy my age. And then he was in all those movies about trying to raise the dead."

"It's a wish that's always with us," I say, but he doesn't hear.

"Remember *Frankenstein*?" he says again. "I saw it in the theater as a boy. Boris Karloff. That was scary for a boy my age. And then he was in all those movies about trying to raise the dead."

I consider showing him the wedding notice again.

Nearly twenty-one years ago, after my mother died at home, my father told me, "Your mother didn't want a hospital. She'd just seen her sister in misery with the tubes and machines and all that coming to nothing."

This week, when we talked on the phone, my sister has told me that his chart says *Resuscitate* where a choice is asked for. Thirteen years ago, nearly eight years after my mother died, my father's heart was stopped during bypass surgery. For a year, each time I visited, he showed me his scar. "The things they can do," he said. Within the next few years, his brother and sister died of cancer. "There has to be a limit on miracles," he said at the time. "Maybe it's one for each family."

When we get home, I look up Boris Karloff's films. Sure enough, there are some that sound as if they repeat the plot of a doctor trying to raise the dead. *The Man they could not Hang* and *The Man with Nine Lives,* for two. The plots feature grave robbing and secret serums for curing cancer and providing eternal youth. The common denominator is Boris Karloff as the mad scientist, not the reanimated body.

35

During the 1950s, a Soviet surgeon named Vladimir Demikhov sewed the heads of puppies onto full-grown dogs. Both heads were alive. The puppies even lapped milk with their tongues, though it ran from their severed throats. This is how we will be revived one day, he said, meaning with the hearts and lungs of others. Tissue rejection killed those dogs in a month or less.

Those puppies must have wondered why the milk dribbled out behind them. Their heads remind me of old dolls, the way their rubber faces, always with their one expression of breast hunger, could be squeezed loose from their pink, sexless bodies.

Those full-grown dogs, on the other hand, must have been aggravated every moment by the nuisance of a second, useless head.

36

I've made a list of the times I might have died, yet, as my mother always said, "Lived to tell about it":

Pneumonia—four bouts, each one relieved by antibiotics.

Being a passenger in a car driven by drunks or speeders—a good many times before the age of twenty-two, surviving each trip unscathed and discovering, months or years later, that several of those drivers eventually killed themselves behind the wheel.

Falling asleep while driving—not me, but the man who'd picked me up as I hitchhiked, a cornfield fortunately level with the highway at the spot where he left the road.

The list doesn't seem extraordinary except for the time that I braked my Volkswagen hatchback hard when a trailer truck I was passing suddenly veered into my lane. The hatchback locked into a four-wheel drift, lurching sideways across the median strip and through two lanes of oncoming, limited-access speeding traffic, somehow missed by all of them before the tires, just as miraculously, caught on the opposite shoulder as I spun and ended up facing sideways.

I took a breath and chose a break in the traffic to cross back to my lanes, swerving into the passing lane where I'd been seconds before. Two miles later I exited and found myself behind that same truck at a stop light. The truck driver climbed down and walked toward me. It was summer. The car wasn't air conditioned. My window was open. He bent down and said, "Fuck, I'm so sorry. You must be sitting in it."

It didn't take his shaken expression to convince me I'd had something like a last-second pardon.

37

In November, I read that another new oldest living person has been certified, beginning her bout with the condensed celebrity of age. As always, the biography opens with the frequencies of cigarettes, beer, and deep-fried dinners. Nobody mentions those faraway villagers who once helped to sell yogurt based on its connection to longevity. The rustic-looking peasants in the television commercials were seen enjoying yogurt while the announcer claimed most of them were over one hundred years old and that some of them were one hundred and twenty or more.

I think of Joice Heth, the slave who nursed George Washington, yet lived to be displayed by P.T. Barnum at one hundred and sixty-one. Her secret, Barnum explained, was thinness, just forty-six pounds on her ancient frame, as if fasting, not yogurt, was the best defense against death.

My father is approaching half his former weight of 210 pounds. No matter what's served, he cleans his plate; he craves a nightly snack. He hoards the cookies and candy he refused for more than eighty years, making himself sick with overeating in his nursing home room. "Like a little boy," he says, and then he weeps.

He tells me the woman two rooms away, just turned one hundred and one, barely leaves her bed, her bald scalp shimmering pink as a wound. "Ten more years of this," he says, "imagine," the future palpable enough to flop belly-first across his bed, the mattress sighing while the well-fed constellation of inevitability blinks on above the horizon, dragging the dark by its hair, shoulders bent against the weight.

I turn on the television and find a football game, but he slumps forward in his wheelchair, staring at a spot on the carpet between his feet. It's no wonder the shrieks of Earth, as scientists say, can be heard from space, such collective terror slithering along our tongues as we struggle to recall even the wrong answers that blink, strobe-like, in the brain until we nearly choke on confusion, our mistaken guesses speeding skyward, humming like the panicked prayers of the dying.

And now, after more than eight decades of devotion to his church, he says nothing about eternal life, not even the back-lot pearly gates set piece of childhood. He says less and less, his sentences shrinking like cheap trousers until, during this visit, we share the long conversation of the unsaid, rehearsing the future.

38

Sometimes there are verifiable revivals. It has been confirmed, for example, that a man in Chile woke in his coffin. Sitting up, dressed in his finest suit, he asked for a drink of water before rejoining his family.

Sometimes, however, one revival comes carrying the direct consequence of loss: My student, years ago, was tagged incorrectly after an auto accident, his parents discovering the dead body of his friend when they were asked to verify his identity. Eventually, they were escorted to a private room so that the parents of the other young man, just arriving with anxiety and joy, would not cross their path. "Inconceivable" was how a colleague put it when we heard how they had to be told that a mistake had been made, the mother and father guided, at last, to confirm what everyone now understood to be the truth.

And sometimes revival can be extraordinarily terrible: Primo Levy relates that during his days in a Nazi concentration camp, he was assigned to dispose of bodies after a gassing. On one of those occasions, a girl rose from the dead tangle of the gassed, and his work crew was saddened past despair because there was never charity in the camp, all of them knowing she would be returned to the gas, unbearably understanding what was coming, her resurrection so dreadful it would madden the living.

39

Some animals have returned from the dead, resurrected after a century extinct like the Cebu Flowerpecker or Jordan's Courser, both of them sighted and confirmed by the radar of science.

It's the work of Thomas, such confirmations, as close as laying fingertips to wounds. Consider the naturalist on Fiji who searched for Macgillivary's Petrel.

His optimism as he set out to lure the lost from extinction's deep privacy. He spent a year sounding its call like a prayer against absence until one morning the long-missing bird flew into his head as if he were the object of desire.

Consider, too, how to present that news, breathlessly beginning, "Listen." What's next to say? Each thick history of belief is crammed with illustrations that depict the loneliness of the single sighting, the man, recently, who claimed he had seen the Ivory-billed Woodpecker sixty years after its case was closed tight by science. Without corroboration, he's become the prophet for improbability, someone with a camera who sits still and loves the silence of expectation while every faint flutter of color turns into the promise that phantoms whisper.

40

My wife and I visit my father a few days before Christmas. He nods off at short intervals, a signal, I'm sure, that something serious is decreasing the amount of oxygen that is reaching his brain. During the four hours we are there, the only thing he responds to is an old album of photos. "Everybody in here is dead," he says, able to name his sister and his three brothers, his two best friends, and three girlfriends, one of whom, near the end of the album, is my mother. His head sinks, one hand resting on her picture. I measure his breathing until he snaps back.

I talk to him by phone on Christmas, calling when I know my sister is there so she will answer and tell him it's me. Twice, as we speak, I am sure he nods off because there is more than a minute without a response, not even a "That's good." Two days later, while I'm interviewing candidates in San Francisco for a position at my university, he dies.

His minister tells me that my father has fallen back into resurrection's arms, his body surrendering its balance to the trust exam of eternity. He is intent on convincing me that all's well, that the dead are always revived. He doesn't ask me if I share that faith.

41

Some scientists speculate that small, asteroid-sized objects would have lasted the longest as the lost satellites. "They would have looked more like Jupiter or Venus in the sky than a satellite," one scientist has said. "They would have resembled very bright stars."

42

After all the post-funeral things are settled, I make two last visits to my father's house, keeping them as short as possible, the asthma attack-inducing dust an issue, now, in every room. What I want most are photographs, especially those that help to deny the *never* of what is irretrievable.

I spend half of that time in my old room rummaging in boxes from department stores that closed decades ago. Inside one from Horne's are photos so unfamiliar that I barely recognize myself from ages six to eleven. After I look at others in the box I can tell that the photographs were taken by an uncle, that they were stored in my bedroom closet after both he and my aunt had died. My father, about ten years earlier, had claimed all of them from another empty house.

My sister, a church choir director, keeps the book of hymns.

43

The moon, recently, was a celebrity, full and a few miles closer than usual, enough to bring two neighbors outside near midnight. A perigree moon, science calls it, the tides heaving up higher as well.

Looking at his watch, one of my neighbors suggested *Auld Lang Syne*, but I was alone with remembering the approach of planet Melancholia in a film I had seen the year before, how, for one perfect night, it was sized exactly like the moon, the sky brilliant with the fascination of malevolence and the approach of oblivion.

44

Today I woke with the coffee maker set to six a.m., its cough driving me out of sleep like a smoke alarm. Within an hour, three birds flew into the living room windows, one of them dead in the iris, the other two missing. A neighbor says it's three flights of the same bird, but I remember the music of those thumps, the variation of size and speed, and I see the colors of the vanished above the trees, shades necessary as water as I stand beneath them, my face upturned to spaces they have left in the sky.

*** I originally came upon some of the odd histories in *Elephants on Acid and Other Bizarre Experiments* by Alex Boese

WEEKEND

From: *The Mayan Syndrome* (Madhat Press, 2023)

After seventh grade basketball practice, you ride the late bus, a trip that lasts half an hour before it reaches your stop that is still nearly two miles from your house, hitchhike distance, but less than half a mile from your parents' bakery. Because it's Friday, you're supposed to go there to help your mother close the shop.

It's 5:30 when you walk inside. Your mother is sweeping the floor behind the counters near the bread slicer. You drop your gym bag and your physical science book on one of the two chairs that sit on either side of the hardworking space heater. "Keep watch," your mother says. "Call if somebody comes in."

Hardly any customers show up this close to closing. The nearby mill that is rumored to be closing has a shift that ends at three. To ease rush hour traffic exiting nearby Pittsburgh, parking is forbidden between four and six. But the pans are always there to scrub, the emptied display ones as well as the heat-darkened ones used for baking. On Fridays, sales are higher and more pans are emptied. Tonight, baking begins four hours earlier than Monday through Thursday. Saturday is the busiest day of the week by far, the "make or break day" according to your mother.

Your mother scalds bakery pans in an ancient sink that sits in the back corner of the preparation room. She never wears the "house-wife-tested" rubber gloves modeled on television. She never passes her hand under the open faucet to feel for temperature, trusting steam to mean there is heat enough to scrub the sugar left by sweet rolls and doughnuts, by coffee cakes and pies, flat pans sanitized and glistening on edge, reflecting the sunset's last light just before she switches to the deep pans for baking pecan rolls and upside-down cakes, fruit and nuts scattered over the greased bottoms so the cakes lift out gleaming with sweetness.

Two customers come in. One buys a loaf of day-old bread for half price. The other chooses the last seven cherry-filled sweet rolls, and your mother, because it is late, charges her the price for half a dozen.

Outside, it is midwinter dark by six. Your sister, who is fourteen, will have dinner made, but your half hour in the bakery is only a preliminary. Since seventh grade began, Friday nights mean working beside your father for three hours and earning a dollar an hour. Shortly after seven, your mother drops you and your father off in front of the bakery and drives to her mother's house. She will peel apples there and slice them for your father to scatter on tomorrow's coffee cakes. It is only a mile. Her sister lives there too, and they can "catch up" for a few hours.

You grease pans and weigh dough to place in pans that shape bread. You measure ingredients. You punch the next batch of rising dough and leave it under a cloth cover to rise again. You stand for three hours in the unheated room that has no foundation beneath it. The low ceiling captures heat from the adjoining room's ovens so that your face roasts while your feet freeze until your mother returns shortly after ten to drop off the sliced apples and drive you home.

You stay up past midnight to watch Chiller Theater. Saturday is the one day to sleep in, and you are in love with monster movies. When you sit on the floor about six feet from the screen, your mother says, "Don't sit so close." You slide back a few inches and wait for her to walk down the hall to her room. You are three years from contact lenses. The new glasses that you wear for blackboard work are in your school locker. When you move close to turn down the volume because she never closes her door, you barely move back at all, sitting twice as close as before. Body snatchers, mummies, and werewolves are exciting, but what you like best are the vampires because they always seem to find women in negligees and sexy dresses to attack. You are twelve and obsessed with breasts. For now, you have settled for making a pledge to yourself to kiss a girl before the school year ends.

Your mother expects your door to stay open all night, but you never hear her leave in the morning at 5:45. Around nine, you hear your father come home. He will get up before three to take your older sister to the bakery to help out, but when you walk into the kitchen, he eats breakfast with you before he goes to sleep.

By ten o'clock, you are hitchhiking to Mt. Royal Boulevard where the friends you've made this year all seem to live in house set on quiet streets a block or two from the boulevard. Since you started working on Fridays, your parents have allowed you to thumb rides as long as they are "local." You will never mention the woman who smoked and slurred her words when she picked you up. You will say nothing about the man who asked if you had a girlfriend, who, when you said "no," asked, "Do you ever play with your friends, you know? Good-looking boys like you should enjoy themselves or let someone do it for them."

You have to be home by five so you can ride back to the bakery with your father. Your mother is washing pans again; your sister is waiting on customers. Your job is to tend a fire that burns a week's worth of cardboard and paper in a depression behind the bakery. In January, even near the fire, you are never warm enough because you refuse to wear a hat or earmuffs, even where there is no chance some classmate will see you.

Your mother makes dinner and serves it at seven. Meat, potatoes, and a vegetable like always. Pizza is unheard of; sandwiches aren't dinner. She washes the dishes by hand, scalding smears of grease before arranging the plates and silver in rubber slots for drying.

You shower and dress and watch a few minutes of Dick Clark's weekly rock-and-roll show before she drives you to the high school for the junior high winter social. After half an hour of excuses and delays, you dance with a girl who some other girl says, "Likes you." Encouraged, you stay on the gym floor with her after the song is over. The second-hand information seems to be true. For the rest of the dance, you think that maybe this is the night that first kiss occurs.

You stay behind to talk with her in the school lobby, but two of her friends stand close by, one of them saying, "Come on, my brother's outside, and he has his girlfriend with him, so you know he's in a hurry to dump us."

Though you are only ten minutes late coming outside, your mother is angry. "Where have you been? It's late," she says.

"I was talking to Nancy Jenkins," you say, and she looks at the three girls who are coming down the stairs.

"They all look like they live out the boulevard," she says.

"They do," you say.

"You be careful. Watch your manners." She doesn't ask which of the girls is Nancy Jenkins.

Your mother says nothing else during the five-mile drive. There is no radio in the station wagon. She follows the boulevard for a half a mile before she turns down the hill toward the highway that is lined with factories and businesses, turning again at the strip mall and trailer court before she drives up the hill where your house sits among others that are small but mostly well kept.

In the driveway, she turns off the engine and says, "I'm glad you had fun, but I have a terrible headache, and there's church in the morning, so no Hit Parade for me tonight. Anyway, I bet your father turned off the TV. Ever since *Gunsmoke* chased George Gobel away, he gets up and makes himself a sandwich at ten o'clock."

Your sister is in her room studying on a Saturday, but sure enough, your father is at the kitchen table as if he'd positioned himself to make her look like a fortune teller. Despite her headache, your mother turns on *Your Hit Parade*. Half an hour later, the #1 song turns out to be *April Love*.

"I'm glad a nice song like this is still number one," your mother says. "I think poor Snooky Lanson left the show because he had so much trouble with those Elvis songs. It's way easier to be Pat Boone."

So easy, you want to say, that Dorothy Collins is singing *April Love* tonight. As if your father agrees, he stands in the kitchen doorway and begins to sing along, except he belts out the words at his own pace, smudging what Dorothy Collins is crooning while you watch her breasts lift when she reaches her arms toward a shadow that suggests her distant lover.

When your father shows no sign of shutting up, what you notice is not how exhausted your mother looks, but how she bites her lip throughout the song as if she wants to scream at him for ruining the performance. You realize there is nothing about the way his voice sounds that would shape the sounds into a chorus that deepened the emotion for any listener, but when your mother stands, catching herself on the arm of the couch, you wish your father would take her hand and dance or at least shut up and hug her, but he keeps singing the last chorus out of sync while she walks down the hall to leave Saturday behind.

In the morning, your mother has eggs ready with the coffee cake that didn't sell yesterday. It's slathered with maple icing, and you tell yourself that it's no wonder it was ignored by customers. "How come the fresh apple ones are never left over?" you say.

Your mother says, "Only the early birds get those."

"They're the best," you say, and she gives you a smile that already looks tired before she stands behind you, places her hands on your shoulders, and squeezes, saying, "Thank you for that," and you try to say something wonderful and manage "You're welcome."

In church, off to the side in the front row, you sit with three friends. All of you are acolytes, but this isn't your Sunday to wear the embarrassing white smock and light candles. As you've been doing for months, you write the times each of you guess for how long the sermon will last on the back of the church bulletin. The guesses, by the rules all of you agreed to, have to be fifteen second apart, and today they range from fourteen to seventeen minutes. You pick fifteen-thirty, but the sermon is only fourteen minutes and twenty seconds, and you remember, too late, it's a communion Sunday when the sermon is always shorter.

None of you are old enough to take communion, that ritual a year away. Your parents and sister all sing in the choir, and they walk down with the others from the loft behind the altar to accept the wafer and the wine. As your mother turns to leave, you notice that she lays a hand on the arm of the woman beside her as if she's been surprised by a moment of unsteadiness or by a spasm of the back pain she complains about some mornings while she hovers over your school day breakfast.

As soon as you get home, your mother goes into her room to lie down. Your sister heats up leftovers for lunch while you read the sports section of the *Pittsburgh Press*. For three hours, with your bedroom door closed, you listen to the new Top 40 countdown on your small clock radio.

For once, you have sandwiches for dinner, cold cuts and cheese your father lays out with sliced tomatoes and lettuce and onions. "Your mother doesn't feel good," he says, but she comes out and sits to nibble on a piece of cheese and a handful of potato chips before she takes the section of the paper with the big Sunday crossword puzzle, the one that seems impossible to finish, into her room.

Before you finish eating, a car horn sounds from the driveway, and your sister rushes off to practice for the church pageant. You watch Ed Sullivan with your father, but when you realize there are no rock and roll singers this week, you decide to listen to the radio again. Your mother's door is open, and she looks as if she's asleep with the lights on, the puzzle lying on the floor. You tiptoe in and pick it up. There are only seven spaces left unfilled. Two of the incomplete answers are French words; two are last names of historical figures. You think of surprising her by finding the answers in your sister's French book and the cheap encyclopedia she bought through a grocery store promotion three years ago, but you know she would be angry that you cheated.

When she opens her eyes and sees you there, she says, "Turn off the light for me, would you? And leave the puzzle where you found it. I still have some work to do on it when I get a chance."

The bakery is closed on Monday, so tomorrow is laundry day. What she will do, the weekend over, you and your sister back in school, your father still asleep. Since it is January, she will feed soaking clothes through the wringer that squeezes everything as flat as cartoon victims before she hangs each item on a maze of clotheslines in the cellar and reminds everyone that "downstairs is off limits."

For the first time ever, you clear the kitchen table, run hot water in the sink, add soap and wash all of the Sunday dishes. You dry them, put them away in their proper places, and think you are learning something, that what people call their jobs is not the hardest thing they do, that whether it is out of love or resignation or some combination difficult to measure, waiting and serving are the work that never stops.

SPARKLERS

From: *The Mayan Syndrome* (Madhat Press, 2023)

1

In late May, after baseball and the blasts of complimentary fireworks that opened nearly overhead, the pedestrian bridge to Pittsburgh, temporarily closed, compresses our crowd of late-night walkers. Someone next to my family mentions the latest terror, children and their mothers pierced by an explosion of glittering spikes after a pop star's concert in England. Faces of young girls illuminate two nearby phones. Ahead of us a father believes his arms have invented safety, yet somewhere, he must recognize, terror dreams our bodies as it decides the exact address for delight. The river's cruise ship passes beneath us, its decks packed with prom goers. The water reflects a swirl of pinwheels; a vendor ignites a fistful of sparklers.

2

For seven summers, the evening of the Fourth of July, I wrote my name in the air with a sparkler. Sometimes I circled them into brief, eclipsed suns or simply threw their violent lace into an arc that spiraled sparks to our lawn. Always, July 5th, I had to find every sparkler gone out and dropped the night before. Up and back, I paced our yard along the narrow paths the mower took. If there was even a hint of leftover nub on a wire, I tried to light it, but none ever burst into sparks. I threw away those wires and never once thought to learn what a sparkler was made of.

3

A sparkler is usually made from a wire coated from one end with a mixture of metal fuel, an oxidizer, and a binder. The most commonly used wire is made of iron and is most often coated in aluminum and magnesium for a yellow/white glow. The fuel is charcoal and sulfur, as in black powder. The binder can be sugar or starch. Mixed with water, these chemicals form a slurry that can be coated on the wire. Once dried, it is a sparkler, some as large as three feet in length in order to burn for several minutes to produce a long-lasting effect. They are non-poisonous if sucked on, but poisonous if eaten, causing gastrointestinal symptoms.

4

Sitting beside my son, I once watched a videotape of the beginning of a rock show at a Rhode Island club called The Station. The room in which a crowd was packed to hear a band called Great White looked so eerily familiar, it could have been one of the clubs I'd watched my son play lead guitar in for the previous three years. I remembered only "Once Bitten, Twice Shy," the band's biggest hit, but my son and I were paying attention to the pyrotechnics they were using, surges of sparks ascending as they began playing. "This is real bad," my son said, just home from touring in most of the venues Great White had played in the weeks leading to this show. He sounded thoroughly spooked. "Using pyro in places like this is crazy," he said, and watching that film, I couldn't argue. Those white-hot sparks set the back wall on fire, the flames running up to the low ceiling and spreading rapidly. "Somebody fucked up bad," my son added as the camera, seconds later, shut off. "Even you would know not to use it. There's no way you can miss the danger."

5

Typical pyrotechnics are made from flammable materials such as nitrocellulose and black powder or a mixture of fuel and oxidizer. A plug placed at one end of the container with a small orifice, called a choke, constricts the expulsion of the ignited pyrotechnic compound, increasing the size and aggressiveness of the jet.

6

When I was five years old, there was a fire in the back room of the bakery my father had purchased less than a year before. "Sparks from an electrical short in the old blue refrigerator that came with the place," my father said. "Hot enough to catch something that burns and there you have it, the place up in smoke." The fire was contained, but it took six weeks to make enough repairs to the back room and the roof to reopen. All of that work was done in the middle of winter. For nearly all of those six weeks the blackened refrigerator sat in the snow behind the bakery. In late January, he baked a cake for a small celebration of reopening. My mother placed one small sparkler candle in the center, and I watched until it went out, wishing for more.

7

I've learned that four-inch cake sparklers burn for about thirty seconds. For birthdays, some cake sparklers are shaped as numbers. Heart-shaped sparklers are sometimes offered as favors for wedding guests. To ignite those sparklers, the guests need to light them at the top where the heart creases in. Most often, the guests are given elongated, sparklers to light and hold while the newlyweds pass by. Those wedding sparklers are advertised as "dazzling," "brilliant," and "unforgettable."

8

Witnesses describing the bomb explosion after the pop concert in England were consistent. First, the red-orange flash, then the ear-splitting boom, then the bodies falling to the ground before a plume of smoke wafted over the crowd. More than one survivor said, "All this sort of debris and embers came floating from the roof."

9

I ran the Great White video again, this time remembering how I watched my son play, early in his career, from the privacy of a side room filled with piles of flammable trash, a room with exactly one way in and out. Watching closely, I checked to see which member of the band first notices the flames. It looked to be the guitar player I knew was dead. As if he was following my eyes, my son said, "It makes you think."

10

A pyrotechnic engineer usually has an undergraduate degree in chemistry or physics, followed by further training in pyrotechnics. Pyrotechnic engineers might work for firework companies or sporting arenas. Because safety is a factor in their work, some states require a licensing exam.

11

When I was eleven, Mrs. Cellander, our next-door neighbor, watched, like I did, a great sparkling puff of newspaper lift and float into her cherry tree from the burn barrel I was tending near where our backyards bordered. She screamed and swore and reminded me I was a careless idiot who deserved to be burned if that tree was damaged. Inside the burn barrel, the fire crackled and sparked as if it wanted to soar. Illuminated by the rapidly burning paper, the cherry tree's branches were thrown skyward like a a cluster of hostages.

12

A spark is a simple, familiar way of describing a spangle of light.

13

The Great White fire, every investigator agreed, could likely have been prevented had those involved paid attention to standard safety practices around the use of pyrotechnics. Less than two years later, a similar pyrotechnic-induced fire destroyed the Republica Cromagnon nightclub in Buenos Aires, Argentina, killing 194 people.

14

A spark from a firework is a particle of red-hot powder ejected from the firework container.

15

Two years before the Manchester, England pop concert disaster, after armed terrorists attacked LeCarillon Bar in France, witnesses said they initially thought firecrackers had gone off before they realized that they were under fire from semi-automatic rifles. "People dropped to the ground. We put a table over our heads to protect us," said a man who was with his wife at the back of the bar. Fifteen people died in the attack on the bar and restaurant, with fifteen severely injured. More than one hundred bullets were fired.

16

Sparks from a sparkler are extremely hot, their temperature anywhere from 1800 degrees Fahrenheit to 3000 degrees Fahrenheit. Last year, in the United States, about 1,200 injuries that were related to sparklers were treated in emergency rooms between June 16 and July 16, what is known as the Fourth of July season. Half of those sparkler injuries happened to children under the age of fourteen.

17

Sparklers leave behind a residue of tiny flecks of burnt iron that is usually not even noticed. Nobody I knew as a boy ever got burned by a sparkler.

18

The most common categories of pyrotechnics are concussion, smoke pot, flame projector, and gerb, which is more complicated and designed to create a jet or fountain of sparks. Various ingredients are added to provide color, smoke, noise or sparks.

19

Ariana Grande, the headliner of the Manchester, England show that was attacked by a suicide bomber, has an enormous fan base among young girls. Video shot inside the venue for that evening's performance showed terrified teenagers screaming as they made their way out amid a sea of pink balloons. Some fans were still wearing the singer and former Nickelodeon TV actress' trademark kitten ears as they fled.

20

By the time my son and I watched the Great White video, we knew that the low ceiling in The Station had been soundproofed with cheap insulation that is not only highly flammable but produces dense, toxic smoke that roiled into the room so thoroughly poisonous those fans had maybe a minute altogether before the odds suggested they were going to die.

21

On a windy, late spring day when I was twelve, I let an open-pit trash fire get away behind the bakery. A couple of burning bags, sparks scattering, tumbled onto the dry, unmown grass. I watched, terrified, as the high grass caught fire and the wind drove the flames toward the bakery. By the time I circled the fire and ran for the back door, the man who lived above the feed store next door scrambled down his back stairs and used a hose he kept for washing his car to extinguish the fire just before it reached the back wall.

22

I ran the Great White video a third time, concentrating on the crowd. A few beer bottles are held aloft in salute to the band. The fans near the front rock in place. The wall behind the band is already on fire, yet a fan in the second row raises a fist in appreciation. One man finally turns toward the camera and gestures toward where the main door must be. Two more patrons turn as the flames reach the roof. And then the camera shuts off, the man doing the filming, I'm sure, heading for the door because it had been noted he was among the survivors.

23

A few months after we watched that video together, before the first time I attended one of his shows in a large arena, my son explained that I should recognize that a bright pinwheel to the side of the stage was a warning that a pyrotechnic concussion was imminent. "Because you're so close to the stage," he said. "So you're ready."

24

On January 27, 2013, at the "Kiss" nightclub in Santa Maria, Brazil, an accident due to the use of pyrotechnics by the performing live show band caused a fire which resulted in the deaths of at least 236 people, while dozens suffered serious injuries from the fire and smoke inhalation.

25

The 2015 terrorist attack in France was coordinated. More restaurants were fired upon. At Café Bonne Biere and La Casa Nostra pizzeria, five people were killed and eight severely injured. Another occurred at La Belle Equipe bar. "It lasted at least three minutes," one witness said. "Then they got back in their car." Nineteen people died in the shooting, with nine in critical condition. Survivor accounts sometimes included "We thought, at first, we were hearing fireworks."

26

Sparkler bombs are constructed by binding together as many as 300 sparklers with tape, leaving one extended to use as a fuse. Because they don't have a timed fuse, there is some chance they could go off in someone's hand.

27

When I was thirteen, a boy I knew blew his fingers off when he lit a pipe bomb he had finished a few hours earlier. "Isn't this cool?" he'd said the whole time he was setting the fuse. "You should make one." He said he was taking it to a family reunion picnic and placing it in the men's room of the county park. His cousins that were around our age, he said, would be impressed because "It would blow shit up."

28

Children were among the twenty-two people killed in the suicide attack after the Ariana Grande concert. Fifty-nine others were wounded, including some who suffered life-threatening injuries.

29

In large arenas, my son's band performed during intermittent pyrotechnics that erupted near where they were standing. The jets of sparks never reached the high ceilings, all of which were constructed of materials that didn't burn.

30

Once, in the middle of a tour, my son forwarded me a photograph of him standing beside a rock guitarist known as Dimebag Darrell, who had co-founded the well-known heavy metal bands Pantera and Damageplan. Both guitarists are relaxed and smiling after their paths crossed while touring. Shortly after my son sent the photo to me, Dimebag Darrell was shot and killed while performing with Damageplan in a Columbus, Ohio club by a man who jumped on stage.

31

October 30, 2015, at the Colectiv nightclub in Bucharest, Romania, pyrotechnics used by the band Goodbye to Gravity accidentally ignited soundproofing foam on a pillow. The fire quickly spread onto the ceiling and the rest of the club. Sixty-four people died, and more than two hundred were injured. Four members of Goodbye to Gravity lost their lives; only their soloist survived.

32

After I played that Great White video a third time, my son said, "Enough," but I watched once more and focused on the man in the crowd who appeared to be oldest, my age maybe. He is near the back, not bouncing in place. When the film ends, even as some people move past him, he still hasn't turned to rush toward the door.

33

Sparklers burn at temperatures hot enough to melt some metals.

34

Somewhere, I think early every day, the acolyte of terror dreams our bodies as it decides the exact address for delight.

35

The terrorists in France also attacked The Bataclan, a 1500-seat theater located at 50 Boulevard Voltaire in the 11th arrondissement of Paris, where an American band Eagles of Death Metal were playing. Eighty-nine people died as the terrorists fired Kalashnikov-type assault rifles into the crowd. At least ninety-nine others were taken to hospitals in critical condition. "We thought it was fireworks," one survivor said, "but then we realized there were men shooting in all directions. So we all lay on the floor and started crawling towards the stage."

36

Because of a sparkler bomb's construction, whoever is in the vicinity when it is lit will not know the direction in which the explosion will go, or whether the bomb will split and break up. It can explode shrapnel with massive force.

37

After the suicide bomber's attack in England, the security editor for NBC News' U.K. partner ITV News, reported that nuts and bolts were spotted in the arena's foyer, but police, initially, would not comment on whether victims had suffered wounds from shrapnel.

38

One afternoon word came down from the venue that someone had threatened my son's band for that evening's show in a city located hundreds of miles away. We talked on the phone several times while security was being tightened and authorities alerted. I tried to reassure him and myself that it was better to have someone openly declare the threat than keep it a secret because that meant it was highly unlikely that anything would happen that night. "But," my son said, "there's the next show and the next."

Telephone

From: *The Mayan Syndrome* (Madhat Press, 2023)

1

I ask my wife if she remembers who, using a specially-designed extension handle, repainted our dining room's cathedral ceiling. "Of course, I do," she says. "He was disgusting. A week later, he called and said he wanted to rape me." As soon as I hesitate to speak, she stares. After I admit I've forgotten that call, she glares.

2

Late in the 1950s, my family's dial phone was heavy and black and sat on a narrow counter just wide enough to hold it between the refrigerator and the electric stove. It was on a party line with other phones—sometimes, when I picked it up, I could hear other people talking. It was thrilling and then it was scary when some stranger would say get off the line whoever you are often punctuated with blasphemies I had been warned never to say because god would overhear and punish me. And sometimes, especially men, they used words that were obscenities, rough and threatening, but carrying my parents' wrath rather than god's.

I never called anyone until I was eight or nine, and then only with permission. My mother, when those calls became more frequent, cautioned, "Watch your mouth; you never know who's listening," citing a trilogy of gossip, government, or God. For a year or two, I did, but only because I didn't yet know the obscenities and none of my calls were like the ones I regularly listened to, most of them women who spoke in stories of complaint and scandal.

What was required of me was silence, even when a woman would say, "Who's there?" or some obscenity from the thesaurus for forbidden phrases. Mostly, they watched their mouths, but some afternoons their voices lowered to tell tales stuffed with polio, leukemia, and deaths by accidents that had missed me for so long I thought of myself, by eleven, as immune. More often, they fed me chemotherapy and catheter, excision and metastasis, words I researched in a dictionary I used during calls, during sixth grade, I made to Nancy Harter, all of them undetected by my mother because they were local, Nancy's house within a radius tighter than the destruction zone of a hydrogen bomb.

Fellatio, Nancy said one afternoon, not watching her mouth, then *cunnilingus,* repeating the proper words for pleasures she had discovered in a dictionary of her own, researching how variations of joy could be brought to the vagina and the penis, both of us not knowing who might be listening. We were excited to expose our mouths, speaking with an untested authority, as if we knew the future of our intimacy, as if our lives were larger through language that named the body's curiosities. After she read the definitions of a new word we were both silent for a few seconds, something like the false endings in songs we loved for a few weeks, a space we seemed to be filling in with expectations before we said the crude words for those acts out loud, learning to translate. What made it more thrilling was imagining that someone was listening.

3

My wife doesn't wait for me to ask how she could identify him. "He tried to disguise it by deepening it and sounding hoarse, but I recognized his voice," she says. "He had just been inside our house. I can quote him exactly: 'Lock your doors because I'm coming to rape you.'" She pauses as if I need to insert an apology, but I have nothing but silence. When she begins again, her voice has risen. "Absolutely, I'm sure about that one. And I had to see him a few more times. At the post office. In the grocery store. It made me sick every time."

4

The morning my daughter was born, my wife, hours from delivery, answered a call that came so early, the late September morning still suppressed by fog, it sounded like an emergency until a man's hoarse voice whispered how hard he was thinking about her soft, fuckable body before he lapsed into nothing but heavy breathing. Over forty years now, our rotary phone an antique, my daughter with girls of her own, but right then, between contractions, my wife said, "I think I recognized him," naming a man who worked for her, somebody she had hired. "Impossible," I said, citing how swollen she must have been the last time they had met, spinning suspicion into accident and driving slowly without mentioning our neighbor, even the day before, watching her cross our just-mown lawn from what I knew was his bedroom window, or how I'd noticed that habit of his for months, often pleased he surely coveted his neighbor's wife. I might as well have called her myself to heavy-breathe I needed men to desire her. And yes, this morning, a man I know boasted how fuckable his daughter had become, then laughed as if confident I'd agree, as if he carried private photographs to share with someone who might confess to calling a woman he knew to covet her with words, excusing himself with self-disgust and rage, trusting such a weak, perpetual penance substitutes for decency day-to-day.

5

My wife's rage, she says, is ongoing. She thinks about it without the sort of prompting I've just given her. That man she was so sure had called has been dead for more than ten years. Whatever punishment she wished upon him is impossible. There is an accusation in her voice, and I have no alibi to put distance between me and shame. I have as much chance of being exonerated as I do of successfully calling the dead to deliver a promise to add punishment to that caller's personal hell.

6

Decades ago, when my younger son was in sixth grade, a policeman called to let me know someone in a town twenty-five miles away had accused my son of making obscene phone calls. "I thought I should let you know and you could handle this before I have to," the policeman said. "Mr. Beaver says it's your boy. He has him on his answering machine. We need you to come in and listen to the tape. Bring your boy, let him listen to himself."

"I don't understand," I said, the sticky film of embarrassment adhering to the entire length of my body. "How does he know it's my son?"

"He leaves his name each time. He tells Mr. Beaver who he is."

I was relieved. "Nobody does that," I said.

"You'll be shocked. I guarantee it. He left his phone number, too. It's a plea for help. Wait till you hear these."

"It's a friend," I said. "It's somebody my son knows trying to be funny."

"Nobody's friend talks like this," he said, and I allowed silence to extend, waiting for common sense to arrive, but "Bring your boy in. You'll see who's mistaken," ended that call.

When I relayed the message to my son, he was expressionless. "You can check," he said. "That guy lives so far away, those calls would be on our phone bill."

"So, there it is," I said. I had a detective for a son.

A few days later, the policeman called back. "You haven't brought your boy in," he said.

"That's right. My phone bill doesn't have a single call to the town where Beaver lives."

"That proves nothing," the policeman said, but he never called again, and soon the incident became a joke among me and my two sons, one of us saying, "Beaver called" to laughter.

7

I remember that house painter—his thick muscular arms, his protruding belly, how the word squat comes to mind when I describe him to myself. He was twenty-five years older than we were, recently retired. Not, in my imagination, a poster-body for a rapist or even a man who fantasizes rape. He was, give or take, the same age I am now.

8

Five years after my son's bout with Mr. Beaver, I received an obscene call of my own, a man's voice repeating the ways he wanted to please one private part of my body, his breath and moans building to a sudden cry that ended in a line gone dead.

Fifteen years before we had Caller ID, I was left to wonder who had confessed such desire. For weeks, each man I knew became a suspect. I listened for the caller's inflections, the clues of his final vowels. I imagined how many times he'd considered calling before that night, whether he knew my wife was at a meeting or it was luck enhanced by persistence. Most often, I wondered whether he'd called before and hung up when she'd answered, that she kept his multiple queries secret because she had deduced their reason.

Regardless, that voice never again found me alone, so much time passing I had to accept it was random, that any man who answered would do, that the caller preferred me to be, not who I was, but what he imagined, someone in love with being wanted, eager maybe, pleased to be objectified, even targeted, as far as I could extend that sentence without self-incrimination.

Though, for months, I left the phone unanswered when I was alone, allowing each caller to leave a message, yet listening for an extended silence that might be longing to hear my triggering voice.

9

From our balcony, the house painter would have looked down at my wife going through the movements of an ordinary late afternoon and early evening. He would have been able to stare, the track lights on the wall below the balcony railing brightly illuminating her body as she passed beneath him. His gaze would have had time to cover every intimate area of her body each time he paused while perfecting the paint on our difficult-to-reach ceiling, leaving not a spot or a corner untouched by the well-practiced, efficient extension of his arms.

ON LOCATION: A VALENTINE

From: *The Mayan Syndrome* (Madhat Press, 2023)

At Griffith Park a few weeks ago, while I tried to convince my granddaughter that hitting a backhand wasn't difficult, she told me that Emma Stone played tennis for a *Battle of the Sexes* scene on a nearby Los Angeles court where her friend takes lessons. "Down by the fountain," she said, meaning the Riverside courts a half mile from where she lives. "The director," she explained, "needed an old-fashioned surface, something that looks like it's in the 70s."

She'd played four times by then, three of them with me, beginning with balls so pressureless they seemed to hover in the air. I told her I was seventeen years older than Bobby Riggs was when he lost to Billie Jean King in the Astrodome, a year younger than Billie Jean was in the present where I was teaching her despite my ruined knees and spinal stenosis and a one-handed backhand that puzzled her.

She wanted to know how hard it was for me to play with a wooden racket, a thing so strange and heavy, its small sweet spot that must have made tennis more difficult. When I said I'd once used a Jack Kramer model, she told me he was the movie's sexist bad guy.

She loved tennis now, planned to use her own money to buy a vintage outfit like the one Emma Stone wears to play Steve Carrell's version of Bobby Riggs. Better yet, she was ready to turn her shoulders early and prepare to swing like Emma Stone, who, like her, had never played until starring in that movie made her learn how Billie Jean King had bounced a ball before serving and how she had held her wooden racket, switching from a forehand to backhand grip.

We were practicing because my daughter had told her I'd coached a college team and spent a few summers as a teaching pro at a country club where successful men, during those 70s, had hired me to teach their wives not to be liabilities in the business of mixed doubles, berating them, sometimes, like minor-league versions of the Jack Kramer she had so much disliked when she'd watched the film.

The court we were using is built into a landscape of rugged, low mountains, a twenty-minute uphill walk from where my wife and I stayed for the month of January. Six times we made that trek, and every time we talked the whole way up and down, most of the time about her current life as a fourteen-year-old.

Two miles above those courts is the observatory where James Dean faced off with the "hoods" in *Rebel Without a Cause*. Two miles below them is the high school James Dean and Natalie Wood, as alienated teenagers, attended in that movie. She is a freshman there, and doesn't imagine herself in the 50s.

My daughter drove me to the Riverside courts a few days later. We stood on the court where Emma Stone pretended to be Billie Jean King winning a tournament held in San Diego. Less than 100 yards away a row of power lines towered up from where they follow US 5 and the roar of heavy Los Angeles traffic.

My granddaughter could walk to that court in ten minutes and play in the footsteps of Emma Stone. She has a forehand now, sometimes a backhand, and less often an accurate serve.

What I kept to myself were the secrets of the once deadly slice of Bobby Riggs, who was born the same year as my father, who, on courts far from Hollywood, taught me what he could from his repertoire of homemade strokes until he handed me to a stranger who changed everything but my backhand, the stroke he said was "a natural."

On the last night of our stay, my granddaughter and I watched *Battle of the Sexes* together, sitting side by side on the couch. She concentrated as if she hadn't already seen it. At last, she said, "Look, there it is, the court," and we watched Emma Stone run across the 70s court, swing her wooden racket, and deliver the illusion of a winning forehand before we said a half hour of goodbyes, we hugged three times, she cried, and I almost did myself.

On Location: New Year's Eve

From: *The Mayan Syndrome* (Madhat Press, 2023)

Because my granddaughter is fifteen, my company is necessary for each mile-long walk to care for two dogs and a cat. Because her street, the last hundred yards of our walk, feels dangerous for anyone. Because the street is really an alley and badly lit. Because there are budget apartments that sit below the narrow street on one side rather than more single-dwelling houses and duplexes like the ones set into the hillside on the right.

The new year is four hours away when we leave the apartment my wife and I have rented for six weeks to avoid winter and visit with our recently remarried daughter. She has saved her honeymoon week until we were available to watch over her daughters. The only complication has been those animals need attention three times a day.

Halfway through those last hundred yards, an empty car is double parked in the alley, the driver's side door open. Lights extinguished, a curiosity so close to her house. My granddaughter veers right, and I drift her way as subtly as I can muster. The next bend takes us into the street's deepest shadows just before the flight of stairs to the door.

"Those apartments are sketchy," she says, when we are inside. The dogs welcome us. They go out the back door and soon return, expecting food. The cat, as always, refuses to be seen.

In the bedroom my granddaughter shares with her twelve-year-old sister, we play records I've sent her for Christmas, used albums of mine from the 70s I've guessed she'd love—Queen, Judy Collins, Linda Ronstadt, Harry Neilson—thinning my collection and building hers. We spend an hour with the music, including an entire side of *Nilsson Schmilsson* that my granddaughter sings softly along to. The dogs, instead of settling, are restless, pacing to windows and back to us. Neither of them barks.

As soon as we walk around the bend, beginning the return trip, we see two police cars by the double-parked car, its door still open, but now a young woman is inside. Except for the policeman who waves to invite us past, whoever arrived in those two marked cars must be inside. "What you looking at, bitch?" the woman says. The policeman's wave shifts into demand. "That's it, keep walking, bitch," the woman calls as we pass him. "Fuck you, bitch," she yells as we clear the scene.

"I wish I hadn't looked," my granddaughter says when we reach the busy highway at the end of her street. "Did you look?"

"Yes."

"But she only talked to me."

I think of comforting or explaining, but settle for, "You'll never see her again." We have nearly a mile for the return walk, but all the rest is where traffic, even on the holiday, is constant. Because we both know there are fewer shadows on the other side, we wait at the first intersection, an awkward one, three streets intersecting the main highway, a series of left turn lights extending the wait. Down the sidewalk on our side, we can see a small crowd has gathered where the apartments have a lower entrance.

"The dogs knew, didn't they?" my granddaughter says, after we have crossed.

"Yes, they must have sensed when the police arrived."

Back in the apartment, we stay up for the bells and sirens and fireworks from a thousand yards spreading toward the city. My granddaughter and I, both terrified of heights, choose to stay inside when my wife and her sister step out on the twelfth-floor balcony. They look like they are in terrible danger, like they could vanish when the railing they lean on collapses. "What do you think she could have done?" my granddaughter says. Before I can answer, she adds, "She didn't look much older than I am," whispering as if it were a secret.

Butterflies, Biopsies, the Lockdown Hosts

From: *The Mayan Syndrome* (Madhat Press, 2023)

> If a butterfly flaps its wings in Brazil,
> it might produce a tornado in Texas.
> from *The Laws of Chaos*

The Butterfly Effect

Once, early in your weekly newsmagazine, a photograph of Haitian women wailing. On the next page, more women who looked to be holding their breath and the hands of men tense with what was identified as "bullet expectations." This was decades ago, the same week you discovered that the wind swirling winter rain along your street might have originated from their mourning, the beating, weeks before, of their arms in the air sending a record warm front north.

You absorbed the Butterfly Effect, how chaos is not chaos, how slaughter in Haiti could flap its wings and churn into your grip on the arm of your son and your hiss through clenched teeth as he fluttered his free arm and wailed and altered, in turn, the future of weather in a country farther east where another father would choose to stun his young son to obedience. That night, after you allowed the dog to walk you into sense, the wind chattered branches that skittered her to a barking panic on your street of sculpted shrubbery where a web of Christmas bulbs, in one nearby yard, might have arranged itself into words if you were properly angled, upstairs, across the street and positioned like an antenna straining for a distant station, like your son behind his bedroom window watching you soft-handle the dog, your breath without its winter clouds, nothing he would believe could join the southern grief of a warm front.

1

Your newest neighbor is a prison guard. His daughter, last summer, came to your door in tears. She sat in your living room and said only that she needed a place to wait, forgetting her key and her curfew time, well past late at twilight. Ten years old, she sipped water your wife offered, her pink shirt covered with butterflies. While waiting for her mother to return her call, she confessed that her father was inside the house, that locked out in the dark was a lesson she was expected to learn, crying on her porch a sentence meant to deter, but this time, a recidivist, she had decided to escape to the closest door that stood open.

2

Your granddaughter's letters from Los Angeles always end with butter-flies. One of her drawings, this time, is half a page large, and you are sketched inside both of its wings. Like a species pattern, you think, blue-masked, with red and white dots along your arms and legs, the butterfly a blaze of orange and yellow, the antennae green.

3

Last December, just before the first report from Wuhan slipped into the newspaper, you postponed an ultrasound appointment because it fell on the same day as the one that completed your follow-ups to back surgery. It had been seven years since your first and second thyroid "growths" had been biopsied, ten months apart, both coming up benign. After five years of annual ultrasounds, all of them declaring "stable," you had been put on a two-year cycle, so long between appointments, you had forgotten the latest one and double-scheduled. The decision was easy. The back surgery was recent, the ultrasound a routine precaution.

Because you have spent most of the winter in California, you have an imaging-center appointment for early March. The ultrasound is quick, almost pleasurable. A few days later, a call left on your phone says that one of the two "nodules" has shown significant growth. For years, they have kept their uneasy truce, but now one has swollen like a militia covertly arming. The message ends by announcing that an appointment for the following week has been made for another biopsy.

4

After your parents moved your family into a new house when you were seven, leaving the three-room rental behind, your father hung two framed butterfly collections on the basement wall. He had received a merit badge for that project when he was thirteen, and now he had room for those butterflies to be displayed. He would live in that house for fifty-six years, the last twenty-one years alone, and those butterflies remained exactly where they began. By the time he moved to a nursing home, those butterflies, all of them monarchs, were seventy-seven years old.

5

Due to the COVID-19 pandemic, the hospital postpones your biopsy. When you call your doctor, an automated message says the office is now closed. Your wife tells you that the postponement is good news, that if the doctor thought your tumor was malignant, he would declare the biopsy an emergency and keep it scheduled. "It's just a precaution," she says, but all you hear are the words *tumor* and *malignant*. All you see is your mother wearing a wig when you came home from college for Thanksgiving. The site of her "troubles" was her thyroid.

6

"We barely know anything about the new neighbors," your wife said after you both watched the girl in the butterfly shirt walk to where her mother parked in her driveway and waited beside her car. "All those years in classrooms taught me that you can't always trust a child's story when they find themselves in trouble."

7

After your granddaughter sends another butterfly drawing, your wife tells you that Denise, a book club friend, loves butterflies. "They buy the butterflies from a farm," she says, "and her husband mounts and frames them." You Google "Butterfly Farms" and discover one is an hour's drive away. Tours are available by appointment. There are presentations about

Monarch butterflies and their life cycle, a "dress-up demonstration representing the anatomy of the butterfly." It is the perfect gift you can give to your granddaughter when she visits, as she does each summer, in August, when it likely will be safer to fly.

8

You research thyroid cancer and discover there are four kinds: Papillary, Follicular, Medullary, and Anaplastic. Papillary is the most common and has the best outlook because it grows slowly. Even when this cancer spreads to the lymph nodes, it responds well to treatment. Follicular and medullary are less common, but their prognosis is good overall. Anaplastic is the fastest-growing type of thyroid cancer, and it doesn't respond well to treatment.

9

Two months pass before your biopsy is rescheduled for the week after your Pennsylvania county and the one in which the hospital is located both go from "red" to "yellow."

10

Your neighbor, the prison guard, hosts a pandemic lockdown party. Five cars arrive. Each one has a prison parking sticker in the upper right-hand corner of its windshield. Though the weather is perfect for late May, clear and warm, all of the couples, neither the men nor the women wearing masks, go inside the house. You don't hear loud music; no one emerges onto the back patio. Because you have been inside that house, you know it is smaller than yours, that twelve adults and the guard's two children make a crowd.

11

You arrive for the cell extraction that will name the future. You tug your mask, that recent habit replacing fingers to the face or the temptation to examine, low along your throat, for invasion's tenderness or pain. When your glasses fog, you take them off and wave them clear while you slow your breathing. At the door to the hospital, you are asked for your name and birthday. Your temperature is taken while you submit to a brief inquest about recent contacts, shortness of breath, and persistent cough. The last question is whether or not three months of stay-at-home has, by now, seduced your restlessness.

Intimacy has been on such an extended leave, you nearly welcome the doctor's blue-sheathed hand, your throat softly touched and swept sideways for a needle so thin the myth of "only a pinch" comes true. You recognize extraction's pressure, the impulse to swallow throughout each attempt.

12

The butterfly farm also offers butterfly releases for special events, including weddings, anniversaries, birthdays, graduations, and memorials. Besides the ones from "mass release boxes," the farm promises special releases from individual envelopes that can be personalized with writing and a small picture.

The advertisement ends by saying that all metamorphic stages and butterfly releases are available, dependent upon season.

13

After each needle extraction, you wait to learn whether the sample has sufficient cells to be useful for a definitive assessment. Four samples are each, in turn, deemed insufficient. As if the pandemic has complicated biopsy, the aisles in your tumor designated one-way like the ones at your grocery store, the cells reluctant to emerge from lockdown because everyone is dangerous.

The doctor and the radiologist apologize while the technician carries your fifth sample to pathology. For now, the doctor says, it ends, because "we don't want to beat you up with more than five extractions." Before you leave, you learn that the chorus of your body's song has only repeated "non-diagnostic, but statistically safe." To be more certain, another biopsy should be scheduled. Though during these times, scheduling is difficult. Though weeks will likely pass.

Which is time enough for uncertainty to startle you from sleep like a dry, persistent cough. Which happens often enough for you to master the art of settling down. Slowly deep-breathing, you tell yourself, each time, that all three of those medical faces would be as unrecognizable as yours if you accidentally meet, unmasked in the open. Your throat will look so common they will never remember the mayhem of your small, ambiguous illness.

14

Your father never mentioned the process for pinning and preserving. The butterflies simply hung there like family portraits, the only ornamentation on the basement walls except for a framed print of a painting of the Titanic sinking that he hung on another wall after your grandmother died and none of your uncles or aunts wanted it.

15

The butterfly farm web site notes that you can purchase from any stage of the butterfly life cycle: eggs, larvae, pupae, or butterflies.

16

When there is another indoor party at your neighbor's house, this one attracting more cars, you write a brief story that you title, *My Father, the Prison Guard*:

> *My father, the prison guard, says his cells have been opened now, the men he watches going home the same way he does. He says the Governor has freed them, not the virus. He has all the proof he needs—the prison is near the state capital and not one of the inmates is sick.*
>
> *My father's friends are guards, too. Three of them visited last week. They brought their wives, but not their children. My father said their names and ours. He said we're not afraid in this house. We're not distancing, not my wife, not my son and daughter. Masks are for thieves.*
>
> *The guests stayed for hours. My mother and the wives, after dinner, sat outside. They drank wine and looked at their phones. They texted their babysitters and told my mother, "Don't tell our husbands."*
>
> *The men drank beer and played poker. They bragged about how they've memorized the odds, how they can read each other's tells. I watched from behind my father. He took a sip of beer when his cards were good. He picked at the label when he bluffed.*

My brother and I stayed up past midnight. We watched a show where the host was at home and the audience was as far away as we were. He made fun of men who refused to wear masks, but nobody was there to laugh.

When they were ready to leave, my father hugged his friends. Each one touched his face and laughed. My father repeated, "Trust is love." He sounded like our priest.

After the house was empty, my father said, "You kids see what strong is? Did you?" He hugged our mother and said, "Say thank you. Say it now before you see how right I am."

This week, every morning, my mother took my temperature. She took my brother's and hers, too, but only after my father left for work. "You keep this a secret," she said. "You tell me if you hear your father cough."

Today, while we ate breakfast, my father cleared his throat and said, "This thing will pass." He pulled the thermometer from his pocket and laid it on the table between our cereal boxes. He told us to take a good long look while he cleared his throat again.

"Ok," he said. He picked it up and pointed it at our mother. "Your mother wants to take my temperature," he said. My mother bowed her head, but she didn't fold her hands or move her lips. He pointed the thermometer at my brother. "I told her to go ahead and try." He pointed it at me. "How's that sound?" he said. "Like I mean it?"

When my mother whimpered his name, he snapped the thermometer. "How's that sound?' he said, his voice hoarse. "Like the end of something?" None of us moved while he stood up. "I have work to do," he said. "That's what they're paying me for. Being there. Somebody they can count on."

17

Stage I-II thyroid cancers are confined to the thyroid. If it has spread to nearby lymph nodes, it is still considered stage I-II when the patient is younger than forty-five. The presence of cancer in the lymph nodes does not worsen the prognosis for younger patients.

Stage III thyroid cancer is greater than four cm in diameter and is limited to the thyroid or may have minimal spread outside the thyroid. Lymph nodes near the trachea may be affected. Stage III thyroid cancer that has spread to adjacent cervical tissue or nearby blood vessels has a worse prognosis. However, lymph node metastases do not worsen the prognosis for patients younger than forty-five.

Stage IV thyroid cancer has spread from your thyroid gland to other parts of your neck, lymph node or distant areas of your body like your lung or bones.

18

After you tell your wife you've missed the age advantage for thyroid cancer by thirty years. she says, "Your age matters more to the coronavirus."

19

To pin a butterfly, first gently press the thorax with the blunt end of a pair of tweezers until you feel and hear it crush. Be careful not to squash the thorax completely. Push a pin through the thorax so that where the wings join it is level with the top of the pinning board. Pin thin strips of card on either side of the body. Place a pin next to the abdomen on one side to keep the body in place while you open the wing. Using tweezers, move it into the position you desire. Press down gently. Be careful not to rip it as you hold the wing in position. Place a piece of unwaxed paper over the wing and pin around the outside. Repeat on the other side. Leave the specimen in a cool, dry place for a week. Keep ants and other pests away by using surface spray in the area near your specimen. Once it is dry, remove the pins and store it in a safe place. Use plenty of mothballs.

20

Your doctor's office is across the street from a nursing home that is shuttered, its parking lot secured from traffic with what appears to be crime scene tape. You park and call the office number to announce your arrival and wait, as instructed, by your car. After ten minutes, the midday sun brings up sweat and you call again. After fifteen minutes, you sit in your car, running the air conditioning and listening to music. You are startled when the receptionist raps on the window, and you step outside, unmasked, so close to her that she retreats. Over six months has passed since the original, postponed ultrasound appointment, more than three months since the ultrasound showed significant growth. The doctor orders a second biopsy. The appointment you have kept lasts less than ten minutes.

21

After five years, survival rates:

> Papillary thyroid cancer: Regional - 99%, Distant - 78%
> Follicular thyroid cancer: Regional - 96%, Distant - 63%
> Medullary thyroid cancer: Regional - 90%, Distant - 39%
> Anaplastic thyroid cancer: Regional - 12%, Distant - 4%

Just below that fourth, dismal prognosis, the site says: Remember, everyone is different. Ask your doctor what you can expect based on your type of cancer and other things that are unique to you.

You don't mention the numbers to your wife, keeping even the good numbers to yourself.

22

One morning, to distract yourself, you weed around the yard's shrubbery. Because you have forgotten to prune, for the second consecutive year, the butterfly bush your granddaughter loves towers far beyond repair, its leaves, during a dry July, gone uniformly curled and brown. Your granddaughter will not witness the result of your shoddy maintenance. The pandemic has canceled her late summer visit, furloughing you from discovery like a wealthy, white-collar felon.

23

The butterfly farm's site declares that although butterflies know when they are touched, it is thought that their nervous system does not have receptors that register pain "as we know it."

24

Your prison-guard story is accepted for publication. In 2021, the emailed contract says, which seems so distant, you simply type "ok, thanks" and click "send" after supplying a virtual signature.

25

A woman who appears to be as old as you are performs the second biopsy. She is cheerful in a grandmotherly way and describes out loud everything she is doing, "Now I am preparing to insert the needle. Soon you will feel pressure. There, now, the needle is doing its work…" She says she does five extractions in a row, sending all of them to the lab after she's finished because this biopsy is being performed in an auxiliary unit of the hospital. Even on the fifth extraction, she says, "Now I am preparing to insert the needle."

26

Your father, at eighty-eight, had his caregiver bring the Titanic print up from the basement and lay it on the dining room table. He asked you if you wanted it, saying it must be valuable because it was an antique by now. You didn't mention that years ago you'd seen that print on the walls of two friends' living rooms, the row boats surrounded by hopeless swimmers in the ocean, the Titanic listing steeply, poised to sink with passengers still on board. He never offered the butterflies, both of which were discarded after he died, no takers for either them or the Titanic, which, two years later, was still on the dining room table after he went to the nursing home.

27

In mid-August, over eight months since the original ultrasound appointment, you are told that the nodule that has grown is benign. The immediate concern is whether it will continue to grow and interfere with swallowing or speech. You are placed, once again, on a six-month ultrasound cycle.

28

In Los Angeles, your granddaughter begins school online. When you talk with her on FaceTime, you tell her about the butterfly farm and promise to take her next summer.

29

Walking home from the community pool on the Saturday before school in your town begins, the neighbor girl passes on the sidewalk. She smiles and waves. At once, you raise your hand to acknowledge her, so pleased you almost call out a question about the masks she will begin wearing to class, what sort of patterns she's chosen for sixth grade.

30

Late in your wife's latest Zoom book club meeting, during the goodbyes from isolation, you hear Denise say to everyone, "Would you like to see our butterfly collection?" You step into the room and watch as she tilts her laptop so the camera shows the dining room wall behind her is nearly covered with hung boxes of butterflies. You count twelve, nine in each box. 108 butterflies that look identical to you. You search the eight other women's faces in the Zoom panels, looking for a match to your wonder. Two go dark.

Denise stands, the room swaying through her camera as she carries the laptop closer to the wall. All of the butterflies seem to have the same deep blue with golden specks in a simple, consistent pattern. "They have names," she says, beginning a slow pan across the boxes. "They're on the back." Four panels are vacant.

"My husband is in self-quarantine," Denise says, "but so far, he's mild." She moves her laptop closer to the wall, holds it steady. You think of an atlas you once owned, how the biggest cities were enlarged in panels. You and your wife are alone with her as she says, "Don't they look as if they could fly?"

You imagine another wall sprouting something like an ivy of boxes before Denise hosts another Zoom book club meeting. What she will show and call beauty's still life while those others at the meeting go quickly dark into their ordinary, private lives. You vow to look up the species. To ask her now seems taboo, an interruption of worship. You imagine her husband busy with a new specimen, carefully restoring something dry and fragile under a brilliant light. While you stare and stare, all that is left of her is breathing.

ACKNOWLEDGMENTS

The following essays were first published in:

American Literary Review: "Sparklers"

Arts & Letters: "Catching"

Ascent: "Hearts"

Brevity: "All of It," "Crosswords," "During the Farm Show Parade," "Hard Candy"

December: "Proximity," "Telephone," "Weekend"

Ecotone: "The Homemade Court"

Five Points: "Shibboleth"

Kenyon Review Online: "After the Three Moon Era," "The Physics of Desire"

Lake Effect: "Hands: A Memoir," "The Woman in White"

Passages North: "Brains"

Pleaides: "Scream: A Panorama"

Shenandoah: "The Ass End of Everything," "The Canals of Mars," "Kicking Ass," "Things that Fall from the Sky"

South Dakota Review: "Butterflies, Biopsies, the Lockdown Hosts," "Headlights"

Southern Humanities Review: "After Arson," "The Faces of Christ"

Sweet: "On Location: New Year's Eve"

Tampa Review: "Potato Chips"

The Citron Review: "On Location: A Valentine"

The Literary Review: "The Pagoda Sightlines"

Woven Tale Review: "Oak Ridge: A Cantata"

The following essays have been recognized with these awards:

"The Darkness Call" won the Robert C. Jones Prize for Short Prose (Pleaides Press, 2018);

"After the Three-Moon Era" was reprinted in *Best American Essays 2020*;

"The Canals of Mars" was reprinted in T*he Pushcart Prize XXV* and again in *The Best Pushcart Prize Essays*, Vol. I-XXV;

"The Ass-End of Everything" was cited as Distinguished Essay by The Pushcart Prize;

"The Pagoda Sightlines," "The Woman in White," "Potato Chips," "Hearts," "Proximity," "After Arson," "Telephone," "Shibboleth," "The Physics of Desire," "The Handmade Court," and "The Canals of Mars" were cited as Notable Essays in *Best American Essay* Volumes;

"The Faces of Christ," "The Pagoda Sightlines," "After Arson," "Shibboleth," and "Brains" were reprinted in *The Cresset*.

ABOUT THE AUTHOR

Gary Fincke has published five collections of essays, including *The Darkness Call*, which won the Robert C. Jones Prize (Pleiades Press, 2018). Individual essays have been reprinted in *Best American Essays* and *The Pushcart Prize*. His short story collections have been published by Coffee House, Missouri, and West Virginia and have won the Flannery O'Connor Prize and the Elixir Press Fiction Prize. Collections of his poetry have won book prizes offered by Ohio State, Michigan State, Arkansas, Stephen. F. Austin, and Jacar.